The Maverick

George Weidenfeld and the Golden Age of Publishing

Thomas Harding

PEGASUS BOOKS

NEW YORK LONDON

THE MAVERICK

Pegasus Books, Ltd.
148 West 37th Street, 13th Floor
New York, NY 10018

ISBN: 978-1-63936-445-9

10 9 8 7 6 5 4 3 2 1

Printed in the United States of America
Distributed by Simon & Schuster
www.pegasusbooks.com

For Hella Pick, the indomitable trailblazing journalist

CONTENTS

List of Illustrations   ix

Introduction   1

CHAPTER 1   Arthur's Diary, 1919   7

CHAPTER 2   The Goebbels Experiment, 1942   25

CHAPTER 3   The Hedgehog and the Fox, 1953   49

CHAPTER 4   A Young Girl's Touch, 1956   65

CHAPTER 5   Lolita, 1959   80

CHAPTER 6   The Group, 1963   95

CHAPTER 7   Herzog, 1965   105

CHAPTER 8   ██████████ 1967   125

CHAPTER 9   The Double Helix, 1968   134

CHAPTER 10 Mary Queen of Scots, 1969   146

CHAPTER 11 The Governance of Britain, 1976   155

CHAPTER 12 Unity Mitford: A Quest, 1976   167

CHAPTER 13 Yoni: Hero of Entebbe, 1979   182

CHAPTER 14 In the Eye of the Storm, 1982   196

CHAPTER 15 Mick Jagger, 1985   210

CHAPTER 16 Catcher in the Rye II, 1987   227

CHAPTER 17 Remembering My Good Friends, 1994   248

CHAPTER 18 Letters from Oxford, 2004   272

CHAPTER 19 Obit, 2016   283

Epilogue 291

Endnotes 297

Bibliography 310

Acknowledgements 314

Index 317

LIST OF ILLUSTRATIONS

Max, Arthur and Rosa Weidenfeld, 1919 (Laura Barnett)

Arthur Weidenfeld, circa 1929 (Laura Barnett)

Arthur Weidenfeld passport, 1937 (Laura Barnett)

Adele Weidenfeld and Laura Eisenstein (Laura Barnett)

Nigel Nicolson, 1959 (Getty)

Isaiah Berlin, 1959 (Getty)

Jane Sieff and George Weidenfeld, 1952 (Laura Barnett)

George Weidenfeld and Laura, 1953 (Laura Barnett)

Barbara Skelton, 1948 (Getty)

The first edition of *Lolita*, with the author on the back cover, 1955 (John Atkinson Books)

Mary McCarthy, 1968 (Getty)

Melbourne Herald, 'We'll Sell "The Group" in Streets', 20 March 1964 (*Melbourne Herald*)

Saul Bellow, 1965 (Getty)

George Weidenfeld (Laura Barnett)

Sandra and George just after their wedding with Laura and Sandra's daughter Averil, 1966 (Laura Barnett)

James Watson with a reproduction of DNA double helix, 1962 (Getty)

First edition book cover, *The Double Helix*, 1968 (John Atkinson Books)

Antonia Fraser, George Weidenfeld and Antonia's mother Elizabeth Longford, 1966 (Laura Barnett)

Harold Wilson and Lady Falkender (Marcia Williams), 1966 (Getty)

Baron Weidenfeld of Chelsea, 1976 (Laura Barnett)

Adolf Hitler and Unity Mitford, circa 1937 (Getty)

George in the 1970s (Gemma Levine)

George and Chaim Weizmann, 1948; George with Moshe Dayan, 1970s (Laura Barnett)

Kurt Waldheim in Podgorica; today Montenegro, 1943 (Getty)

Mick Jagger (Getty)
George with Ann Getty and Arianna Huffington, 1980s (Laura Barnett)
George with Pope John Paul II, 1990s (Laura Barnett)
George with Chancellor Kohl (Daniel Biskup)
George and Annabelle's wedding, Jerusalem, 1992 (Laura Barnett)
George with Mathias Döpfner, 2006 (Annabelle Weidenfeld)
George on the dance floor at grandson Rowan's wedding, 2008
    (Henriette Olbrisch)

'There are at least ten George Weidenfelds and I love every one of them.'

Barbara Walters

'George cannot be described, indeed, as other than an international institution.'

Chaim Herzog

'George sees everyone he meets as a potential book.'

Beatrix Miller

INTRODUCTION

It was a grand, boisterous, lavish event and, at the centre of it all, as was usual for such happenings, was the publisher, George Weidenfeld. Known as Arthur on his birth certificate, Turli to his parents, Lord Weidenfeld by the newspapers, and simply George to his friends, the publisher at turns listened intently, recounted an uproarious story, laughed warmly, shared some shocking rumour about a notorious person horrifyingly, wonderfully ensnared in scandal, before offering to refill a glass and inviting the listener to write a book: 'It will be a huge success,' he would purr.

It was 1987 and the dinner party was held in Ann Getty's sumptuous apartment on Fifth Avenue. The nine-storey building stood across the street from Central Park, just a few steps from the Plaza Hotel, one of New York's best addresses. Ann, who was married to the oil baron Gordon Getty, was the chief investor in George's publishing venture. With her fiery red hair, angular cheeks, dimpled mouth and mischievous smile, she easily drew attention. Sitting next to Ann was the former Secretary of State, Henry Kissinger. Next to him was the TV presenter Barbara Walters and then the journalist Arianna Stassinopoulos, later known as Arianna Huffington. There were sixteen people in total gathered around the enormous round table, each adept at climbing the New York ladder.

'Who is that over there?' Donald Trump whispered to Juliet Nicolson, gesturing towards a man quietly eating his asparagus. Trump lived in the same building and was friends with Ann Getty. Juliet Nicolson worked as an editor in George's firm Weidenfeld

& Nicolson and was the daughter of the firm's co-founder. 'That's the journalist Bernard Levin,' Juliet whispered back. 'He doesn't say very much,' Trump replied, *sotto voce*. 'Well, he is a clever man,' she added, giggling. 'Oh my God, is he?' Trump said, in mock awe.

Juliet was thirty-three years old and had recently arrived from London. She looked fabulous in the glamorous evening gown she had borrowed from the New York frock rental store where the firm had an account used by its female employees. Trump was probably pleased to be sitting next to Juliet, she was his junior so he didn't have to lose face asking who was who. It was unlikely that she would put him down.

The food was prepared by Ann Getty's personal chef and served by a team of professional waitresses hired in for the event and dressed in black trousers and white shirts. The table was covered with crisp white linen, the finest silverware and plates, as well as vintage glasses purchased from Sotheby's, one of Ann Getty's favourite auction houses. Just recently she had asked Juliet to bid on a diamond bracelet for her. When the young employee had protested that she was in the middle of a paperback auction, Mrs Getty had told her to go at lunchtime. 'What's the budget?' Juliet had asked, now resigned to her task. There was none. 'Just get it!' her boss confirmed.

In between the main course and dessert, George pushed back his chair and rose to say a few words. At five foot nine, he was not a tall man, but his bulk more than made up for any lack in height. He looked handsome in his tailored dark suit, well-knotted tie, with dark brown eyes and hair pushed back from his high forehead. Having thanked their host for her graciousness and hospitality and congratulated her on the exquisite deliciousness of the food, he reminded the guests that they were gathered to support the writers' charity PEN. George looked around the room and was greeted by smiles and nodding heads. In reality, as everyone there knew full well, this was much more than a charitable event. As with all of the publisher's get-togethers, this was also an occasion to network, to make contacts and to forge closer business and social relationships.

On one level, the story of George Weidenfeld is a tale of rags to riches, in the mould of Dick Whittington. It is the fable of a young man who flees Nazi persecution in his home country of Austria, arriving in London without money or contacts and barely able to speak English. Faced with assorted temptations and challenges, including anti-Semitism, he not only masters the new culture, but acquires fame and fortune. By his life's end, he has become a fully fledged member of the Establishment: Lord Weidenfeld of Chelsea.

This story also provides a window into the twentieth century, via its literature. Through his publishing house, Weidenfeld & Nicolson, George released some of the most significant titles of the last hundred years, including *Lolita* by Vladimir Nabokov, *The Double Helix* by James Watson and *The Group* by Mary McCarthy, as well as huge bestsellers, such as Keith Richards' memoir *Life*, Vikram Seth's *A Suitable Boy* and *I Am Malala* by Malala Yousafzai. His list of authors was astonishing: Truman Capote, Joan Didion, Henry Miller, Edna O'Brien, Clare Tomalin, Gore Vidal, Antonia Fraser, Martin Gilbert, Norman Mailer, Margaret Drabble, Lyndon B. Johnson, Moshe Dayan, Henry Kissinger and Carlos Ruiz Zafón, to name just a few. This, then, is a book about books, an investigation into publishing, including its dark arts. Who gets to be published, who doesn't, and why? How do editors deal with celebrity tantrums, libel and other challenges? Why are some books successful and others not? In other words, how publishing actually works.

More than this, George Weidenfeld's story provides an insight into some of today's hot-button cultural conflicts. Protecting freedom of speech while avoiding hatred and offence. Safeguarding the right to publish but adhering to national security and libel laws. Providing ever-greater access to information without infringing on people's privacy. As well as one of the greatest contemporary questions: should the value of information be judged by the quality of the product and its contribution to society or by the size of its audience and, as has become so important today, its engagement. And, perhaps most pressing of all, should information be curated, as George would have argued strongly in the affirmative, saying that an editor and their team add huge value to a book or other literary product. Or conversely, as the likes of Facebook or Twitter might argue, should information be made available unfettered and unmediated? These difficult issues were frequently faced by George; indeed, time and time again over the decades, he was at the very heart of the cultural reckoning.

There is also George's very public private life. His marriages to four women. His relationships with his female staff members. This again has strong echoes of some of our most difficult challenges, raising the question about whether we can apply the values of today to decades past and, if we can, how the judgement of those who came before reflects on us now.

Perhaps most intriguingly, there is George's inner life. On the surface, he was known as one of the world's greatest networkers, his parties legendary. His book of contacts unrivalled, including the private telephone numbers of kings and queens, prime ministers and presidents, celebrities and rock stars. And yet, at his core, the publisher was from the very start deeply lonely. In this time of endemic isolation, when so many chase 'likes' and 'friends' on social media only to feel rejected and unseen, this story is, therefore, also a personal one, about a man who just wanted to be seen, to belong, to feel safe.

A brief note on the structure of the book. This is not a traditional cradle-to-grave biography. Instead, I chose to explore George's life through the books with which he was associated. This, however, prompted a question: which books? After all, during George's long connection with Weidenfeld & Nicolson, the firm released more than 6,000 titles. Therefore, a longlist had to be made, a difficult task, and then a shortlist, even harder. In the end, I settled on nineteen books that I felt provided the best insights and narrative arc for his long life. Some may say I have failed to give sufficient attention to certain key texts, for instance those by Israeli states- men, various academics or European literary titans. Others may argue that I should have moved beyond George's publishing career and focused more on his paramount love for Israel, his fascination with opera or his prodigious philanthropic work. To those I ask forgiveness.

Finally, let me speak about the genesis of this book. One day, out of the blue I received a call from the chairman at Weidenfeld & Nicolson who asked if I might be interested in writing a biography of George Weidenfeld. When I suggested that I might not be the best candidate given that I had never met the publisher, I was told that was exactly why I had been chosen. Also, the chairman said, George and I shared the same background: our families had both fled the Nazis (his from Austria, mine from Germany) and both arrived in England as refugees in the 1930s. Shortly after agreeing to write the book, I heard that George's family supported the project. His wife Annabelle, daughter Laura and other family members kindly shared artefacts, letters, photographs and official documents, as well as their memories. Yet, to be clear, this is not an authorised biography. I have control over and take full responsibility for its contents.

Coming into this project, I was aware that there have been a series of recent scandals in the publishing world. Hachette in the United States refused to publish the film director Woody Allen's autobiography after staff threatened to walk out. Employees at Simon & Schuster threatened similar action if that publisher distributed a book by former Vice-President Mike Pence. Norton published then dropped Blake Bailey's biography of Philip Roth, after allegations of sexual abuse surfaced against the author. In other words, publishers were increasingly vigilant about the potential impact of their books on their reputation. Therefore, when I started this book, I asked if Weidenfeld & Nicolson would allow me to include anything I found, warts and all. They said yes. Anxious that there would be no misunderstanding, I asked again. What would happen if I unearthed information about George that might taint the company's reputation? What if I found something out that was so bad it posed an existential threat? They reassured me once again and, to their great credit, Weidenfeld & Nicolson have not asked me to make a single cut or deletion.

At one point during my research, I looked up the word 'publisher' in the *Oxford English Dictionary*. I learned that it had two meanings. First, 'One whose business is the issuing of books, periodicals, music etc.' The other definition: A person 'who makes something public'. For George, both senses apply. A man who brought a large number of remarkable books into being. And a man who tried to reveal himself to and thereby connect with other people, to make himself public. Neither effort, however, was without its complications or challenges.

CHAPTER 1

Arthur's Diary

1919

'The writer: It is he that we serve and are served by.' – GW

Arthur George Weidenfeld's life started with a book. His mother, Rosa, decided to chronicle his first few months in a journal. Keenly aware that money was tight, she thought it best to reuse something she already had. After a brief search, she found an old black- and green-striped notebook. She could just about read the faded word 'Register' written in thin brown ink on its front cover. Inside, the lined pages were blank. Rosa turned to the first page and made an entry. It was a description of Arthur's birth that had taken place just eight weeks earlier.

'I wanted to have you at home at Gumpendorferstrasse 111,' Rosa began, addressing her son who she hoped would one day read the journal, 'Doctor Grubel from the 2nd District visited me at home and told me that I needed to go to hospital immediately. It was a dangerous situation for me, but more so for you.' Gumpendorferstrasse 111 was where Rosa lived with her husband Max. It was a cramped, dark sets of rooms located on the ground floor next to the rear staircase. The building was situated in a Jewish neighbourhood within Vienna's 6th District, far away from the opulence and finery of the city centre. There was no running water available inside the apartment, the privy was in the courtyard. It was small for the growing Weidenfeld family, but the rent was cheap and it was all that they could afford on Max's salary.

'Together with my mother and the midwife Frau Marder,' Rosa

continued, 'I took a cart to the sanatorium.' They arrived at the hospital in the early morning. There the doctors discovered that the baby was breech and encouraged Rosa to push, but after many difficult hours there was still no progress. Exhausted by the effort and in considerable pain, Rosa was given strong sedatives. She fell asleep for a while. Outside the hospital gates, Max and his brother Josef waited anxiously for news. In the early afternoon, Max was invited to go inside to see his wife. 'Your father was off-balance and confused,' Rosa recorded in her journal, 'We both thought that this would be the last time we would see each other.' On his way back outside, Max was stopped by a hospital official. If a choice had to be made, would Max want the mother or the baby to survive? Without hesitation, Max said the mother, Rosa.

Meanwhile inside, a team of doctors struggled to save both the mother and her baby. Rosa was by this time barely conscious and yet still she continued to push. Finally, at 6 p.m. on 13 September 1919, after a herculean effort, the baby was born. Rosa fell immediately into a deep sleep. When after many hours she awoke, she was told about her baby. 'How great was my joy when you my sweet arrived healthy and with all your parts intact,' Rosa wrote. 'You weighed 3.3 kg. I couldn't believe it! Everyone said I would get a girl because I had a high belly. But I always hoped to have a boy. I was happy when I woke up and was told it was true, you were a boy!'

A little over a week later, the family gathered in Max and Rosa's apartment at Gumpendorferstrasse 111. The baby's two grand-mothers were there, Laura and Adele, as were his grandfather Jacob and Uncle Josef. Some of the relatives had been unable to make it as the trains were not yet back to normal, even though it had been a year since the end of the Great War. In charge of the proceed-ings was his great-uncle, Rabbi Horowitz, one of the many rabbis on his mother's side of the family. They were all dressed in their finest clothes. The men in dark suits, some wearing wide fur-lined hats, others skullcaps. The women in dark ankle-length dresses and necklaces. For this was a special occasion, a day of celebration.

The family was split in two. The women were crowded into Rosa's room. They had lit candles and were singing a song. There were tears of joy in their eyes. The baby was with the men in Max's room. They were also singing, led by the rabbi. Waiting for the moment when he would be blessed. For, as it was written in Leviticus chapter 12, verse 3: 'And on the eighth day the flesh of his foreskin shall be circumcised'. Finally, the moment came. With Uncle Josef holding him, Rabbi Horowitz reached down and in a swift slashing movement, completed the task. '*Mazel tov!*' cried the men. '*Mazel tov!*' echoed the women from the other room. And so it was that Max and Rosa's baby boy was issued into the community.

In her journal, Rosa described the *bris* that had just taken place. 'You looked like an angel in your blue silk dress and bonnet,' she wrote, 'it was a present from your grandma Adele.' She then moved on to introduce her son to his relatives. 'You have to know that you are part of a very Jewish family on both Papa's and my side.' Her family, she continued, offered a particularly rich cultural legacy: for hundreds of years they had produced rabbis respected for their wisdom and insight. 'To be part of this family,' she added, 'you will have the chance to be an important man.'

On the next page, Rosa explained how they had come up with his name. For a while they struggled with what to call him. Should he be named Saul after her great-grandfather, another famous rabbi, or Abraham, after the grandfather on his father's side? They decided against both these names as neither sounded sufficiently Germanic. Max's sister and brother wanted him to have a biblical name like Gideon, but Rosa's parents rejected this suggestion saying it sounded too old-fashioned. 'We had to find a European name that would give you no problems,' Rosa wrote. She then explained that his father, Max, had been given a hard time, first at school and later in the office, because the name on his birth certificate was Mordche. 'This sounds to people who are not Jewish very exotic,' she wrote, 'some think it is ridiculous.'

When, after a number of days, they still hadn't come up with a name, Rosa said enough was enough. She and Max sat down around a table, poured two glasses of wine, put out a plate of sweet pastries, and agreed they would not get up until they had resolved the matter. After two hours, they made a decision. They would call their son Arthur George Weidenfeld. This was why, on the front cover of the old notebook, beneath the faded word 'Register', Rosa had written the following words in bold brown script: 'Tagebuch Arthur', or *Arthur's Diary*.

As she continued to chronicle her son's first few months, Rosa did not restrict herself to writing about religious ceremonies and baby names. 'You are born my little boy in a very very interesting time,' she wrote in one entry. 'After five years of murderous war, Europe is full of sorrows, most of all in our land. Poverty is a real problem. As is the cold. Never in world history have we had such a terrible winter as we are now experiencing.' She then reported that 'One of our biggest challenges is to find heating materials so that you are kept warm. It is necessary to stand for hours to get a small amount of wood for huge sums of money.' In another entry, she wrote that 'Thousands of people die because they don't have enough to eat. A lot of children perish every day. Because of this we thank God for each moment we are blessed with you. There are so many families who are grieving.'

She also recorded her thoughts on the political situation. She wrote that Austria 'is now a lowly beggar republic', adding that they had to acknowledge the unpleasantness of being defeated. Like the majority of Vienna's population, Rosa and Max were keen for Austria to expand its borders once again. This would be a key part of Arthur's heritage: an empathy for the sufferings of others and a love for Austria.

Two days after Christmas, Rosa added another passage:

Today, for the first time, you were put in a dress, which Aunt Ida brought as a Chanukah gift, along with two shirts, as befits a big boy. All men who like to poke fun at women should have to walk around in dresses once in their life. Hopefully you won't belong to the category of men who believe themselves superior, who tease women to their heart's content. There are certainly corrupt and bad women who must be avoided, just like all bad people! But that doesn't mean we should condemn the world of women all together. Don't forget that many of the best moments in life are created by romance and this is thanks to women. Being subjected to the daily struggles, men become spoiled and materialistic. Interactions with women – only those in whom 'something eternally feminine' is expressed, as Goethe put it – are intoxicating and refine the mind.

'Socialisation is naturally one of the most important female tasks,' she continued. 'I don't want to influence you my little boy – but should you judge women objectively as human beings, you will agree with me, I think. We are not angels; we have our faults! Maybe by the time you grow up, women will play a different role than they do now.'

A month later, Rosa, Max and four-month-old Arthur visited a studio in Vienna to have their photograph taken. At 500 kronen it was expensive, yet despite their having little income the family felt it important to capture their image for the future. To the left of the picture stood Max, in a jacket and tie, starched white shirt, high forehead, cropped curly dark hair, sporting a modest moustache. He is looking directly at the camera, with an expression of wary determination. The reason for this look is that he is holding his son firmly to his chest – right hand under Arthur's bottom, left hand gripping the baby's neck and head – to stop him from squirming as the shutter remained open to complete its long exposure. For his part, Arthur is also looking at the camera, dressed in a white gown, chubby and round-faced, mouth ajar, tiny tongue out, pupils glistening in the bulb's flash. To the right is Rosa. She is wearing a black dress with a wide, white, cross-hatched collar, her thick brown curly hair neatly tied up, her face youthful, with high cheekbones, a small nose and rounded chin. She is turned towards her husband and son, staring adoringly at Arthur, her smile warm and relaxed. 'Today I wanted to get you photographed,' Rosa wrote in her diary. 'You screamed a lot.'

Max, Arthur and Rosa Weidenfeld

As Arthur was growing up, he was taught how to read Hebrew and learned about his family's religious heritage. In particular, he was directed to the family tree filled with rabbis going back to the sixteenth century that hung on the apartment wall and which was a great source of pride. Of these, his mother told her son, the most famous was Isaiah Abraham Horowitz (also known as the 'Holy Shelah'), who in the 1600s had been chief rabbi in Prague, before moving to Jerusalem where he led the Ashkenazi community. During his time in Israel, Isaiah Abraham Horowitz wrote a book that became highly influential among European Jews. In it he stressed the pursuit of joy and positivity, even in the face of adversity and evil.

Judaism was important to Arthur's parents. A year before his birth, they had married in Vienna's oldest synagogue on Seitenstettengasse. For the high holy days, they attended the huge synagogue on Tempelgasse, which could hold up to 2,000 people. They fasted, as was the custom, during Yom Kippur, the Day of Atonement. On Friday mornings, they prepared food for the weekend, and then in the evening gathered with other family members for Shabbat dinner. Unlike Rosa's ancestors, however, they did not keep kosher at home. Nor did they want their child to attend a Jewish school. Instead, when he was six years old, Arthur was sent to a non-religious elementary school in the local community.

Max worked as a salesman for the Phönix insurance company. Based in Germany, it had a regional office in Vienna, selling contents and life-insurance policies. During the First World War, Phönix had expanded quickly, partly by selling 'war participant' insurance, providing compensation to those who lost loved ones during the conflict. Max worked hard and for long hours, and was rarely back at the apartment before his son was asleep. Rosa was a homemaker. But she yearned to get out of the house, visit the museums with their fine pictures, play cards with friends, have some time for herself. So when Max received a raise, they hired a nanny from the countryside.

Many decades later, Arthur would return to this home and his memories of the nanny as part of a documentary about his life. By this point, the building had been demolished and replaced by a more modern, concrete structure, but the intense feelings remained. When asked about his nanny, he calls her 'That slut from the country', before adding, 'She meant nothing to me.' He pauses for a beat, smiles enigmatically, then continues, 'She always locked me away – whenever she had a lover – and my mother was not there.'

The interviewer appears shocked. Arthur has just told him that he was repeatedly locked in his room as a small child, so that his nanny could have sex with her boyfriend.

'You noticed that?' asks the interviewer.

'Yes,' Arthur says, 'I noticed that.'

'It wasn't a happy place?' asks the interviewer.

'Not a happy place, no,' Arthur replies quietly.

The pair turn, and walk away from his childhood home.

In 1926, when Arthur was seven years old, Max began earning sufficient income for the family to move. They rented an apartment closer to the city centre, on the border between the 8th and 9th Districts. Filled with wide boulevards and elegant, tall, nineteenth-century apartment buildings, the neighbourhood was home to various well-known Viennese figures, including the author Stefan Zweig and the psychoanalyst Sigmund Freud. It was also mixed, comprising both Christian and Jewish families, suggesting that the Weidenfelds were not only more affluent but also trying to assimilate. They lived at apartment 17 on the fourth floor of Alserstrasse 47, a six-storey building with a stone facade and an internal courtyard, which allowed light into the rear rooms. Unlike their previous apartment, this one had high ceilings, parquet wooden floors, an inside toilet – though shared with the neighbour – and plenty of light.

Now that Arthur was older, his parents felt there was no need for a nanny, so in the afternoons after he returned home from elementary school he was left to his own devices. Arthur loved to read and luckily Max had an extensive book collection, including the complete works of Shakespeare, Dante, Goethe and Molière. There were also plays by the German Friedrich Hebbel and the Spaniard Lope de Vega, as well as short stories by several Italian authors. At the centre of his father's library was a nineteenth-century roll-top desk. On this, Arthur set up dominos and chess pieces and, as he read a novel or a play, he would move the pieces around. This helped him keep track of the characters. And so the hours passed. Arthur, by himself in his father's library, going through one book and then the next, the occasional click as he moved a queen or a pawn or a domino piece across the wooden desk.

'The most significant fact about my life,' Arthur later remembered, 'is that I was an only child. The warm love shown to me by my parents was a bit of a double-edged sword. On the one hand, I became used to being cosseted. On the other, I felt misunderstood, as my parents were unable to convey the sense of conviviality that I so passionately longed for. I was alone a great deal of the time.' He then added, 'I had a deep fear of loneliness and that is something from which you always want to escape. I can't bear to be alone, especially in the evening, even if I'm at home. I want people to come and see me, to chat with me. I just don't like being by myself.'

At the age of ten, Arthur started at the Piaristen high school, which was a five-minute walk from the family home. Max and Rosa had been attracted to this conservative institution because of its traditional focus on Latin and Greek, along with the opportunities to learn English, French and Italian. Each day, the students were obliged to attend prayers in the Catholic church next to the school. There, under the high dome adorned with garishly painted biblical stories, the pupils sang hymns and participated in the service. An observant and curious child, Arthur saw the similarities between the Christian and Jewish traditions and rituals, giving him a lifelong fascination with Catholicism and freeing him from an attachment to his family's religious practices.

According to his school reports, Arthur was an excellent student, scoring the top grade 'very good' in German language, religious studies and history. He was less successful in mathematics, for which he consistently received lower grades. In addition to academic studies, the students engaged in physical activities, including gymnastics and fencing. Arthur also took part in several school productions; he enjoyed putting on costumes and performing in public. Overall, he loved being part of this new community. The boisterous but curious children. The attentive and well-read adults. After school one day, he told his parents that he wanted to be an actor. They appeared supportive. This gave him a sense of excitement, that anything was possible.

In September 1932, Arthur turned thirteen years old. It was now time for him to take part in his bar mitzvah. Although the records were lost in the later destruction of Vienna's Jewish archives, it is likely that the ceremony occurred in the same synagogue where the Weidenfelds attended high holy days on Tempelgasse in the 2nd District. One Saturday morning in the autumn of that year, Arthur would have stepped up to the *bimah*, or altar, at the front of the great hall, dressed in a newly purchased suit and, with the rabbi standing nearby, would have read from that week's passage from the Torah. This was a difficult task as the text had

Arthur Weidenfeld

no vowels but, given that Arthur had a proficiency for languages and had prepared for some months, there is little doubt that he would have performed admirably. Upon finishing his reading, those gathered in front of him, including his parents, grandparents, aunts and uncles, would have cried out '*Skoiach! Skoiach!*', or 'Well done! Well done!' Arthur was now considered a man.

In the early 1930s, Austria was gripped by political turmoil. The end of the First World War had culminated in the collapse of the Habsburg Empire, its territory shrinking to around 40 per cent of its former size. For the first time in 650 years the country was a republic. Its first chancellor was Karl Renner, a Social Democrat, who, in the interests of national unity, had formed a grand coalition with both left- and right-wing parties. After a period of relative stability, however, Austria had been rocked by hyper-inflation and high unemployment, ushering in a decade of great political uncertainty. Street fighting erupted between monarchists and republicans, socialists and fascists. The government struggled to maintain order.

As he moved into his teenage years, Arthur became increasingly aware of this political maelstrom. At home over dinner, his parents frequently discussed the current situation. Rosa and Max supported the Social Democrats, who were friends of the Jewish community and, like the majority of the population, were in favour of Austrian and German unification. Arthur adopted his parents' positions, and then, as he experienced the outside world, made them his own. One day, from their apartment's front window, Arthur saw a parade of young men march by. The wide avenue on which the Weidenfelds lived, Alserstrasse, was a main thoroughfare that ran from the periphery to the city centre and was commonly used as a route for political parades. The marchers wore improvised uniforms – white shirts, military trousers, black boots and swastika armbands. As the procession passed by, he heard them shout '*Deutschland erwache!*

Juda verrecke', or 'Germany awake! Judah perish!' When Arthur asked his father who these people were, Max said they were Nazis.

At the end of January 1933, news arrived in Vienna that Adolf Hitler had been appointed chancellor in Berlin. Within a short space of time the Nazis seized control of the state apparatus in Germany. They then enacted a series of anti-Semitic laws: Jews could no longer work in the civil service. The number of Jewish students at German schools and universities was restricted. Jewish lawyers and notaries were barred from working on legal matters. The news from Berlin caused much discussion within the Weidenfeld household. After all, Hitler (Austrian by birth) had for many years said that he wanted to absorb Austria into a greater Germany. Arthur wondered, could the anti-Semitic laws be passed here? Max reassured his son. He worked closely with members of the government through his insurance work. He knew them to be reasonable people. Things would all settle down, he said. The Austrians would never allow the Nazis to take power.

Despite his father's calming words, Arthur perceived an increased sense of threat as he moved around Vienna. In restaurants and cafés, he saw posters announcing upcoming Nazi rallies and political meetings. Walking along the pavements, men sneered at him and called out 'Look at that Moshe', a pejorative name for a male Jew. One day, on the way into a lecture hall to hear a Jewish speaker, Arthur's way was blocked by a group of young Nazis. They pushed and shoved him, all the while screaming 'Fucking Jew! Fucking Jew!'

Over the next few months, Arthur became increasingly conscious of his fellow students' political affiliations. From the badge they wore in their lapel, he was able to tell which faction they belonged to: Republican. Monarchist. Fascist. Zionist. For Arthur, it was this last group he found most exciting. With the support of his parents, he visited Palestine with a Jewish youth group during the summer holidays and was swept up by the centuries-old culture and history. On his return home to Vienna, he read the writings of Theodor Herzl, the renowned Austro-Hungarian journalist who had so eloquently called for the creation of a Jewish homeland. Inspired, Arthur signed up with a Zionist youth group and began attending their meetings.

In the summer of 1936, Arthur graduated from the gymnasium with top marks. It was time for him to go to university. He was vaguely thinking of becoming a lawyer, so he applied to study law at the University of Vienna. He also applied to the Diplomatic Academy as an external student. Although he knew that as a Jew he could not join the diplomatic service, the academy offered excellent language courses which interested him. To attend both colleges at the same time was unusual but, given Arthur's outstanding grades, both admission offices accepted him; clearly they thought the young man was up to the task.

Shortly after celebrating his seventeenth birthday in September 1936, Arthur started his university studies. In the first few days he applied to join a Zionist student fraternity. As part of his initiation as a provisional member, he became the 'fag', or servant, to an older boy called Cis Hecht, helping him with odd chores, like fetching food or cleaning his clothes. Six months later, he was told that to achieve full membership, he had to provoke a student from another fraternity into fighting a duel. So it was that one Saturday morning in the spring of 1937, Arthur and Cis Hecht went to the university campus and watched students in uniform march around a fountain. Some were attached to a Nazi fraternity, others to the Social Democratic group, still more had the colours of the Communists. As they observed the parade, Hecht told Arthur to approach one of the Nazis and provoke him. When Arthur looked puzzled, Hecht said this was a test. Now understanding what he had to do, and not a little nervous, Arthur continued to monitor the parade until he singled out his target. He then walked up to a young man – a veterinary student named von Stieler – and told him his shoelace was undone. When von Stieler saw that this was untrue, he became irritated and demanded a duel. Arthur accepted the challenge and declared that he would meet von Stieler at Café Landtmann at three o' clock in two days' time to discuss the details. He then clicked his heels, turned and returned to Cis Hecht to share the news.

The following Monday, Arthur duly met von Stieler at Café Landtmann, a coffee house located a few steps from the University of Vienna campus and famous for playing host to student artists, intellectuals and musicians, including the young composer Gustav Mahler and the poet Peter Altenberg. After bowing to each other, Arthur and von Stieler sat down and went through the established protocol. Von Stieler demanded to know if Arthur would apologise for his rudeness. When Arthur declined, his opponent declared that they would therefore need to duel. Von Stieler said he had just one more question: was Arthur an Aryan? When Arthur said he was not, von Stieler stood, bowed again, and walked away. Arthur was grateful, as he really did not wish to fight, but Cis Hecht said that this was not the end of the matter. There were three stages he must complete. First was the private offence. Next was the insult in front of many people. The third was the duel.

A few days later, Arthur tracked down von Stieler at a restaurant where he was known to eat lunch. He walked in and shouted, so that everyone could hear, that Herr von Stieler was a coward. The second stage had been accomplished. Soon after, they met again at Café Landtmann. Von Stieler wanted to know, for the second time, if Arthur would now apologise. Arthur replied that he would not back down, because he wanted to prove that Jews were also gentlemen.

The duel, with swords, took place several days later. Arthur and von Stieler were joined by a medical aide along with two seconds, whose job was to look out for police since fighting in public was frowned on by the authorities. Technically, von Stieler was the better swordsman; he was also taller, which was an added advantage. But Arthur had a surprise. He was left-handed, which he was not obliged to reveal until twenty minutes before the start of the fight. Upon a signal from one of the seconds, they began to duel. Arthur was cut on the left shoulder and on his forehead. With a thrust and a parry, he drew blood in return. Back and forth they went, their swords slashing and slicing. After ninety-two rounds, the duel was declared a draw. It was over. Arthur bowed to his opponent and walked away, his honour intact.

'When he returned home heavily bandaged from a duel which he had kept a deadly secret,' Rosa later wrote, 'Max and I had the worst suspicions but he was under oath not to tell.' It was, she continued, 'my most anxious moment'. The following morning, the medical aide who had attended the duel called them by telephone and said there were no grounds for concern. Their son had fought bravely against a superior opponent. Please, he begged, do not hold either the fight or his silence against Arthur. Reassured, Max and Rosa forgave their son and never spoke about it again. Soon after, he informed them that he had been inducted as a full member of the student Zionist group.

Just before sunrise on Saturday 12 March 1938, German tanks rolled across the Austrian border. Shortly after, airplanes from the Luftwaffe landed at Vienna's airport. Hitler's annexation of Austria, or *Anschluss*, had begun. Four days later, on Wednesday 16 March, the Weidenfelds heard a loud knocking at their apartment door. It was only 7 a.m., so they wondered who it could be so early in the morning.

When Arthur's father opened the door, he saw two officers from the financial police authority standing before him. They announced they were there to arrest him for fraud. Without being given time to pack or make other arrangements, Max was taken to the courthouse jail and placed in an underground cell. He was charged with corruption and would be held pending further inquiries.

As soon as she was allowed, Rosa went to visit Max in prison. She brought him clothes, food and newspapers. He was also visited by his secretary, Helen Hoschek, from whom he learned that other people at the Phönix insurance company had been picked up. They were also in jail and had been charged with fraud. It was unclear what Max's role was in all this. Not long after his arrest, he was moved from the courthouse jail to a prison on Elisabethstrasse. Several weeks later, he was moved to another facility. The questioning never stopped. They wanted to know about the insurance company. Who were the clients? Where did the money go? What was Max's involvement? Then, on 10 December, Rosa and Arthur heard that Max had been transferred to the Metropole Hotel on Morzinplatz. This was terrible news. Shortly after the *Anschluss*, the Metropole Hotel had been taken over by the Gestapo. It was renowned for being a place where Jews were not only brutally interrogated, but also tortured. Many did not survive the ordeal.

During his interrogations, Max was repeatedly asked about how the Phönix insurance company operated. Wasn't it true that bribes had been paid? The Gestapo had been told that money had been given to various political organisations – the Social Democrats, the Communists, even the Nazis. Who had he given money to? Max said he didn't know anything about such things. Yes, he was a director, but his was just one of the company's smaller divisions. He had never been involved at the op level. Frustrated, the Gestapo interrogators sent the prisoner back to his cell. They would try again tomorrow. They were confident they could break him.

While his father was in jail, Arthur heard more worrying news. He was told that as a Jew he could no longer attend classes at either the University of Vienna or the Diplomatic Academy. There was one glimmer of hope: if he could find a way to keep up with the course work then he could sit the exams at the year's end. To have any chance at success, he would need books, lecture notes and papers delivered to his home. Luckily, one of his friends called Kurt Waldheim offered to help Arthur out. Nevertheless, he could see the writing on the wall. The situation in Austria was likely to get worse.

Arthur now told his mother that he wanted to leave the country. Rosa fully supported her son's decision. The question was, where should he go? Jerusalem was one option, but recently the British government had prohibited Jewish refugees from entering Palestine and Rosa worried that something might happen to Arthur if he tried to evade the British patrols. She said that Max was already in prison, she didn't want to now lose her son. In the end, they agreed on London. It was also closer than America.

Over the next few days, Arthur set about making arrangements to leave the country. First, he had to obtain a travel permit from the 8th District administration as he was just eighteen years old – three years below the age of maturity. This was issued without a problem. Next, he needed an exit visa from the Nazis. At the time, the authorities were encouraging Jews to leave the country, so again this was relatively straightforward and, as he was a young man without assets, he did not have to pay the onerous flight tax that was due from older people. Finally, he had to secure an entry visa to the United Kingdom. Typically, this was more challenging but fortunately Arthur had the names of two cousins in London who were willing to provide a guarantee, so the necessary form was stamped and handed over.

Just before he was due to depart, Arthur visited his father in prison. Max had lost considerable weight and looked pale and exhausted. In the small, dank cell, he shared a few pieces of parental advice with his son. One of these was not to drink alcohol or smoke cigarettes (though Max rarely drank, he was a chain-smoker). After just a few minutes, Arthur was told it was time to go and he was escorted out of the prison.

At the end of July 1938, Arthur was accompanied to Vienna's

main railway station by his mother and several members of the family. He wore a suit and a hat and was carrying a small suitcase. After one last goodbye, he boarded the carriage and took his seat. As the train pulled out of the Austrian capital, heading west, Arthur was unsure if he would see any of them ever again.

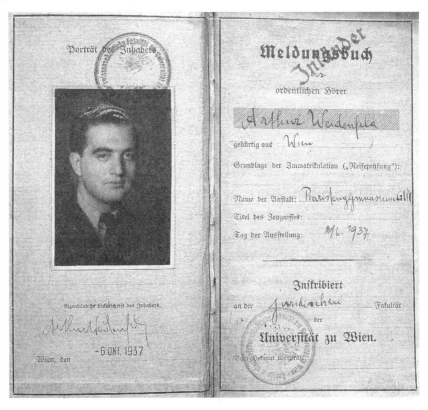

The passport Arthur used to leave Austria

CHAPTER 2

The Goebbels Experiment

1942

'Every publishing decision is an act of faith and hope.' – GW

Arthur arrived in England in August 1938. His journey had been long. From Vienna, he had taken a train to Zurich, then another to Paris, where he stayed a few days. Next on to Calais, from where he had taken a ferry to Dover, and finally another train to London.

Among the belongings in his bag were documents he thought might prove useful in establishing his new life. His birth certificate and Austrian passport. His school and college reports. He had also brought letters of support from people who knew him in Vienna. One of these was from the director of the Diplomatic Academy. 'Mr Weidenfeld has shown much talent and diligence and has achieved good results,' wrote the director. 'As he intends to continue his studies abroad, the Executive can recommend Mr Weidenfeld most thoroughly for any support that could be granted to him.'

After dropping his bag at a crowded and noisy boarding house at King's Cross, Arthur explored his surroundings. 'I found the strange mixture of metropolitan grandeur and almost village-like modesty baffling,' he later recalled, adding, 'in the summer of 1938, I had no idea what the future would hold for me. Should I continue with my studies? Should I learn a trade? Should I try to leave for a distant land, with my parents' fate uncertain?'

A few days later, hungry for better accommodation, he moved in with Mr and Mrs Smythe, a civil servant and his wife, along with their two children. The family belonged to the Plymouth Brethren, a nonconformist church in North London. His room was more spacious, the street quieter, and the family gracious and friendly, for all of which Arthur was grateful, but it was still a bitter, lonely and worrying time. From newspaper and radio reports, he understood that the situation in Austria was worsening. The Nuremberg Laws were being strictly enforced there: Jews could not work in legal or medical professions; nor could they employ so-called Aryans. Jews had to register their assets with the government, including property, bank savings, paintings and life insurance policies. Jews could not travel on public transport. And, as acts of humiliation, Jews were being forced to wash pavements and public toilets.

Then, on 10 November, Arthur learned even worse news. Journalists reported that during the previous night, ninety-three synagogues and houses of prayer in Vienna had been destroyed by roving crowds of Nazi thugs. In addition, more than 6,000 Austrian Jews had been arrested and deported to detention camps. Among the synagogues set on fire and ruined was his family's on Tempelgasse. The Torah he had read from during his bar mitzvah, the seats where his family had sat, the synagogue's archives and world-renowned library, all were lost in the conflagration. Later, the pogrom that also swept Germany would become known as *Kristallnacht*, or night of the broken glass. Arthur was now desperate to help his parents escape Nazi-occupied Austria, but there was little that he could do from London. His frustration was made worse by the slowdown in letters arriving from Vienna. One evening he returned to his room, collapsed on the floor, and prayed for his parents' survival.

With his father still in prison and his mother trying to secure their exit from Austria, Arthur redoubled his efforts to find steady work in London. He was now spending most of his time at the Regent Palace Hotel near Piccadilly Circus, sitting at a table in the grand foyer among the throng of other European refugees, chatting, networking, hoping for a lucky break. There, sipping on loganberry juice, flirting with the waitresses and other young women, and with popular tunes like 'The Teddy Bears' Picnic' playing in the background, he wrote speculative articles about Austrian and German politics for newspapers in London and Amsterdam, hoping they would print his work and pay him a fee.

Early in the morning of 20 March 1939, a few days after Hitler's troops occupied Czechoslovakia, Arthur was at breakfast with the civil servant in his North London home. His host opened *The Times* and saw an advertisement announcing that the BBC was looking for linguists to work in their monitoring department – a new service that listened in to European radio broadcasts. Arthur must apply, the civil servant encouraged. When Arthur protested – he was too young, his English was poor, there were many other refugees more suitable with PhDs and professional qualifications – his host persisted. That afternoon, Arthur asked a woman at the Regent Palace Hotel to type up his résumé and a covering letter, which he posted to the BBC. Several days later, he was invited in for a French language test. Three weeks after that, he was given an interview – during which they asked him if he had ever belonged to the Nazi Party. He replied that of course he had not, for he was a Jewish refugee. Then he was asked what his main interest was. 'History,' he replied. When he was pressed on what kind of history, he replied 'turning points' and quoted an English historian who had written: 'So often at turning points of history the people who live through those times are the last to know when and where history turns.' The following week, he received a letter telling him he had the job.

A few days later, and ten months after his arrival in London, Arthur finally received a message from his parents. To his enormous relief, they were on their way to join him. Arthur would later learn what had happened. While his father was in prison, he had refused to disclose information about pre-occupation allegiances with certain people. This had earned him the appreciation of a senior member of the local Nazi Party who would otherwise have been compromised. Word was sent that Max was to be 'protected'. It was on this basis that he had avoided torture and was finally freed. Having organised Max's release, this Nazi encouraged Arthur's parents to leave the country as soon as possible, which they did, travelling by train into the foothills of the Alps, and then, with the help of a guide (who robbed them of their money), they hiked through the Brenner Pass and into Italy. At the end of June 1939, they arrived in London. George met them at Victoria Station. He was both excited and relieved to see them. After warm embraces, he accompanied them to North London and introduced them to Mr and Mrs Smythe (the kind Plymouth Brethren family), with whom they would stay until they found more permanent lodgings.

On his first full day in England, Max set off to introduce himself to the contacts he'd been given back in Vienna. He was a confident man, and his résumé was impressive. Yet despite numerous meetings, he failed to secure a job. His English was not fluent enough and he was unfamiliar with this new insurance market, let alone the business culture. It was a painful awakening. Meanwhile, Rosa struggled even more. Her English was close to non-existent, and she found Londoners aloof and cold. Such challenges were to be expected for newly arrived refugees such as the Weidenfelds. More disorientating was their growing fear and worry about their relatives left behind in Vienna. When would they arrive? And if they did not, what would happen to them? On Max's side, there was his mother Adele, brother Josef and sister-in-law Elly. On Rosa's side, her elderly mother Laura and sisters Eugenie and Regina, along with Eugenie's husband Fritz. Arthur, for his part, was experiencing a mixture of emotions. While he was of course concerned for his other relatives, he was thankful that his parents were safely in London. Most evenings on his way home from the Regent Palace Hotel, he would pop by to say hello to his parents. His mother would ask him about his day while he played a card game called Tarok (using tarot cards) with his father. Each Friday evening, they would share a Shabbat meal together.

Three weeks after their arrival in London, Rose and Max received a letter from Rose's mother and sister. It stated that they were leaving Vienna by 'train tomorrow' and should arrive in Liverpool the following day at 10.45 in the morning. At first, this sounded like positive news, but then they looked at the date the letter had been sent: 6 July 1939. That was more than a week earlier. Arthur's grandmother and aunt should have arrived by now. What could have happened?

The family's anxiety was heightened still further when they received a letter from Max's brother Josef. He had managed to find a way out of Austria and was now being held in a refugee camp in France. The problem, Josef explained, was that he had lost contact with his wife. 'I don't know where my Elly is and that causes me painful days and sleepless nights,' he wrote in pencil on a page of light-blue cross-hatched paper torn from a notebook. 'Help me, please, help me to find her.' After begging Max to send word of his situation to their mother back in Vienna, he closed with these difficult words: 'I am quite broken through.'

It was at this point, in the middle of family anguish, that Arthur had to start his new job with the BBC. One warm summer's day in 1939 he took a three-hour bus ride from North London to Evesham in Worcestershire. He stepped off at a bus stop just outside of town and headed towards a pair of ornate wrought-iron gates marking the entrance to Wood Norton Hall. After his papers had been checked, he was pointed up the gravel driveway towards the manor house. At first there was nothing to see, the buildings were so well hidden behind trees and bushes. Arthur continued walking; then, around a corner, the house came into view. It was a rambling Victorian manor house, its facade a mixture of red brick, cream stone, and black and white Tudor stripes. On the grounds nearby had been built a number of temporary shacks, painted dark green, presumably additional accommodation for his soon to be co-workers.

Arthur walked up to the tall oak front door, where he had his papers checked again. He was told to hang his hat and coat on a row of pegs along the wall and then go into the main hall and find one of the small tables that filled the room. There were more than twenty men and women already there, all sitting at the tables. From their accents he could tell they were from all over Europe, probably refugees like him. Soon, they were instructed to place a pair of black headphones on their heads, listen and note down anything of interest on the sheets of paper laying on the table. It took a moment for his ears to adjust, to block out the crackle and other background noise; then he realised he was hearing the familiar sound of German radio. Eight hours later, Arthur and the others were told to put down their headphones and summarise what they had heard. This report would be sent to London. Later that evening, after having dinner at the canteen, Arthur was shown to his room, located in an outbuilding not far from the main house. He was now working for the BBC Overseas Intelligence Department.

The next morning, Arthur turned up for his shift and, as the day before, spent eight hours listening to German radio. He followed the same routine the next day, and the day after that. He put the headphones on in the morning and then, with few breaks in between, took them off in the evening. There was a report of an attack by Poles against a railway station in Upper Silesia. A Spanish newspaper story that viewed Hitler as peaceful in his intentions. A notice that German citizens must black out their windows. After a while, it all blended together. It was hard to remember what day it was.

Occasionally, however, it was hard to forget. At 2 a.m. on 4 September 1939, Arthur was tuned in to Zeesen radio, a station that broadcast on long wave to the entire German nation. Just a few hours earlier, Neville Chamberlain had declared war on Germany following their invasion of Poland. This was the Nazis' official response. 'The war party in England has gained superiority and plunged Britain into War,' read the presenter in German. 'As twenty-five years ago, the argument was used that there was no intention whatever to destroy the German people, just its regime. Then they said that they were opposing one man, and nevertheless England inflicted a hunger blockade upon innocent women and children. Today England betrays Europe.'

Over the next few weeks, Arthur continued to monitor German radio broadcasts. This changed when a supervisor learned that he could speak other languages, and soon he was monitoring Italian and French radio as well as German. A few months later, he was invited to provide commentary to BBC radio programmes broadcast from Wood Norton. 'I loved the work,' Arthur later recalled, 'and plunged into it with great zest, intent on mastering the job and improving my English by concentrated reading.'

Early in the morning of 15 May 1940, while Arthur was still asleep in Evesham after a late night listening to German radio, his parents experienced a shock in North London. There was a knock on the front door. When Max went to answer it, he was surprised to see a uniformed police officer on the doorstep. Arthur's father was told to pack an overnight bag and report immediately to the local police station. When he checked in a few hours later, he was instructed that he was to be held until further notice. This followed Prime Minister Winston Churchill's policy of rounding up all potential 'enemy aliens', resulting in more than 8,000 Austrians and Germans living in Britain being interned, most of whom were Jewish refugees. The irony that Max was being held because of the nationality of his birth, even though he was the victim of Nazi persecution, was not lost on the Weidenfelds.

The family was now split up. Arthur remained working for the BBC in Wood Norton, Rosa was by herself at the flat in London, while Max was shunted from one English internment camp to the next, ending up on the Isle of Man. Arthur was worried about his father. Having escaped custody in Nazi Austria less than twelve months earlier, he was now being incarcerated in Britain, the adopted country where he had sought refuge.

Four months later, on 10 September 1940, Max was released from internment, and returned to be with Rosa. The experience had been difficult for the former insurance salesman from Vienna. What confidence he had built up since his arrival in England was all but lost. 'My parents were now the innocent babes,' Arthur later said. 'I became their guardian and provider.'

In March 1941, Rosa received a letter from her sister Eugenie. She and her husband had managed to obtain a visa to enter the United States. They were now living in Cambridge, Massachusetts. Their sister Regina had escaped to Switzerland, where she was convalescing in a sanatorium. Meanwhile, their mother Laura was still in Vienna. Eugenie said that she had recently received three letters from their mother, who reported that 'she is keeping quite well'. It was still not clear why Laura and Regina's attempt to leave Vienna had failed two years before. Now that they were in America, Eugenie continued, she could, 'thank the Lord', help their mother by sponsoring her emigration. She had signed the necessary papers and sent these off to Vienna. The next problem was obtaining a ticket. She knew that Rosa and Max didn't have much money, but luckily she had saved up and, if she had to, she would sell her wedding ring. 'The feeling to help her is worth everything,' she wrote.

But as the days went by, no more letters came from Rosa's mother. Nor was there any communication from Max's mother, Adele. There were no last-minute calls from either of Arthur's grandmothers that they would soon be arriving in Liverpool, London or New York. There was only a worrying silence.

In the late summer of 1941, two years and many thousands of hours of listening later, Arthur Weidenfeld was transferred to London to work as a correspondent and commentator for several BBC radio programmes. He now helped produce more than twenty current affairs shows a week, each of these no more than five minutes in length. Sometimes he was asked to speak on air, including the time he was asked to recite a speech given by Hitler, in the voice of the Führer, as the producers could not locate the original audio recording. According to contemporary accounts, he was an excellent mimic.

One day, before going live on air, a pipe-smoking producer told him that 'Arthur' was too difficult a word to say on the radio. Did he perhaps have a middle name? From this point forward, the young man from Vienna went by the name for which he became so widely known: George Weidenfeld.

Life in London was very different from what it had been at Wood Norton with its manicured lawns and bucolic pastoral views. Much of the city was in chaos following months of devastating air raids. Buildings had collapsed, rubble filled the streets. George encountered people who for so long had been gripped by fear having endured the horror of daily attacks. At their peak the previous winter, more than 300 firebombs had been dropped per minute, killing more than 25,000 people and injuring about the same number. And while the sound of sirens wailing was now rare, George carried a gas mask everywhere he went and was always aware of the location of the nearest bomb shelter in case the alarm was raised.

Meanwhile, from the newspapers which he read assiduously each morning, George kept up to date with the latest developments overseas. Germany had overrun most of Western Europe. Yugoslavia had surrendered to the Nazis and British forces had retreated from Greece to Egypt. Then, in a dramatic twist, Germany in June 1941 had invaded its former ally the Soviet Union, provoking Stalin to announce a 'scorched-earth policy in response', escalating the global conflict. The United States was yet to enter the war; the Japanese attack on Pearl Harbor was still six months away. In a radio broadcast that was transmitted around the world, Winston Churchill asked that America show its support by sending arms to Great Britain. 'Give us the tools,' the prime minister boomed in his whiskey- and cigar-coarsened voice, 'and we will finish the job.'

Despite George being back in London, there were no more games of Tarok or comforting Shabbat dinners with his parents, for Max and Rosa were now living in Stroud, Gloucestershire, away from the danger and chaos of London. They went back to communicating by letter. George told them that he was doing a 'brilliant' job at the BBC, but didn't feel that he 'fit in'. By return, Max informed his son that he had found a position teaching classics at the town's secondary school. Rosa was giving piano lessons to local children, while keeping house, doing the shopping, cooking, cleaning, washing, and writing letters to her mother in Austria. It had been four months since anyone had heard from her. It had been even longer since word had come back about Max's mother.

Through his work at the BBC, George's social circle widened. He had lunch regularly with George Orwell and shared office space with the writers Norman Collins, Edmund Blunden and William Empson, all of whom were attached to the Overseas Service. He worked with the Oxford academics Richard Crossman and Patrick Gordon Walker, both of whom would later become members of a Labour cabinet. He met exiled politicians from Norway, the Netherlands, Czechoslovakia, Yugoslavia and Free France, and from these contacts he was introduced to still more interesting people. Through General de Gaulle, for instance, he met the painter Feliks Topolski and the philosopher Raymond Aron. And so, George's network grew and grew.

When he was not occupied by his duties at the BBC or checking in with his parents, George began work on a book idea. An avid reader since a boy, he wanted to share what he had learned while working at the BBC. His idea was to try and answer the following question: how was it possible in such an advanced culture as

Germany that a right-wing faction had so quickly taken power? The answer, he felt, could be found in two new communication technologies: amplified sound, which the Nazi Party had used so powerfully in the streets and stadia of Berlin and Vienna, and broadcast radio transmission, which is where he spent his working days. George was gripped by the subject, and he could see its potential appeal. This would be more than a story about the Nazi propaganda machine. It would demonstrate that for the first time in human history, anyone with a mastery of sound and speech could galvanise the masses. He was convinced that the book could have a large readership.

Between shifts, over lunch in the canteen or during a cigarette break outside, he told his colleagues about his idea. His excitement was contagious. He found that speaking about the subject with others helped clarify his thinking. He identified new angles, new dimensions to the project. One of those he conversed with was Derrick Sington, a thirty-two-year-old BBC editor who had previously worked for the *Manchester Guardian*. George quickly decided that Sington should help him write the book. First, George hated typing – he didn't have the dexterity for it – while his handwriting was close to illegible. He worked best dictating his thoughts to someone else. Second, and this was important, George was not very patient. Sitting passively listening to the radio all day was one thing – he could zone out from time to time and nobody would be the wiser – but he couldn't imagine sitting down hour after hour writing and rewriting the book. Sington, on the other hand, was an aspiring writer and seemed to have an appetite for just this kind of work. Indeed, four years later he would go on to write a bestselling book about being one of the first British officers to arrive at Belsen concentration camp. Third, and perhaps most significantly, Sington had a deep sympathy for the oppressed, something that George both shared and admired. He anticipated that it would be pleasurable to work with this man.

Sington responded favourably to the invitation so, over the next few weeks, the co-authors worked on the book. George did most of the research, Sington the majority of the writing. Making use of the readily available transcripts of German radio broadcasts, along with copies of Nazi leaflets and other propaganda sheets that had made their way into the BBC archives, they soon had a first draft. They then set about revising the manuscript until they thought it good enough to show to someone. It was at this point that George sent a book summary along with several early chapters to John Murray, one of Britain's most established publishing houses. Founded in 1768, it had published some of the world's greatest writers, including Jane Austen, Arthur Conan Doyle, Charles Darwin, Herman Melville and Lord Byron. Several weeks later, a letter arrived for George. The editors at John Murray would be delighted to publish the book, and they enclosed their standard contract. At the time, it was extremely rare for an author to be represented by a literary agent, so such a direct approach was typical. The contract ran to a single page and detailed the key terms: the transfer of rights from author to publisher, the amount that would be paid and a commitment to publish the book within a defined period of time. George read the contract carefully. Unlike other people who found such matters tedious, he saw great meaning in each of the words on the piece of paper. This was more than a transaction, it was a meeting of minds, a handshake to take action, an agreement to bring a work of art to the wider public. This was his first taste of publishing and he found it thrilling.

Throughout the rest of autumn 1941 the novice authors continued work on their book. They took in comments from the publisher and added their own improvements. When finished, George sent the final manuscript to the offices of John Murray. This was a nerve-wracking endeavour given it was his only copy. Two years into the war, the postal service was struggling to keep up with the enormous volume of correspondence between those stationed abroad and those back home. A few days later, much to George's relief, the publisher sent confirmation of receipt. The text would now have to be typeset and the pages designed and laid out. This would take some time as much of the work was done by hand.

At the end of December a parcel arrived in George's pigeonhole. He removed the brown paper wrapping and, to his great excitement, saw that it contained his book. A book that he had created, one that was forged in his mind. It seemed an impossible idea. There was something else though as well. It was handsome. The publisher had done a fabulous job in designing the book jacket. It was bright yellow with what looked like a black tyre tread running vertically up the left-hand side of the cover. To the right was the title in bold black lettering:

The Goebbels Experiment:
A Study of the Nazi Propaganda Machine

Further down the page were the authors' names: Derrick Sington and Arthur Weidenfeld. He would have preferred it if they had used 'George', the name he was now going by, and that his name had come first – after all, the book had been his idea – but Arthur was his legal first name and he understood that publishers often chose to arrange names alphabetically for co-authored books. Such minor concerns were quickly put aside, and George was soon showing the book off to his colleagues at the BBC.

The book was published on 1 January 1942. To George's dismay, none of the major British newspapers covered its release. There was no great debate about the clever arguments that it made. There was no buzz, hubbub or excitement of any kind. How would the British public know about the book if it was not reviewed in the most popular newspapers? When *The Goebbels Experiment* was published in America the following year, however, it did attract attention. But it was not the kind that George had hoped for. The book received harsh treatment from the critics. Most notable, and perhaps most hurtful, was the *New York Times*, given that it was considered by many to be the American newspaper of record. On 27 February 1943 the reviewer William E. Schlamm wrote that *The Goebbels Experiment* was 'a promising candidate for a prize for the most unnecessary book of the year', adding that the book is 'liberally sprinkled with factual errors' and 'even if the combined talents of Swift and Poe had been added to the team the book would have still remained a collection of trivia'. In short, the book was a 'failure'.

Many years later, George would say that he was proud of *The Goebbels Experiment*. 'Yes, I wrote a book when I was twenty-three years old', he told a Swiss journalist. 'It was, and remains, something like a handbook on Nazi propaganda.' Nevertheless, at the time, George learned some useful lessons about the book industry. He discovered that he loved the process of publication. The coming up with the idea. The debates about how best to organise the material, followed by discussions about structure and tone. The selling of the project to the publisher. Then the making of the deal. What he didn't enjoy at all was the hard work of writing. The sitting down in one place, hour after hour, typing the words and then, most dreaded of all, the editing. Going back over the sentences, over and over. Crossing out, marking up and retyping. To George, this felt like torture. As for the critics, he wasn't sure what was worse, being ignored or being savaged. He wondered if he might be able to carve out a role for himself in the publishing business that didn't involve being an author.

Over the next two years there was no word from, or about, either Laura Eisenstein or Adele Weidenfeld, George's two grandmothers. With every story that appeared in the newspapers – describing the next Nazi atrocity, reporting the latest massacre – their darkest fears deepened. In March 1945, Aunt Eugenie wrote to her sister Rosa saying that she hoped their mother was still alive. Perhaps Laura was being held in Theresienstadt in Czechoslovakia, she said, which she heard was treating Jewish people better than the other camps. This was conjecture. She had no idea where their mother was.

The family continued to write letters to the authorities, asking them to trace the whereabouts of George's two elderly grandmothers. Each inquiry came back with a response, but none contained any substance. The British Red Cross, for instance, was typical. An administrator wrote to the family saying they had no further information and that they had forwarded the inquiry to their sister organisation in Geneva. This disappointing update was softened only slightly by the kindness of the bureaucrat's final sentence, 'sympathising with you in your anxiety'.

In May 1945 the war in Europe came to an end and, one after another, the camps were liberated. As with millions of other families, the Weidenfelds checked and rechecked the lists of survivors and displaced people that were collected and disseminated. The family maintained their hope, writing again and again to the Red Cross and other humanitarian services, asking for the whereabouts of George's grandmothers. In the end, the reports they received were inaccurate, incomplete and unconfirmed. Finally, the family accepted the terrible truth. Although they didn't have official confirmation, George, Max, Rosa and the other members of the family understood the heartbreaking reality: neither grandmother had survived what was now being described as the Holocaust. To make matters worse, they didn't know where or when or how they had died. This meant that it was impossible to visit their burial site. Or mark their death on a certain day. Like millions of other Nazi victims, the two women had simply disappeared.

Before the war, approximately 192,000 Jewish people lived in Austria, the majority residing in Vienna. Within two years, approximately 117,000 Jews would flee Austria. By 1942, there would only be about 7,000 Jewish people still living in the country, most married to non-Jews. In all, more than 64,000 Austrian Jews would be killed in the Holocaust.

Adele Weidenfeld   *Laura Eisenstein*

The family would find out what happened to George's two grandmothers many years later. According to the official records, Rosa's mother's full name was Debora Laura Eisenstein. She was the widow of Moshe. Her maiden name was Goldberg. Her last known address was apartment 2, Lilienbrunngasse 8/11, Vienna. In January 1942, at the age of seventy-seven, she was rounded up along with hundreds of other mostly elderly Jews and for a few days kept in a holding facility in the city. Then, on 6 February, she was marched to the Aspangbahnhof railway station, assigned the number 953, loaded onto a cattle cart, known by the bureaucrats as Transport No. 16, and then, at 5.40 p.m., the train pulled out of Vienna. The transport consisted of approximately 1,000 Jews. The average age of the deportees was fifty-four. Four days later, on 10 February, the train arrived at the Skirotava station in Riga, Latvia. The young and the healthy, around 300 people, were marched through the snow to a nearby ghetto. The remainder, including Rosa's mother, were transferred to waiting buses. Inside the vehicles, Laura Eisenstein and the others were murdered by gas.

The full name for George's other grandmother, Max's mother,

was Jetty Adele Weidenfeld, née Hauptmann. In mid-September 1942 she was taken from her home at 2 Untere Donaustrasse – a ten-minute walk from where Rosa's mother lived – and a few days later, on 23 September, put on Transport IV/2 from Vienna to Theresienstadt camp in Czechoslovakia. She was prisoner number 806. That same day she was put on another train, this time to Treblinka in German-occupied Poland. She was now known as prisoner 1718. Upon arrival in Treblinka, she was forced off the train and marched to the gas chamber. Of the 2,005 people deported from Theresienstadt to the camp that day, one person survived. Adele did not. She was seventy-four years old.

In the months after the war's end, George continued to work at the BBC. He also provided occasional advice to those setting up and overseeing the Nuremberg Trials. He shared his knowledge about German propaganda and, in particular, how the Nazi Party used information to help ordinary Germans to overcome their pangs of conscience. Such input, while interesting, took up little time. What really kept George busy was a new business idea.

Working as a journalist and commentator for the BBC made George feel insecure. He didn't like being told what to do; he wanted to be his own boss. 'I yearned to start something myself,' he later recalled, 'and turn my condition of being English but not of the English into an advantage.' The way forward, he decided, was to start a monthly literary magazine. He wanted it to be the British equivalent of the *New Yorker*. First, he secured commitments from the team who would help him put the magazine together, including fellow émigré André Deutsch; publisher of the *Architectural Review*, Hubert de Cronin Hastings; the academic Harold Laski; as well as the editorial advisor Lance Beales, who had helped Allen Lane launch Penguin Books. He next asked Stephen Spender if he would like to be the magazine's literary editor, but the poet declined as he was soon to leave for the United States. Instead, George hired Philip

Toynbee, the raffish, heavy-drinking former communist, who was well connected to London's bohemian writing community. With commitments from the team in his back pocket, George then set about raising the funds to pay them. Mostly this came from people he had met while working at the BBC, though George secured less money than he had hoped for. Finally, he rented three cramped, decrepit and extremely cheap rooms on the top floor of a building in Manchester Square in central London. The infrastructure for the magazine was now in place.

By this time, George was sharing a flat at 34 Devonshire Place near Regent's Park with three others, including Diana Athill, who had also worked for the BBC during the war. One day, the house-mates were gathered in the kitchen and the question of what to call George's new magazine came up. They brainstormed various ideas, made a list of favourites, crossed out those already taken, and ended up with their agreed choice: *Contact*. At some point during the conversation someone asked George for his central ambition. 'Very simple,' the would-be publisher replied, 'to be a success.'

Success, however, would not prove easy. George soon learned that a major obstacle stood in his way: paper was unavailable for new periodicals because of rationing. The only way forward, he was told, was to distribute the magazine under the umbrella of a book publisher, for book publishers were still allowed unlimited reams of paper. To appear legitimate, Contact Books Limited, as the company was now to be called, would also need to release a few book titles each year.

With the first issue of *Contact* almost ready to be sent to the printer, George urgently looked for a suitable book manuscript. In this he was lucky. Through Lance Beales he was passed a manu-script on the coal industry written by a government statistician. The text was dry, overly long and turgid, but it had one major quality – it was ready to print. This is how it came to be that, in late 1945, the first title to be published by Contact Books Limited was *New Deal for Coal*. Fortuitously, for both the company and its publisher, the author would become Britain's prime minister two decades later – Harold Wilson.

In April 1946, a few months after Wilson's book had been released and following a series of delays, the first issue of *Contact* was published. The cover featured a close-up of the eye of the Labour politician Ernest Bevin, above which was the issue's title *First Spring of Peace*, and below, to make absolutely clear that this was not a magazine, were stamped the words: 'A Contact Book'. Inside, readers found a 1,500-word feature on the British Foreign Office by Richard Crossman, who had produced anti-Nazi propaganda broadcasts for the BBC during the war. There was also a conversation between the British journalist Kingsley Martin and the renowned American radio broadcaster Ed Murrow, along with a piece by the German refugee Sebastian Haffner, provocatively entitled 'The End of Europe?'

A few weeks later, a second issue was released, *Britain Between East and West*. A third issue, *Points of Contact*, was made available more than a month later. There were articles by the Hungarian-born author Arthur Koestler on the Jewish underground and another by the British novelist William Sansom on the new jiving dance craze. A third was penned by Philip Toynbee's father, Arnold, and entitled 'My View on History'.

Sometimes, when the writing offered was outstanding, George and his colleagues didn't have the sense to accept it. This was the case when George Orwell submitted his iconic essay 'Politics and the English Language'. The essay was rejected not because it lacked 'intrinsic excellence', George Weidenfeld later recalled, but because he felt it did not fit in with the magazine's 'purist formula'. He had been, he admitted, 'high handed'.

These first issues of *Contact* received some attention from the media. The *Winnipeg Free Press*, for instance, praised the magazine's physical aspects: 'The layout is interesting, the experiment in combination of type and arrangement succeeds in being both attractive and impressive.' The *Observer* called the text 'first rate' but said the layout was 'fussy' and the typography 'designed to discourage'.

George Orwell – likely remembering that he had been rejected by the magazine – was more critical. In his London Letter column for the American *Partisan Review*, he wrote that *Contact* was 'the kind of streamlined, high-powered, slickly got-up, semi-intellectual magazine which you are familiar with in the USA, now beginning to appear here also'. He added that people might have their suspicions of the magazine because they were uncertain who was providing the funding. Perhaps, he continued, the money might have come from the fraudster and publisher Clarence Hatry (which George strongly denied).

It was a rocky start. Money was short, publication dates were irregular and repeatedly pushed back. Although the magazine was attractive in its stiff, hardbound cover, the pieces inside were frequently inconsistent and rambling. More than 3,000 people subscribed to the magazine, but this was insufficient to cover the costs. Investors came and went. Creditors wrote angry letters demanding payment. If they didn't find money soon, the magazine would fail.

On 2 August 1946, George met Nigel Nicolson for the first time over lunch. The encounter had been arranged by Philip Toynbee, the literary editor at Contact Books. George was wearing a tailored suit. For his part, Nigel arrived wearing the uniform of a captain of the Grenadier Guards; he had not yet been demobilised from the army. They sat around a table at the White Tower restaurant on Percy Street in London. An auspicious place to meet, the White Tower had long been popular with the avant-garde, frequented by the painter Augustus John in the 1930s (when it was called the Eiffel Tower), as well as George Bernard Shaw and the Prince of Wales (before he became Edward VIII). At times, the lunch was gossipy and hilarious. At others, intellectual and exhilarating. They swapped ideas on who were the day's best writers. The pressing problems facing the new government. The Nuremberg war-crimes trials still taking place in Germany.

Nigel Nicolson

George's words fell on fertile ground. Nigel was impressed by George's acute mind and daring, as well as the fact that he was without conceit or snobbishness. The subject of employment was not taken up till the meal's end. Nigel said he would be happy to start as an assistant editor right away and, most importantly, that he might even invest in the enterprise. This would partly be his own funds, he added, but he might be able to persuade family members also to invest. George was delighted and they shook hands.

Before making a commitment, Nicolson felt he had to consult his father, the former politician, diarist and now journalist, Harold Nicolson. Nigel wrote to his father asking for advice. At this time, Harold was in France reporting for the BBC on the Paris Peace Conference. Harold wrote back that he would look into George and would report back. He told his son to listen to the radio. If he mentioned 'Brighton', then his investigations were positive. If he used the word 'Bognor', then Nigel should decline the invitation to work with George. A few days later, Nigel was sitting next to the radio when he heard his father start his broadcast. 'I was thinking the other day of the people of Brighton...' The following day, Nigel let George know he would accept his offer. George was thrilled. Nigel would start on 1 January 1947 on a salary of £500 per year.

Part of the allure of bringing in Nigel Nicolson was the association with his famous parents and the extensive contacts that they brought with them. His mother, Vita Sackville-West, was perhaps even better known than his father. Novelist, columnist and poet, she was the inspiration for the main character in *Orlando*, a novel written by her friend and lover Virginia Woolf. Although Harold had given his tacit approval to Nigel's association with George, his support was not unqualified. 'Although he had met George and liked him,' Nigel later wrote, 'there was a strong streak of anti-Semitism in [Harold's] nature and even more in Vita's [...] Once she said to me that she couldn't understand how I'd ever consented to enter in a partnership with "that Jew".'

Based at the two-room office in Manchester Square, George, Nigel and the rest of the editorial team worked to put out the occasional *Contact* magazine. George's role was to be the troubleshooter, organiser and attractor – persuading people to contribute articles and essays. Harold Macmillan wrote a piece, as did Alan Pryce-Jones, Raymond Mortimer, Cyril Connolly and Nigel's mother Vita. Nigel was the assistant editor and proof-reader, he supervised the layout and artwork. To attract attention to the magazine, new authors and subscriptions, George hosted a series of well-lubricated parties, all paid for out of the company's meagre coffers. Nigel became 'scared of George's extravagance' and his fears were realised when George told him that the firm was rapidly running out of money. Sales were poor. The magazine was in trouble. It was now that Nigel reluctantly agreed to prop up the firm by investing £16,000, nearly all his savings. His mother put in £5,000, and Nigel's brother Ben a further £2,000. As part of the deal, the company's name was changed from Contact Books Ltd to George Weidenfeld & Nicolson Limited. Later, Nigel would write that some people believed that he had been used as a 'respectable front' for George's ambitions. 'It was not quite like that,' he added, 'but almost.'

George's relationship with Nigel soon moved beyond the professional. Not long after the company's financial crisis had been resolved, George introduced Nigel to the actress Olga Davenport, who at the time was married to the economist Nicholas Davenport. She said she was attracted to Nigel and invited him to bed. According to his unpublished private diary, Nigel was 'terrified, being totally ignorant what to do'. So he asked his business partner for advice. They met at the Guards Club in Pall Mall where George told Nigel 'exactly how to behave, how much to drink, the fore-play, the consummation. It was the most extraordinary interview of my life, and how odd he must have thought it.'

Over the next few months, George began talking with Nigel about a new vision for their company: he proposed they move away from the magazine to focus solely on books. The British publishing industry was at this time dominated by firms that had been in operation for decades, particularly John Murray, Macmillan, Allen & Unwin, William Heinemann, Bodley Head and William Collins. In addition, there was Penguin Books, which had demonstrated remarkable dynamism and fresh ideas, particularly during the war when they had sold millions of paperback classics to military personnel posted abroad. Key to Penguin's success had been that their books were affordable and beautifully designed.

George's idea was to publish authors whose voices were normally shunned by mainstream publishers: the mavericks, the scandalous, the subversive. Among these were authors who had recently arrived from Germany, Austria, France, Eastern Europe and beyond, including female writers whose work was rarely promoted, particularly in non-fiction. The old, stuffy British publishers were little interested in such talent. But George was. He believed there was a potentially massive audience to be found.

George also thought there was an opening for a new type of publishing executive. Those leading the established houses tended to shy away from the limelight, preferring to sit behind their Victorian desks in their tweed jackets, drinking coffee, thumbing through manuscripts or reviewing their warehouse stock. Allen Lane, the founder of Penguin and the man widely considered to have revolutionised the industry, was a case in point. According to his biographer, Lane was 'solitary by nature', 'aloof' and a 'loner', a person who 'loathed making speeches', was 'buttoned up', avoided politics at all costs, and shared an equal passion for books as for farming. The very opposite of George Weidenfeld. The Austrian-Jewish refugee had a bottomless appetite for social engagement. He saw books as a way to impact the political discourse. And rather than being stuck behind a desk, his natural habitat was the cafés and restaurants where the artists and intellectuals hung out, the salons and parties where the edgiest writers of the day could be found.

George had big ambitions both for himself and his books. It would take an extraordinary amount of effort, faith, and of course more money to satisfy those ambitions. Although worried about the finances, Nigel Nicolson thought the plan exciting. Later, he would write, 'I had hitched my wagon to George's star and felt no regrets.'

CHAPTER 3

The Hedgehog and the Fox

1953

'I think the most exciting experience in a publisher's life is to make a discovery; the discovery of talent or genius.' – GW

'Dear Isaiah. Just a line to say how much I liked reading your essay on Tolstoy,' George Weidenfeld wrote to the philosopher and Oxford don Isaiah Berlin on 8 December 1952. 'I would indeed be very happy to publish it,' he continued, 'and if you are agreeable, I would try to bring it out by the end of March.'

George was sitting behind his desk at his office located at 7 Cork Street. This was the new headquarters for George Weidenfeld & Nicolson Limited. It was a narrow, four-storey, red-brick building located a short walk from the Burlington Arcade in Mayfair. Unlike today, when Cork Street is filled with glass-fronted galleries featuring breathtakingly expensive art, in the early 1950s, the street was lined with run-down and mostly vacant buildings. Inside number 7, the rooms were dark and cramped, the carpet threadbare and stained. The ground floor was used to store books, ready to be sent out to shops and critics. The first floor was home to George's office (with a view over Cork Street), along with a small room at the back which the publisher hoped to fill with one or two brilliant young editors. The second floor belonged to Mr Killingback, the production manager, responsible for designing the books and preparing the manuscripts for the printers. Given that the text would be printed using hot-metal type and a letterpress, this required great attention to detail and patience. There was little room for error. The third floor was, at least for now, empty. George intended to populate this space with publicity and marketing staff when he could afford them. The top floor, the attic, housed books they had been unable to sell, remainders, boxes of leaflets, press releases, financial reports, and other detritus from the publishing industry.

While the office was drab and unkempt, George was smartly dressed, in a suit, white shirt and tie. He had followed his father's advice not to smoke cigarettes. On the desk in front of him, a glass of apple juice. George rarely drank coffee and never alcohol, again following his father's advice to abstain. Now aged thirty-three, he had retained his youthful looks, though both his face and torso were a little plumper than before.

On the other side of the desk sat George's secretary, Gloria Richardson, efficiently taking down his dictation. His handwriting remained indecipherable. 'If, then, you are agreeable,' he continued in his letter to Isaiah Berlin, 'I shall send you a more detailed letter indicating the format, number of pages and suggested terms.'

Following George's suggestion, the company had shifted its focus from magazine to book publishing. George Weidenfeld & Nicholson Limited had released its first five titles in November 1949. These included Maxim Gorky's *Unrequited Love and Other Stories*, Benito Mussolini's *Memoirs*, Hjalmar Schacht's *Account Settled* and Goethe's *Truth and Fantasy from My Life*. This was the first time these titles had been published in the UK. The fifth book was an original title, *Truth Will Out*, by the foreign correspondent and feminist writer Charlotte Haldane. The books were well received. The *Spectator* said the Mussolini book was a 'revealing picture', while the *Manchester Guardian* called Haldane's book 'lively and exciting'.

On 10 November 1949 the launch party for these books had been held at Brown's Hotel on Dover Street in Mayfair. Through Nigel's contacts and George's networking, they had managed to assemble an impressive array of guests. Those attending ranged from the writers Peter Quennell, Rose Macaulay, W. Somerset Maugham and Raymond Mortimer, to the publisher Hamish Hamilton, the literary agent Spencer Curtis Brown, the businessmen Sir Simon Marks and Israel Sieff, and the politicians Violet Bonham Carter (Liberal) and Richard Crossman (Labour). George Orwell was also present, apparently his criticism of *Contact* now forgotten. Trays of canapés were passed around, along with flutes of champagne. In all, more than a hundred bottles of cheap bubbly had been drunk that night. For his part, George had a glass of milk. The party cost nearly £300, an enormous sum for the fledgling company. When George asked Nigel's father whether he thought this book launch to be a milestone in their progress or another nail in their coffin, Harold Nicolson had answered 'a golden nail'.

In the year following the launch of the company in 1949, George Weidenfeld & Nicolson Limited had released eight more titles, including reprints of European classics by authors such as Baudelaire and Flaubert – which in Britain was unusual at this time – as well as a handful of originals, including books by Alan Ross and Herbert Wendt. None of these had proven commercially successful, which had exacerbated the precariousness of the company's finances. As for Nigel Nicolson himself, he was not involved with the publishing house's day-to-day operations. Instead, his time was now mostly filled with politics, having recently been elected as a Conservative member of parliament for Bournemouth East and Christchurch. In their increasingly heated conversations, Nigel had made it clear to George that neither he nor his family would be investing additional funds.

Things had come to a head on 10 January 1951, with the resignation of the company secretary, Martin Zander. 'I made it abundantly clear that the Company was insolvent,' Zander had written to George Weidenfeld. 'I reminded you that this had been predicted way back in the summer and I said that if a winding-up was to be avoided immediately then steps would have to be taken to obtain finances to cover the loss of the 1950 operations and working capital of 1951.' He had then continued, 'You are the only person who can say whether there are any "reasonable prospects" of the creditors receiving payment. I repeatedly told you that I knew of no such prospects. Unless, therefore, you are reasonably certain of being able to put the finances of the company in order by say, January 31st, my advice to you is to call a meeting of the creditors and to place the fate of the company in their hands.'

By the time George was writing to Isaiah Berlin, in December 1952, the company had published twenty-nine books. The most recent included a Peter Quennell guidebook to Sicily, Harry Sacher's history of the founding of the state of Israel, a volume by Juliana Crow on indoor plants, and a second book by Charlotte Haldane. The company's finances, however, remained precarious. George had persuaded a few more friends to inject small amounts of money into the firm, but George Weidenfeld & Nicolson Limited was once again fast running out of cash. They needed a bestseller, a hit.

The understanding that certain books sold better than others had been around for centuries, going back to titles that attracted huge audiences, such as Goethe's *Sorrows of Young Werther* (1774), Gilbert White's *The Natural History of Selbourne* (1789), and Harriet Beecher Stowe's *Uncle Tom's Cabin* (1852). With the arrival of enforceable copyright laws in the middle of the nineteenth century, publishers were better able to prevent other firms from releasing their books. This spurred an increased interest in which titles sold best. In January 1890, for instance, an advertisement appeared in the *American Bookseller* journal proclaiming that *Confessions of a Nun* by Sister Agatha had sold 32,000 copies in four weeks, adding 'Booksellers do not fail to keep this book. It is the best seller on the market.'

A year later, in October 1891, the British journal *The Bookman* published a list of 'best-selling books'. The editors announced that from this issue they would provide 'statements by representatives and leading booksellers of the volumes they have found most popular during the month (15th to 15th)'. For this first outing, they compiled reports from three shops, including one in Edinburgh and two in London. The top title for this initial list was Rudyard Kipling's *Life's Handicap* published by Macmillan, a collection of stories based in colonial India, which, *The Bookman* reported, sold most in two of the shops and second-most in the third. This was probably the world's first bestseller list.

Four years later, in 1895, the inaugural bestseller list in the United States was launched by an American version of *The Bookman*. In 1912 the New York-based magazine *Publishers Weekly* started releasing its own bestseller list. Twelve months later, this list was divided for the first time into fiction and non-fiction titles. On 12 October 1931 the *New York Times* inaugurated its own bestseller list. The information had been gathered from four of the city's booksellers but was buried halfway down the paper's Book Notes section and given little fanfare. Top of their fiction list was *The Ten Commandments* by Warwick Deeping. The non-fiction books were headed by *Ellen Terry & Bernard Shaw: A Correspondence*. By 30 November the *New York Times* list had been given its own title – 'Best Sellers Here and Elsewhere' – and reports were taken from Detroit, Chicago, San Francisco and other cities around the country. By the time George Weidenfeld & Nicolson Limited entered publishing in the late 1940s, the term 'bestseller' was an established concept in both America and Britain.

George had first met Isaiah Berlin just after the war. Both were Jewish European refugees – George from Vienna, Austria, Isaiah Berlin from Riga, Russia (now Latvia). They enjoyed a common cultural background, as well as an appreciation for intellectual discourse and the collecting and sharing of gossip. Since their first meeting, they had worked on a number of projects, but never a

Isaiah Berlin

book. In 1951, Berlin's essay on Tolstoy had been printed in shorter form in *Oxford Slavonic Papers*, an obscure academic journal. The elegance of the writing and the originality of thought had caught George's eye. It was a lot to gamble on, which is why in his letter to Isaiah Berlin, George also suggested that the number of footnotes be dramatically cut down. For, to make a profit, a publisher had to pay for the cost of printing which, inevitably, was higher the more pages the book contained. To generate significant income, the book would also require a team working hard behind it – editors, designers, marketing professionals, publicists – which George still didn't have. He needed more staff, which required more money, which George had even less of. Yet if the publisher had one thing, it was belief. Belief in his vision, and belief that he could persuade others to come along with him.

Having completed his letter to Isaiah Berlin, George asked his secretary to send it off. All he could do now was wait and see whether the philosopher could transform his essay into a publishable book and, just maybe, a bestseller.

*

Not long after sending his letter to Isaiah Berlin, George attended a dinner party and was seated next to an elegant woman named Elizabeth Pakenham. Up till now, she was known partly for losing a series of parliamentary elections, and partly for being married to Frank Pakenham, First Lord of the Admiralty. Soon they were talking about publishing and George explained that he was building a list of up-and-coming authors and that his editorial department needed 'a bright young girl'. She also needed to speak several languages fluently, he added, and be good with people, plus shorthand and typing. 'Look no further,' Elizabeth Pakenham replied and recommended her daughter, Antonia, who had just graduated from Oxford. Persuaded by the mother's confidence, though surprised she didn't mention anyone else except her daughter, George said he would like to meet the prospective candidate.

A few days later, Antonia joined George for lunch. To the young Oxford graduate, the publisher looked like the French king Louis XVI with 'enormous rolling eyes, like gooseberries', and while he was in his thirties, he 'looked no particular age'. Over lunch they talked about the naval review that had recently taken place following the coronation of Elizabeth II. There was no discussion of her taking up a possible editorial position and Antonia didn't pluck up the courage to ask. A few weeks later she called the publishing house to see if a job might be available. 'My name is Antonia Pakenham and I wondered...' Before she could finish her sentence, George's secretary Gloria said, 'You'd better come in on Monday.' Clearly, they had been waiting for her to call.

On 14 September 1953, Antonia started with Weidenfeld & Nicolson – by now the company was still officially titled George Weidenfeld & Nicolson Limited, though people generally referred to it without the 'George'. Arriving the same day was Nicholas Thompson, an old Etonian who had also just graduated from Oxford and had been taken on as editorial director. A typical day at the small publishing company started at ten in the morning.

The men wore suits and ties, the women plain skirts, blouses and high heels. Antonia was envious of Gloria, who she considered sophisticated. 'She was a very attractive woman,' she later recalled, 'and she certainly attracted people in the office.' George was a blur of activity. When he was in the office, he was usually on the phone at his desk, an ordinary black rotary Bakelite device, speaking different languages, dictating letters to Gloria. Around 12.30 he would sweep out to lunch with a prospective author, book critic or cultural grandee. Because George never drank alcohol, these were not boozy affairs, at least for him. He would then sweep back around 3.30 p.m., returning excitedly to announce that he had secured a thrilling book commission, or a significant commitment to review one of their books, or an invitation to a VIP dinner or book launch by a hot author, or some other fabulous soirée.

Given the small staff, each employee held multiple roles. George handled acquisitions, along with contract negotiations, finances and foreign sales. Nicholas Thompson was responsible for editing, publicity and personnel. Along with her editorial work, Antonia also had to prepare and place advertisements in newspapers and magazines. If the telephone rang, which it often did, it was answered with a crisp 'Regent 322'. If a cable was received, it was sent to 'NICOBAR London'. Things did not always go smoothly for the new recruits. One day Antonia received a call at home from George. 'You've done it again,' he said, albeit sweetly and without recrimination, 'you've spelled Nicolson with an H.'

Not all of Antonia's acquaintances were happy about her working for an Austrian-Jewish refugee. 'Isn't it sometimes, well ... difficult working with George Weidenfeld?' they might ask. Such anti-Semitism baffled her and made her angry. The publisher, according to Antonia and others who worked for him at this time, was a kind boss. Never cross. That is not to say his patience was never tried. One day, for instance, Sonia Orwell (who also now worked at the company and was George Orwell's wife) reported that she had seen

Antonia walk into the Academy cinema with her boyfriend in the middle of a workday. When George called Antonia in to see him, he had a pained look on his face. He kept trying to persuade her to hone her story. 'It was a foreign film, wasn't it?' he suggested, 'you needed to see it for work?' Finally, she picked up the clue and confirmed that her outing had been publishing-related.

Sometimes, Antonia would be sent out to help authors edit their books. On one such afternoon, George asked her to visit Feliks Topolski, the Polish-born expressionist painter, at his artist's studio near Waterloo Bridge. When she arrived, she saw that the studio was filled with easels, brushes and other painting paraphernalia. There were also several cushions scattered around the room. After working on the book for a while, the painter, who was in his forties, asked if she would like to lie down with him. She said, 'Absolutely no.' To which he replied, 'No? What a pity. George Weidenfeld said you would.' She gathered her belongings and hurried out of the studio. When she returned to the office, she couldn't pluck up the courage to ask George if the painter had spoken the truth.

Throughout the autumn of 1953, the company focused their efforts on their lead new title: Isaiah Berlin's essay on Tolstoy. One of the most pressing issues they faced was what to call it. There had been heated discussions back and forth. Berlin proposed *Count Tolstoy and Count de Maistre*, or perhaps better, *Tolstoy's View of History*. Both of these had struck George as too academic and therefore unappealing to a general reader, the market he hoped to target. Berlin came back with *Tolstoy and the Science of History*. Again, George said no. Finally, a totally different approach was proposed. George suggested they call the book *The Hedgehog and the Fox*. Berlin approved. George's idea for the title came from a question that Berlin had posed at the very start of his essay: Which kind of person are you: a hedgehog or a fox? The former, he suggested, were people who were single-minded, to the point of obsession. The latter were more open-minded, able to go with the flow. Tolstoy for example, he said, presented himself as a hedgehog but was really a fox.

The key to the book's success, at least in George's mind, was timing. For many years now the publishing calendar was rigidly set. The highest volume of book sales accrued between mid-September and Christmas. If *Hedgehog*, as it was now being called within the office, was to save the company, it had to be sent to the printer in early September. With just days to go, Berlin was sent copies of the typeset manuscript along with a note from George. 'I really hate to trouble [you] about the Tolstoy proofs,' wrote the publisher, 'but do you think I could have them by the end of this week as the printer is very concerned and it would be a pity to miss the Autumn season by a hair's breath.' Four days later, the corrected proofs were returned to Cork Street, confirmed by a cable sent from a grateful publisher: 'Proofs received regards George.' Shortly after, the book was sent to the printer.

On 16 November 1953 the book was published. George sent another cable to Isaiah Berlin to congratulate him. On 17 November the publisher received a reply from the author. 'Thank you for your telegram; I await the long gossipy letter with unconcealed impatience, and I tremble about THE HEDGE HOG's fate.' The next day, George provided an update. 'My Dear Isaiah. I feel very guilty at not having written to you before.' Then continuing, 'Your book came out on Monday with two magnificent reviews preceding and coinciding with publication – Schlesinger's piece is in [the magazine] Encounter No.2 and Noel Annan's review on the [BBC] Third Programme.' But Isaiah Berlin, like so many authors, remained nervous. On 5 December he wrote again. 'Dear George. Do write. And do send me some reviews – all I hear is distant fragments of rumours of what has been said.'

On 9 December, George wrote once more, this time attaching reviews. 'You will also be pleased to hear that sales have been good,' he began. 'We sold over 1,000 copies in the first three weeks, and shall almost certainly have to reprint before spring.' Typical of the positive reviews was the one published in *The Times*. 'The intellectual brilliance of Mr Berlin's performance is to be admired,' it gushed. The book was 'immensely impressive'. George had exactly what he had been looking for: a bestseller. What made the book so desirable was the new parlour game that it created. At dinner tables across the country, guests were now asking each other, 'Are you a hedgehog or a fox?' The book had become that very rare thing, a crossover phenomenon, a fad.

Other books on the publisher's Autumn 1953/Spring 1954 list also attracted attention. One of these was written by a little-known science-fiction writer who had been first published in America. His name was Isaac Asimov, and the book was called *Foundation*. Over time, this story would prove a huge success, though in the short term its publication brought in little revenue. Also noteworthy were two books by former Nazis. It was extremely rare at this time, less than a decade since the war's end, for English-language publishers to give a platform to senior Nazis. Publishing giants in America (Knopf, Henry Holt and Random House) and in Britain (John Murray, Heinemann and William Collins) were worried about being seen as sympathetic with the enemy's appalling murderous actions and their toxic ideology. George didn't believe this was a problem as long as the books were set in context. Included in Weidenfeld & Nicolson's 1953/1954 catalogue, therefore, was *Hitler's Table Talk*, a series of monologues given by the Führer. The book was edited by the Oxford academic Hugh Trevor-Roper, who added an introduction, providing context and historical background. *Hitler's Table Talk* sold well. Also in the catalogue was *The Secret Front: The Story of Nazi Political Espionage* by Wilhelm Hoettl, which provided an insight into the German secret service. This book featured an introduction by Ian Colvin, who had been a journalist in Berlin before being expelled by the Nazis. Four years after Nigel Nicolson had given up his savings to help kick-start the company, Weidenfeld & Nicolson was beginning to make a name for itself.

Over the next half-century, George Weidenfeld and Isaiah Berlin would continue to exchange letters. In one of these, the publisher acknowledged the philosopher's role in his early success. 'I shall never forget that you backed, and in some measures identified yourself with us,' he wrote to Berlin, 'at a time when our publishing programme was hardly existent, and our organisation untried.'

Isaiah Berlin returned the favour when, many years later, he submitted a personal note to an anthology compiled for George's seventieth birthday. It is worth quoting in full:

> George's love of life, his eager and unquenchable curiosity, his exuberant sense of pleasure and capacity for giving it to others (together with a scintillating irony free from all rancour, bitterness, intolerance or self-righteousness) is a source of vitality without parallel in a society in some need of it. He is one of the sharpest social observers of his time with a marvellous, highly exhilarating sense of social farce; indeed, his sense of the ridiculous at its most inspired is a genuine expression of creative imagination. With all this he has a firm sense of reality, and is deceived neither about others nor about himself. His immense social success has not entailed a compromise with his basic loyalties which have remained unaltered despite all temptation during his rise to fame and fortune. Gaiety, rich social fantasy, acute social realism, and love of life may not be everything; but they are a very great deal.

In private, however, Isaiah Berlin – who was known for his scathing caricatures – presented a different portrait of the publisher. 'Why, in Aristotle's sense has his personality no weight, only lightness?' he asked the philosopher Bernard Williams about George Weidenfeld, continuing 'Is there a total absence of a moral centre?' Later, to the Israeli diplomat Yaacov Herzog, Berlin described George as having 'no genuine moral substance' and 'a total lack of anything resembling integrity or moral steadfastness'. Again, to the American magazine editor Leon Wieseltier, 'He is quite an interesting man, but integrity is not, perhaps, his central quality – and social life and life are synonymous for him.' To Rowland Burdon-Muller, connoisseur of the arts, 'I always enjoy meeting George W: always. But I feel a little like a respectable person with an addiction to bordels: or the old Folies Bergères: or pornography. Pleasure, yes, but with some slight shame to follow.' And finally, to Svetlana (known as 'Lana') Peters, daughter of Joseph Stalin, 'While some authors are very pleased with him others complain that he promises more than he can deliver – not out of a conscious desire to deceive, but because his thoughts move on to something else, he forgets what he has promised and when reminded seeks to escape.'

Was Isaiah Berlin being sincere when he submitted his contribution to George's birthday book? Or perhaps he was being more honest when writing privately to his friends? Either way, it is likely that George was aware of the two-facedness, making him not only cautious about the philosopher, but raising questions about what others said about him behind his back.

While *The Hedgehog and the Fox* had proved a commercial triumph, it was not sufficient to rescue the company's fortunes. Impatient for success, George thought hard about how to quickly generate income. Should he bring English translations of contemporary European writers to the insular British public, such as Vladimir Dedijer, Erich Kästner, Lali Horstmann and Jorge Luis Borges? Perhaps it was best to focus on biographies and memoirs? What about high-quality volumes of pictures by famous photographers such as Cecil Beaton? In each of these areas he tried his hand and was commended by the critics, but the company finances were not greatly improved.

George started thinking about a new strategy. Weidenfeld & Nicolson would release a series of books in cooperation with a number of foreign houses. These titles would require considerable investment in colour printing, picture research and elaborate production. The publishers would share the costs and therefore reduce the risks. The idea had been deployed before by those who produced coffee-table books about nature and art. George now brought this into the fields of biography, history and memoir. The approach, which was later called a 'co-edition', would prove profitable for the company, and Weidenfeld & Nicolson would be lauded for being a pioneer in the field. However, when the concept was launched in the mid-1950s, it added a further strain to the resources of the young firm. By the summer of 1956, Weidenfeld & Nicolson was yet again facing financial catastrophe. The accountants told George and Nigel that they would soon be unable to pay the salaries of their forty employees, let alone the printers they would require for their next books. They desperately needed further investment. To have a hope of pulling this off, they had to make the company attractive. This meant diluting the existing shareholders' equity.

On 8 August 1956, George had lunch with Nigel Nicolson and two advisors at the Connaught Hotel in Mayfair. This was at the height of the Suez Crisis, and the first part of the lunch was spent discussing the news. Under Prime Minister Anthony Eden, the government had agreed to freeze Egypt's financial assets in British banks. Willie Williams, the American sprinter, had just broken the men's 100 metres record, finishing in 10.1 seconds. A terrorist explosion in Cali, Colombia, had killed more than a thousand people. Eventually George, Nigel and their advisors got around to the topic at hand. George had found three possible investors. In return for investing £13,000 each, Nicholas Thompson (editorial director at Weidenfeld & Nicolson) and Anthony Marecco (who had been a junior counsel during the Nuremberg Trials) would receive 13,000 shares. Patrick Barrington, a short-term partner in the company, would invest £6,500, receiving the equivalent in shares. George, who would invest nothing, would receive 16,000 shares. Nigel's older brother, Ben Nicolson, would receive 2,000 shares for his previous investment of £2,000, while Vita's investment of £5,000 would be considered a loan to be paid back with interest over time. The condition, however, was that Nigel's original investment of £16,000 would be wiped clean.

As part of the restructuring, a parent company was created, called Weidenfeld Holdings Limited, which would own various subsidiaries. The next company down the hierarchy was Weidenfeld (Publishing) Limited. This owned a variety of entities including George Weidenfeld & Nicolson Limited, which would produce the general fiction and non-fiction books, and Weidenfeld & Nicolson (Educational) Limited, which would focus on academic books. To the public, the company was generally known as 'Weidenfeld & Nicolson'.

When Nigel strongly protested that this restructuring resulted in his investment being totally lost while George was receiving shares for nothing, his partner was shocked. 'I remember the look of utter anguish that passed over George's face as I said this,' Nigel later recorded in his unpublished private memoirs. The two advisors then pointed out that without George the company had no hope of success and would be unable to attract investment. Finally, as a face-saving exercise, Nigel proposed they pay him one penny for every share he received. Even this was rejected. Nigel was next told he would not even sit on the board of the new parent company, Weidenfeld Holdings Limited, though he would remain a director of its subsidiary, Weidenfeld (Publishing) Limited. Eventually Nigel agreed to the deal. 'It was an utter humiliation,' he later wrote. He felt 'embarrassed' and 'ashamed', not even telling his wife when he returned home that evening.

'People say, I know, that George behaved badly to me,' Nigel later wrote in his memoirs, 'but that's an accusation I have never levelled against him. I gave him too little help, through my incapacity in business matters, and a lack of editorial imagination and persuasive gifts. He was a brilliant man, and has remained a faithful friend, and my name remained linked with his in the most successful publishing firm to be founded since the Second World War.'

Nigel added one further thought on the matter. He wrote that George promised he would 'leave to my children a sum of money in his will which presumably amounts to the £16,000 which I'd lost'. Nigel was hopeful that George would keep this promise.

CHAPTER 4

A Young Girl's Touch

1956

'Our industry has not advanced very far in measuring,
appraising, predicting what the public wants.' – GW

Romance had long been an important part of George's life. A couple of early loves during his teenage years were followed by his first sexual encounter at the age of seventeen when, in his words, he was 'seduced' by a thirty-eight-year-old married woman from Milan. The rate of encounters appeared to increase following his arrival in London. By 1948, George would boast to his friend and housemate Diana Athill that he had had numerous 'conquests'. He told another close friend that when he could not sleep, rather than counting sheep, he would list the names of his sexual partners. Yet, despite such licentiousness, by the summer of 1951, he decided to settle down.

He had first met members of the Marks and Sieff family – owners of the Marks & Spencer retail empire – before the war. In the years since, he had spent more time with them, enjoying the warmth and mutual reliance of this Jewish clan. So it was that when Teddy Sieff heard that George planned a visit to Paris, he suggested the publisher look up his daughter Jane, then studying at the Sorbonne. For their first date, George and Jane met at the Palais Garnier to see the opera *Don Giovanni*. Over the next days, they went out a few more times. He liked her. 'She was refreshingly unspoilt,' he later recalled, 'and had a contagious enthusiasm for everything French.'

A few days later, George returned to England, promising to stay in touch.

Then, on 11 September 1951, the Sieff family experienced a tragedy: Jane's mother Maisie, long prone to depression, committed suicide. Jane returned to London to be with her father and, in the weeks after, she spent increasing amounts of time with George. They drew even closer. On 11 December, exactly three months after her mother's death, Jane's engagement to George was announced in *The Times*. They were married at the Bayswater synagogue on Petersburg Place in London on 31 January 1952. George was thirty-two years old; Jane was just twenty. Nigel Nicolson was the best man. Pictures of the smiling newlyweds were featured on the front page of the *Birmingham Gazette* and other newspapers across the country. It was, in many ways, an odd pairing. While he was gregarious, well-travelled and loved to socialise, she had seen little of life and lacked confidence. She was also still in grief. George and Jane did, however, share a passion for intelligent conversation and an appreciation for art and creativity.

Jane Sieff and George Weidenfeld

Soon after the wedding, the couple moved into the five-storey, cream-coloured Georgian house at 11 Chester Square near Buckingham Palace, purchased with money from Jane's family. This was a massive improvement on the publisher's previous digs, the flat-share on Devonshire Place.

Many commented that George's marriage to Jane was advantageous for him, both socially and financially. This proved correct. Through Jane's family, George gained entry to the inner circles of the British Jewish community, and from Jane's father he received an ongoing contract to publish a series of books which would be sold exclusively in the Marks & Spencer shops, which underwrote Weidenfeld & Nicolson's cash-flow needs. For George, the union provided one other benefit. As an only child, with just one first cousin, he came from a small family. Marrying into the Sieffs, George would later say, provided him with a profound sense of belonging and security. He enjoyed meeting Jane's uncles, aunts, cousins and numerous other relatives. More than this, while he had no need to attend synagogue or take part in the religious events still important to his parents – Passover, Hanukkah, the breaking of the fast at the end of Yom Kippur – George loved feeling that he belonged to a Jewish clan.

The relationship with Jane seemed to have an impact on George's personality. 'You have changed a lot since your marriage,' wrote Nigel Nicolson on 29 October 1952, nine months after the wedding. 'Warmer, kinder, more gentle, less impetuous.' He then asked George to pass on his 'warmest congratulations' to Jane, adding 'I shall of course say nothing about this.' Apparently, George had told him that his wife was pregnant.

Seven months later, 2 June 1953 – the day of Queen Elizabeth II's coronation – Jane gave birth to a baby girl. They named her Laura, after George's maternal grandmother. She was given two middle names: Miriam, for her great-aunt, and Elizabeth after the sovereign. George was, he later said, 'beside myself with joy'.

George Weidenfeld and Laura

Yet despite Nigel's effusive words and the arrival of the newborn, the marriage was stumbling. While George was fond of his wife, he was either too busy with work or hosting extravagant and noisy social events to express it. 'All this was compounded,' George later confessed, 'by casual infidelities on my part which she was aware of despite my attempt at discretion.' Soon, Jane took her eighteen-month-old daughter and moved in with her father. Two years later, she left for Paris with Laura. In 1956, George and Jane were divorced. Not long after that, she remarried.

George remained at the house on Chester Square. He was embarrassed that the wedding which had been so publicly celebrated had now publicly failed. He was anxious that Marks & Spencer would no longer order books from his publishing house, thus losing a major source of income for his business. Most of all, he was devastated to be divorced from the Sieff family clan. George would later tell his daughter that this period, including his next liaison, was the 'worst time of my life'.

*

In the aftermath of his broken marriage to Jane Sieff, George's attention turned to a young writer named Barbara Skelton. He was impressed by her intelligence, thought her a good storyteller and particularly funny. 'She was strikingly good-looking with a honey-coloured complexion,' he recalled, 'with reddish-blonde hair and slightly slit eyes.' He added, 'Her voice was unforgettably distinctive – there was melody in her speech and a faintly accusatory and doubting tone in her questions.' George had just agreed to publish her manuscript, the novel *A Young Girl's Touch*, which would be included in his spring catalogue.

At this time, Barbara was married to Cyril Connolly, another of George's authors. Cyril was perhaps best known for his books *Enemies of Promise* (1938) and *The Unquiet Grave* (1944), as well as for co-founding *Horizon* magazine. Barbara and Cyril's relationship was facing its own difficulties. Cyril informed Barbara that he was having an affair with Caroline Freud, wife of the painter Lucien Freud. 'In that case,' Barbara had replied, 'I shall have to find somebody.' This didn't seem to worry her husband. 'So long as he is a gentleman, I won't mind,' he said. 'Whom do you consider a gentleman?' she asked, 'Weidenfeld?' Cyril thought about this for a moment, then responded, 'Too continental. But so far as a continental Jew can be a gentleman, he fits.' He then added, 'I would prefer him to most people.'

A few days later, Barbara moved into a spare room at George's house on Chester Square, and they consummated their affection. Shortly after that, she confessed to her husband that she was falling in love with the publisher. Realising that his marriage was now in real danger, Cyril said he would stop seeing Caroline Freud, 'I realise it was making you unhappy,' he told her. For her part, Barbara resolved to end things with George. 'But W.,' she later wrote, 'was very tenacious. Whenever I refused to see him, he elicited sympathy and support' from mutual friends, arguing that he was 'rescuing' her from an unhappy marriage.

'Could I really give up W?' Barbara wrote in her diary. 'How is it I can be in love with someone whose podgy hands and doughy pallor intrude like flaws or speckles in an otherwise perfect photograph?' Sensing her conflict, her husband became depressed and grumpy. 'He would like to kill W,' she continued in her diary, 'and it would break his heart if we separated. It would break mine too.' Yet her feelings for George would not go away. She rushed to London 'in a fearful state, haunted by W'. When she arrived at his home, she found him obsessed by mundanities such as the radiator's thermostat setting and what kind of refrigerator he would purchase since the old one had been taken by his ex-wife, along with much of the furniture. Frustrated and confused, she left after ten minutes.

News of the love triangle spread among George's circle. The fact that he was having an affair with the wife of one of his authors, who he considered a friend, and that he was also about to publish her novel, was frequently remarked upon. The high-powered and celebrity-rich social set they moved in was divided, splitting partly for Cyril and partly for George. There seemed to be little sympathy for Barbara. Two people who socialised with Barbara and George were Antonia Pakenham and Hugh Fraser, the Conservative MP who Antonia had recently married. Barbara was generous with her attentions. 'She practised her skills on Hugh,' Fraser later wrote, 'like a pianist who cannot resist an opportunity to try out an instrument in her neighbour's house.'

As for George, he was finding it hard to control his emotions. Although he viewed Barbara as a 'deeply unhappy woman' and 'neurotic', he found her very sexy. A 'madness' now came over him. He wrote letters to her and delivered flowers to her house in the country. He sent urgent cables requesting that they meet. He called her at home and, if Cyril answered, George would hang up. Barbara wrote to him saying telephoning was a 'mistake' and asking that he not do it again. Meanwhile, Cyril, upset and distracted, was

Barbara Skelton

finding it impossible to work on his next book – to be published by George the following year. Barbara was also conflicted. Loyal to her husband, embarrassed by the gossip and the rumours, compelled despite herself. 'When I see George with his new grey overcoat, and with his alert stride and bright brown eyes,' she wrote in her diary, 'I am terribly in love.'

When Cyril was beset by fibroids and admitted to hospital to have them removed, she sat by his side hour after hour. Later, in her diary, she noted that they had spent much of their time discussing her affair with George: 'How he would always be unfaithful; how Jews get so unattractive in middle age.' Cyril compared George to the toreador in Bizet's *Carmen*, only, in this case, 'the lover is a Jewish businessman'. What he didn't say, because there was no need, was that at the end of the opera, the toreador Escamillo's love interest – Barbara in the analogy – is stabbed by his jealous rival Don José and dies.

George now became unrelenting. He sent desperate, begging cables to Barbara. Sometimes three telegrams arrived in one day. Some of these provided updates on the progress of her novel – the proofs were complete, the manuscript had been sent to the printer, the finished copies were on their way – others pleaded with her to return his phone calls. He was madly jealous that Barbara was spending so much time with her convalescing husband. In her diary, she noted that George was 'wildly frustrated and impatiently awaiting our reunion'.

As Barbara began to withdraw, George stepped up his campaign. He asked his new secretary, Anne Bassett, to contact Barbara and share that she had never seen George so smitten before and that, highly unusually, he spoke of Barbara as a 'real woman'. George and Barbara then spent Christmas together at a hotel in Madrid. The publisher was at turns euphoric, 'I love you more than I ever loved anyone else or shall, I think, love anybody,' he declared to her. 'I want you as a person, as a woman, as a wonderful human being and as a wife.' At other times, he was depressed: 'What a miserable, ill-fated pair!' he told her. 'I think I need a month to think everything over,' he continued and asked, 'Suppose I should want another woman! How will you take it?'

They returned to England, each to their own home. Immediately, George sent Barbara a cable begging her to join him that coming weekend, adding that she would be greeted by 'Red roses red carpet a breakfast tray Sunday and real honest love'. He waited for a response, but none came. George told his parents about the tempestuous affair. His father, concerned, asked if the relationship was just based on sex. George tried to explain by saying that Barbara was his Mrs Simpson. His mother Rosa, more of a problem-solver, counselled that if he truly wanted to win Barbara's love, he had to stop giving her mixed messages. He needed to be consistent.

George sent Barbara more telegrams, one after the other, but still she did not reply. Frustrated by her silence, he began telephoning again, but Barbara refused to accept his calls. The publisher's health began to deteriorate. He struggled to get out of bed. He experienced headaches. He lost his appetite. He found it hard to work. By letter, he told Barbara that he was experiencing a physical and mental collapse and that his doctor had given him sedatives. At last, she sent a response:

THINK CAREFULLY NOT HYSTERICALLY AVOID
LATER REGRETS MISSED OPPORTUNITIES
THINKING TOO LOVE BARBARA

One of the 'later regrets' haunting George was that if he was to marry Barbara, she would first have to divorce Cyril. The one sure way to obtain a divorce at this time was for the applicant (in this case Barbara) to admit to cheating on their spouse by providing the name of their lover, or 'co-respondent' (George). If this became public, which it surely would, the shame could damage the publisher's reputation, something that was crucial to his success. After all, George's divorce to Jane Sieff had only just been approved. To be the cause of a second divorce would be a real blot on his character.

Nevertheless, George's 'madness' won out. He had a lawyer draft divorce papers for Barbara, admitting that he was the co-respondent, and signed them. 'I do not want you to go back to Cyril,' he told Barbara by phone, 'I am not afraid of the divorce scandal. Whatever happens will happen! I love you and want you.' But she resisted. He called again and again, saying that he had to see her, that he had some urgent business to discuss about her soon-to-be-released novel. Again, she refused to meet him. Instead, she flew to Tangiers in Morocco where she joined her husband, Cyril. Telegrams followed. George continued his campaign of persuasion, apologising for his behaviour and asking her to return to London. 'Your words become meaningless,' she cabled back, 'your pleas unconvincing.' Then, by mail, a letter arrived on official Weidenfeld & Nicolson letterhead inviting her to work at the firm as an editorial associate on a salary of £500 per year, a not inconsiderable sum. She accepted the offer, but said she would carry out her duties from Morocco and suggested he send her some manuscripts to read.

Still, George persisted. There were more letters, more cables. Barbara finally relented. In March 1956 she flew to Gibraltar where she met him. They spent several days and nights together at a hotel. Later, when she saw Cyril, he said that he was 'tired of being the Comic Cuckold'. She said that she was also unhappy and encouraged him to divorce her. It was now that Barbara moved back in with George at Chester Square. She felt pleased to be living together, but disliked the interior decoration. 'The gaudy, paisley wallpaper lining the stairs had been hung upside down,' she wrote, 'he had filled his house with ugly furniture, a set of twelve highly polished fake Victorian dining chairs and a lot of Peter Jones occasional tables.' For his part, George was disappointed in his lover's skills as a hostess. 'She wasn't particularly interested in my work or in being a striver,' he later recalled. 'She did not share my interest in business.' Particularly irksome for George, Barbara wore tennis shoes to his publisher's dinner parties, or would get up and leave during the middle of a meal without explanation. For her part, Barbara was disgusted by George's personal habits. One night, she sat next to him in bed as 'He sat about rubbing sweat from his brow with an anguished expression on his face, the lips sucked in a receding point and the nose a distinguished beak.' She had brought food with her and offered it to him. This 'he snatched from my hand without showing any appreciation, all the time saying, "Where's this?" or "Where's that?" with his mouth full before I'd had time to eat'.

Over the next twelve months, Barbara went back and forth between Cyril and George. She had secret meetings with the publisher, during which he talked of marriage. 'I am terrified of being seen,' she wrote in her diary, 'yet I do not have the courage to tell W. that I do not want to marry now.' By this point, George had put on more weight, no longer the svelte figure of his youth. In her journal, Barbara noted that he had become concerned about his appearance. 'Never stops staring at himself naked in the mirror, half in wonder, half in doubt.' At one point, he turned to her and said, 'I'm thinner, don't you think?'

Finally, the court papers went through and Barbara was divorced. Soon after, her novel A Young Girl's Touch, about the social adventures of a female civil servant during the Second World War, was published by Weidenfeld & Nicolson. Ian Fleming, the creator of James Bond, referred to its release in his Atticus column, though he appeared more excited by Barbara's 'slim figure' and her red convertible Sunbeam Talbot 'flashing through the meadowsweet round a blind corner' than the book itself. Tatler was more positive, saying that Barbara 'sustains the mood of the story – which is not totally shocking – extremely well', though adding that 'her grammar is odd'. The rest of the press remained mainly silent. 'Not nearly as bad as I thought it would be,' she noted sourly in her diary.

George and Barbara were married in August 1956. The wedding took place at Caxton Hall, a red-brick registry office on the corner of Palmer Street in Westminster frequented by celebrities and high society. George's secretary Ann Bassett was the witness.

The marriage was a disaster. Barbara was repelled by George's 'distressed bird-face [...] eyes bulging while he chewed at his lower lip'. He came to view her as 'a difficult person who couldn't bear to see others happy'. She became tired of his busy schedule, he of her constant disappointment. Barbara later recalled a conversation from this time. 'You want to ruin me,' George sniped, 'destroy me. Everyone warned me!' To which she replied, 'Why did you break up my marriage then...?' He responded, 'Everyone said you were unhappy...' She shot back, 'I was not unhappy.' George replied, 'Then why didn't you stay with your husband...?' To this Barbara said, simply, 'Because I was in love with you.'

They stopped sharing a bed. They stopped having dinners together. At one point, George's father came by. George said he was worried about the financial stability of the company. Then, looking at Barbara, he added, 'God knows what sort of year it's going to be.' 'Mustn't give up hope,' advised Max, adding that his son needed to 'do the best you can.' Later, George told Barbara that he felt isolated around her. This was his deepest fear.

While George's private life was consuming, he continued to have energy for his publishing firm. Perhaps of all the books he released at this time, the one that had the greatest impact, at least for the publisher, was written by a little-known Harvard academic named Henry Kissinger.

Like George, Henry Kissinger was Jewish, and had experienced Nazi terror in Europe, in his case Germany. In 1938 his family had fled overseas, briefly to London. Kissinger had then settled in New York, worked for American intelligence during the Second World War, and was now a member of the faculty in the Department of Government at Harvard University. They first met at a lunch in London, when Kissinger was trying to win friends and funds for an international summer school. After the meal was over, George had asked, 'Are you, by any chance, working on a book that we could publish?' Kissinger replied, 'As a matter of fact I have a manuscript in my briefcase; it hasn't yet found an American publisher.' The text was based on his doctoral thesis, completed in 1954. Later, George learned that it had been turned down by ten American publishing houses.

Back home, George sat down and read Kissinger's text. It told the story of Klemens von Metternich, the Austrian Empire's foreign minister in the period following the Napoleonic Wars. Although the history would be unfamiliar to most British readers, the publisher was impressed by the acuteness of the analysis and the brilliance of the writing style. The book made for compelling reading. It was also relevant. In an era gripped by anxiety about nuclear war, Kissinger appeared to be arguing that current statesmen had a lot to learn from Metternich who, with the help of the British Foreign Secretary, Viscount Robert Stewart Castlereagh, had constructed a world order that resulted in peace in Europe from the Battle of Waterloo in 1815 to the outbreak of the First World War.

Entitled *A World Restored: Metternich, Castlereagh and the Problems of Peace, 1812–1822*, the book was published by Weidenfeld & Nicolson in 1957. Kissinger's portrayal of Metternich provided an early insight into his world view, including the principle that disorder, and the instability that comes with it, is worse than injustice. The book also revealed that Kissinger believed the real heroes of history were the conservatives who attempt reconciliation and gradual change, not the revolutionaries.

Although not many copies of *A World Restored* were sold – fewer than 500 – the book received widespread praise and solidified George Weidenfeld's relationship with Henry Kissinger. In time, this would also provide his entry into the wider American political and diplomatic community. Weidenfeld & Nicolson would go on to release many of Kissinger's books, including the bestsellers *White House Years* and *Years of Upheaval*. Many years later Kissinger would thank George in a letter for 'a lifetime of friendship, encouragement and support'.

Beyond the commercial and social advantages of the relationship, choosing to release Kissinger's first book, at a time when no American publisher would go for it, also demonstrated one of George Weidenfeld's key traits: his remarkable perspicacity.

In June 1958, two years after getting married, George and Barbara filed for divorce. The newspapers had a field day. HUSBAND NO.2 CITES HUSBAND NO.1, crowed the *Daily Herald*. While the *Daily Mirror* went with the headline THE TWO LOVES OF A NOVELIST, and then reported: 'An author who named a publisher as co-respondent in a divorce case two years ago, was himself named as co-respondent by the publisher yesterday involving THE SAME

WOMAN.' Meanwhile, *The Times* ran the more succinct: FORMER HUSBAND CITED.

'Ours was a passionate, heart-rending, hopeless relationship,' George later remembered, 'governed by alternating cycles of physical obsession, glimmers of hope, deep depression, and profound guilt on both sides. While it lasted I thought of little else, it seemed like a suspension of real life.' He then added, 'I knew no good could come of my relationship with Barbara, but it was an addiction, which dwarfed everything else.'

By the summer of 1958, the thirty-eight-year-old George Weidenfeld was twice divorced. He was once again single.

'When my mother first met my father,' recalls Laura Barnett, the daughter of George Weidenfeld and his first wife Jane Sieff, 'she felt swept off her feet, yet uncertain. She was in love with him and admired him as a man of the world, a man of letters and ideas.'

'When they were married, although a highly intelligent and attractive young woman, she felt rather out of her depth,' Laura continues. 'Running a household, forever entertaining and mixing with his friends. She also feared she would let him down and he would tire of her. In the constant stream of entertaining, she wished for some time alone with him. Yet, according to my mother, they only ever had two meals tête à tête during their married life.'

Laura was just three years old when she and her mother moved to Paris. As part of the divorce agreement, she stayed with her father for two holidays a year. An early memory centres around one of his visits to France, in 1959. 'Strangely enough,' she says, 'it long had the power to upset me.' She remembers her father coming to Paris when she was six years old. During his stay, they had tea at the Hôtel Ritz. A few days later, she was shown a newspaper with a photograph of her father. The caption said George was in Paris for her, which made her feel proud, though strangely the author of the article had given her an unfamiliar nickname, which was confusing. She later discovered that her father had come for a book, and that the unfamiliar nickname was not her own, but the title of this book. She found that very upsetting. 'It left me with a sense of great disappointment,' she says, adding, 'interestingly, to this day I haven't read the book.'

The book's name was *Lolita*.

CHAPTER 5

Lolita

1959

*'I happen to think that a work of art must not
be suppressed and that an artefact of calculated
corruption should be prosecuted.' – GW*

Lolita was originally published as a limited edition in France in
September 1955, four years before George Weidenfeld's trip to Paris
and his daughter's confusion. The book was released by Maurice
Girodias of Olympia Press, a company known for specialising in
pornography, but which had also built a reputation for publishing
challenging literary titles. The first print run had been 5,000 copies
and the book received little attention.

Over the next few months, a handful of copies of *Lolita* were
smuggled into England. A single copy made its way into the hands
of Graham Greene, who reviewed it favourably in the *Sunday
Times*. This was followed soon after by a scathing article in the
Sunday Express, which denounced the book as 'sheer unrestrained
pornography'. Shortly after, the British Home Office ordered that
all copies entering the country should be seized.

When he first read *Lolita*, George knew immediately he wanted
to publish it. His partner, Nigel Nicolson, was not so sure. Nor
were Nigel's parents. His father Harold 'hated' the book and said it
would be 'universally condemned', while his mother Vita 'saw no
literary merit in it at all'. As for Nigel himself, he told George that
he was not convinced they should proceed with publication. George
was unrelenting. He took legal advice, however, and learned that

publication in England would be extremely hazardous. Under the current law, they would likely lose the case, which would result in huge losses. Any copies that had been printed would have to be pulped, not to mention the enormous editorial, marketing, publicity and legal expenses incurred up to that point. Such an outcome would be calamitous for Weidenfeld & Nicolson, placing its future in serious jeopardy. As luck would have it, the lawyers said, the Labour politician Roy Jenkins was right then guiding a new obscenity bill through Parliament. Under this new law, if the government blocked publication and the case went to court, then the publisher would be able to argue the literary merits of the book by calling authors, academics and reviewers to testify. If this bill was enacted, then just maybe, George might have a chance. The effort would still pose an enormous risk but, for the publisher, it might be worth it.

In the decades leading up to the proposed publication of *Lolita*, governments had frequently cited 'obscenity' as the reason for preventing controversial books being published. In the United States, the Federal Anti-Obscenity Act of 1873 had been used to ban Chaucer's *The Canterbury Tales*, John Cleland's *Fanny Hill*, Boccaccio's *The Decameron* and Voltaire's *Candide*. In Britain, the legal test for obscenity derived from a 1868 case known as *Regina v Hicklin*, in which a judge ruled that obscene material tended 'to deprave and corrupt those whose minds are open to such immoral influence'.

In 1928 the British government had relied on the *Hicklin* case to ban Marguerite Radclyffe Hall's lesbian novel *The Well of Loneliness*. Opposition to the book was whipped up by the media, particularly the *Sunday Express* whose editor wrote, 'I would rather give a healthy boy or a healthy girl a phial of prussic acid than this novel.' That same year, D. H. Lawrence's *Lady Chatterley's Lover* was also deemed to violate the obscenity laws and was commercially published in only an expurgated version. Six years later, the publisher Boriswood was prosecuted for obscene libel and severely fined for releasing *Boy*, a sexually explicit novel by James Hanley.

A more positive outcome, at least as far as publishers were concerned, befell James Joyce's *Ulysses*. First published in 1922 by Shakespeare and Company in Paris, the novel was deemed by many as scandalous and unfit for print. In 1923 a total of 499 copies were shipped to England, only to be seized by Customs and Excise and incinerated. In the United States, Joyce found it hard to get a firm to take on the risk of publishing his book. Finally, the challenge was taken up by the co-founder of Random House, Bennett Cerf. In 1932, after a copy of Joyce's book was seized at customs, Cerf and his lawyers persuaded the US District Court to allow them to publish *Ulysses*. The judge concluded that the book was 'a sincere and serious attempt to devise a new literary method for the observation and description of mankind'. The success in America emboldened the young British publisher Allen Lane and, in 1936, he had released a limited edition of *Ulysses* in England. The director of public prosecutions decided that given its price, the book 'was not likely to get into the hands of anyone likely to be corrupted by it and that probably the best course was to do nothing'.

Bennett Cerf and Allen Lane's success with *Ulysses* in the 1930s demonstrated that some books with risqué content could be published. What was not clear, however, was where the dividing line fell between what was and what was not acceptable to the authorities. Nor was it certain how the mood of the public or the press had changed in the years following the end of the Second World War.

Over the summer of 1958, with the lawyers saying that the new bill had a good chance of passing through Parliament, and with Nigel Nicolson's tenuous but nervous agreement, George reached out to the author, Vladimir Nabokov, in New York and asked for permission to publish *Lolita* in the United Kingdom and across the Commonwealth. By the end of November, they had reached an agreement on the general terms and Nabokov wrote to George saying 'an English edition of *Lolita* is nearing signature'. In his reply to the author in New York, George said, 'May I take this opportunity of telling you how inspired and moved my colleagues and I feel by the book and how determined we are to see that it launches with dignity and success in this country.' Publication of *Lolita* in Great Britain seemed a little closer, but then, by the year's end, George's plans started to unravel.

When word began circulating in the press that Weidenfeld & Nicolson intended to release *Lolita*, Nigel's political colleagues pressed him to change course. At one point the Conservative chief whip Ted Heath (and later prime minister) begged him to cancel publication. Nigel asked him if he had read the book. Heath said he had. 'Did you think it obscene?' Nigel asked. 'As a matter of fact I thought it very boring,' Heath replied. 'If it is boring it cannot be obscene,' Nigel said, which he later admitted was not a very good argument. A few days later, the Attorney-General, Reginald Manningham-Buller (called 'Bullying Manner' behind his back), stopped Nigel in a dark corridor in the bowels of the House of Commons. 'If you publish *Lolita* you will be in the dock,' he said, jabbing a finger at him. 'Even after the Obscenity Bill has been passed?' asked Nigel. 'That won't make any difference,' responded the country's top lawyer. 'The book is thoroughly obscene. I've given you a clear warning.'

On 16 December 1958, a week before Christmas Eve, Roy Jenkins' new Obscenity Bill was debated in the House of Commons. Midway through the proceedings, Nigel stood up to speak. First, he acknowledged that he had an interest in the matter as a director of the firm Weidenfeld & Nicolson, which was planning to publish *Lolita*. Then he moved on to the substance of his speech. 'The question could be asked,' he declared, 'Is an obscene work of art a contradiction in terms? I would answer the question by saying, no, it is not. It is quite possible for a work of art to be obscene.' He then went on to say that the book had already been published in America, where over 250,000 copies had been sold. *Lolita* had also been published in France and Italy. 'The question arose whether it should be published in England. That was the question which my colleagues and I had to answer,' he continued. '*Lolita* deals with a perversion. It describes the love of a middle-aged man for a girl of twelve. If this perversion had been depicted in such a way as to suggest to any reader of middle age or, for that matter, any little girl – could she understand it – that the practices were pleasant and could lead to happiness, I should have had no hesitation in advising my colleagues that we ought not to publish this book. But, in fact, *Lolita* has a built-in condemnation of what it describes. It leads to utter misery, suicide, prison, murder and great unhappiness, both to the man and to the little girl whom he seduces.'

At this point, Emrys Hughes, a Welsh Labour MP, rebel and general troublemaker, tried to interrupt, but Nigel brushed him aside and moved on to his conclusion. 'I asked myself whether the loss to literature in this country through the non-publication of *Lolita* was greater than the risk which one ran of offending certain people by its publication.' Pausing to take a breath, he then said, 'In the end, I came to the conclusion that it was probably right to publish this book.' Nigel had for the first time publicly declared his support for the publication of *Lolita*.

George must have been pleased. Over Christmas, he reached out to his growing network of authors, some of whom he published, and some not. He asked them to add their names to a letter in support of *Lolita*. Just before heading off for a trip to Holland, then France, he sent the letter to the editor of *The Times* – the British newspaper of record. He had succeeded in gathering the names of some of the most well-known intellectuals of the time, including the authors Iris Murdoch, Stephen Spender and Peter Quennell, along with the philosopher Isaiah Berlin and the publisher Allen Lane. Somehow, he also managed to persuade the editor of the *Times Literary Supplement*, Alan Pryce-Jones, and the totemic critic V. S. Pritchett to add their names as well.

The letter was published on Friday 23 January 1959. 'We are disturbed by the suggestion that it may yet prove impossible to have an English edition of Vladimir Nabokov's *Lolita*,' it began. 'Our opinions of the merit of the work differ widely, but we think it would be deplorable if a book of considerable literary interest which has been favourably received by distinguished critics and widely praised in serious and respectable periodicals were to be denied an appearance in this country.' George had done well.

But any sense of progress was halted when, that same evening, Nigel took part in a hustings near Bournemouth on the south coast. Towards the end of the meeting, he was questioned by a member of the audience, a Mr Hall, who asked, 'what people should think of a man who was considering publishing an obscene work?' Taken aback by the directness of the question, Nigel paused a moment, before answering that it would be a pity if England were to be the only country where a work praised as literature could not be published. 'Before making any final decision to publish this book,' he added, 'we shall take public opinion into account and explore methods of testing public opinion.' With that, the tension in the room dissipated. According to a journalist from *The Times*, the meeting ended with the singing of 'For he's a jolly good fellow'. But the MP for Bournemouth and Christchurch had not carefully thought through the consequences of his calming words.

When he read the report of his partner's political meeting, George immediately understood he had a serious problem on his hands. It sounded like Weidenfeld & Nicolson was having second thoughts about publishing *Lolita*. Still abroad in Europe, he placed an urgent call to his secretary back in London and asked her to send a cable immediately to the Nabokovs at Cornell University in Ithaca, New York:

Do not be misled by Saturday's Times report of Nicolson's Bournemouth meeting. Stop. Our decision to publish Lolita unaffected by all difficulties. Letter follows. Weidenfeld

Two days later, another letter was published in *The Times*. This time from Douglas Woodruff, editor of the Catholic paper the *Tablet*, in response to the letter signed by Iris Murdoch and her literary friends. He argued that writers and artists had a responsibility to 'bear the claims of public decency in mind in a way that the author of *Lolita* chose not to'. Then Woodruff added his most cutting point: 'If literary merit, such as will always be argued for, is to carry complete exemption, that will mean the claims of public decency are to count for nothing at all against the claims of liberty and art.'

That same day, a slightly rattled George Weidenfeld arrived back in London and immediately wrote to his author in New York. He started the note with 'Dear Mr Nabokov', for they had not met and still addressed each other formally. George now reported that the letter to *The Times* from Iris Murdoch and her other signatories was 'obviously very helpful' but that the rejoinder by Douglas Woodruff was 'the first seriously argued thrust of counter attack'. The key to a successful publication, he continued, would be the passage of the new Obscenity Bill through Parliament, which he hoped would occur sometime that autumn. 'I need not explain to you,' he added, 'how enormously the chances of victory, in the event of prosecution, would be increased if we could produce in court as witnesses the formidable array of literary personalities who signed the letter in *The Times*.' George then addressed Nigel Nicolson's meeting near Bournemouth. He assured Nabokov that even if his partner had inadvertently given the impression that they might delay publication of *Lolita*, this was not the case. 'It is almost impossible to know exactly what was said in the heat of an angry political meeting,' he said smoothly. 'This of course does not represent our policy and we are going ahead with our plans to bring out the book as soon as possible.' He then said he was looking forward to meeting Nabokov in person, and signed the letter.

A month later, at the end of February 1959, George arrived in New York. He stayed at the Gladstone on 114 East 52nd street, three blocks from Rockefeller Centre. This was the same hotel in which Marilyn Monroe liked to stay when she visited the city. Over the next week, George met with Nabokov and his wife Véra several times. They discussed how best to ensure a successful publication of *Lolita*, as well as plans for Nabokov's other books. A week later on 10 March, Véra wrote to George: 'We both very much enjoyed meeting you. We are sending you our best regards.' Upon his return to England, George wrote back to the Nabokovs. 'The battle for *Lolita* is raging ferociously in the lobbies, debating room and ministerial cubbyholes of the House of Commons, in the press, on TV and in counsels' chambers (though not yet in the law courts).'

Meanwhile, the pressure on Nigel Nicolson was intensifying. Ever since Weidenfeld & Nicolson had announced its intention to publish *Lolita*, there had been calls from his Conservative constituents for him to step down. Now, with its publication more likely, this pressure became overwhelming. Already vulnerable because of his voting record, particularly his opposition to the death penalty, Nigel announced that he would not seek re-election. So as not to trigger a by-election, which his party wished to avoid, he would continue as an MP until the next ballot that would take place at the end of the year.

Over the spring, while the furore continued, and they waited in hope that the House of Commons would approve the new

Obscenity Bill, George and his team attempted to identify a printer brave enough to take on the government's censors. Typically, a publisher worked with a limited number of printers. This was not just a matter of economics – the higher the volume, the lower the cost – but also of art. Each publisher had their own particular preferences when it came to the making of a book. What font might be used: Helvetica, Penumbra or perhaps Futura. Which paper stock: light, heavy, clean-edged, rough-edged? The type of board used to bind the book. The kerning (the space between the characters) and the leading (the space between the lines). Whether a ribbon was to be added to bookmark a page. Or perhaps attractive endpapers pasted onto the inside of the front and back covers. Each of these required numerous choices and, over time, the publisher and printer formed a creative partnership. It was also a matter of trust. The printer was unable to read every book that ran through their machines, thousands a year, so they relied on the publisher for guidance in case there were potential problems.

The task of finding a printer was given to Nicholas Thompson, editorial director of Weidenfeld & Nicolson. He approached one printer and then another. Each turned him down. Some of the responses were defensive and short. Others, embarrassed and awkward. One of those who declined was Richard Clay, managing director of Clay and Company, the largest printer in England. 'From a purely personal point of view, the inconvenience which would be caused in the event of there being a case brought by the DPP [Director of Public Prosecutions] would be something which I could not risk,' wrote Clay, continuing 'quite apart from the fact that, should the prosecution be successful (my impression is that there is a bit of a witch-hunt going on in some of the higher legal circles) I should find it extremely inconvenient to be incarcerated, even though it would be at the taxpayer's expense!'

Finally, on 8 May, George had something positive to report to the Nabokovs. 'I am at last able to give you some really constructive news about *Lolita*,' he wrote. 'Having had over thirty refusals from printers, I am happy to tell you that Shenval Press, whose head James Shand is a good and reliable friend, has now agreed to print *Lolita* as soon as the new Obscenity Bill becomes law.' A month later, on 15 June, he wrote again, informing the author that the bill had passed through the House of Lords with an amendment, though, George reassured him, the amendment 'does not affect *Lolita* in any way'. As a sign of his confidence, George had now sent the book to the printer and begged them to be 'extremely circumspect and discreet', lest the newspapers got hold of the story that the book was being printed before the bill was passed. In another letter he told Nabokov that it would be disastrous if there was more publicity during the next fortnight, which might give their enemies a chance to filibuster the bill beyond the present parliamentary session. However, George concluded, 'we have gone a long step further towards L Day'.

Frustratingly, the printing was held up again by a strike that broke out over the summer. When it ended in the first week of August, the book finally went to press. Two weeks later, a handful of sample copies arrived at the office at 7 Cork Street. George and his colleagues gathered around to look at the newly minted book. It looked stunning. The dust jacket was an attractive but modest apricot colour. On the front was printed the title 'Lolita' in large capital letters, beneath which ran a white line and, under that, the author's name. Nothing more. The back cover had a large photograph of Nabokov looking straight at the camera, daring the reader to pick up the book. Beneath his picture ran a short biography of the author, ending with his passion for collecting butterflies. The spine had the book's title, the author's name and then, at the bottom, much to George's pride, the publisher's logo: 'Weidenfeld & Nicolson'. They were now ready to put the second phase of the plan into action.

The first edition of Lolita *with the author on the back cover*

Originally, the idea had been to sell *Lolita* to several bookshops and inform the authorities who, they hoped, would then react by either doing nothing or banning the title from further sale. Instead, George opted for an approach more under his control. In the last week of August, he had three Weidenfeld & Nicolson employees purchase copies of *Lolita*. Copies of the sales receipts were then sent to the Attorney-General and the Director of Public Prosecutions, with a note: 'If you want to prosecute us for an obscene publication, do so [...] if we win the case, we will publish the full edition the following day; if we lose it, we will destroy the entire edition.' A few days later, the Attorney-General acknowledged he had been sent the receipts, but nothing more. A week went by, then two. Still no word. The situation remained unchanged even after George leaked the scheme to the press, which, according to Nigel Nicolson, 'caused a great deal of amusement, and seemed to most people eminently fair'.

By the end of October, they now had a decision to make. Two months had passed and still there was no response from the government. Around 20,000 copies of *Lolita* had been sent to bookshops around the country and these booksellers were anxiously awaiting the go-ahead to put the books on their shelves. Vladimir and Véra

Nabokov had flown in to London for the publicity tour and were staying at Brown's Hotel in Mayfair. Should they publish?

So it was that on 1 November 1959, George met with Nabokov and his wife at the White Tower restaurant in Bloomsbury. Also present were Nigel Nicolson, the critic V. S. Pritchett and the Labour politician Roy Jenkins. Nobody argued for delay, they were too committed now. It was full speed ahead.

Four days later, on 5 November 1959, Guy Fawkes Day, more than 200 people gathered at the Ritz Hotel in London, waiting for the news. The crowd consisted of prominent actors, musicians and authors, as well as dozens of eminent journalists, editors and lawyers. At the centre of the proceedings was George Weidenfeld. Never still, moving from one small group to another. Making introductions. Catching up on the gossip. Suggesting that whoever he was speaking with might consider writing a book. Around him, the room was humming with anticipation. They were waiting to hear whether the government would finally allow *Lolita* to be published. The press was already calling it one of the most important books of the year. If George was able to make *Lolita* a success, it could transform the fortunes of his fledgling publishing house.

Then, around 10 p.m., one of the hotel's staff members called George to the phone. There in an alcove he picked up the receiver and asked who he was speaking to. The man on the other end of the line would only say he worked in the Home Office. George was impatient to hear the news. After some pleasantries were exchanged, the civil servant eventually got to the point. 'This is highly irregular,' said the man, 'but I am a great supporter of your cause.' A few moments passed, then he continued. 'You can go ahead. The DPP has decided not to prosecute.'

George walked back into the ballroom and announced the news. The crowd cheered loudly. Champagne glasses were clinked, hands were shaken, backs were slapped. Vladimir Nabokov stood to one side smiling. His wife Véra rubbed away a tear with a handkerchief.

George then excused himself and placed two more calls. First to the office, telling them to relay the news to the bookshops. *Lolita* could immediately be sold. A second call was made to James Shand, the printer, thanking him for his loyalty and urging him to run off as many copies as possible.

The publication of *Lolita* attracted enormous coverage in the press. The *Western Mail* said it was 'among the most interesting books to appear in the last decade'. Elizabeth Harvey in the *Birmingham Post* called it 'brilliant writing' and 'a work of art'. The syndicated journalist Harry Thompson described it as 'the most controversial novel of the century', while the columnist David Holloway noted in the *Daily News* that 'No book in my lifetime has caused more pre-publication fuss than *Lolita*.'

Not all the critics were so effusive. On 12 November, a week after *Lolita*'s publication day, *The Times* ran an anonymous review under the modest headline NEW FICTION. They said that *Lolita* 'is not a book to be proud of', adding 'its construction is much looser than its morals and it is written in a style which sets the teeth on edge'. After admitting that Nabokov was writing in the person of the main character, Humbert Humbert, *The Times* then added, 'Nobody is likely to be corrupted by this book, but very few readers are going to be much entertained by a study of mania which is neither objectively clinical nor emotionally engaging.' Given the book's subsequent longevity, the reviewer was probably grateful they remained unnamed.

The first print run sold out immediately. As did the next and the next. This was so unusual that the *New York Times* ran a story under the headline LOLITA'S A SELLOUT IN BRITAIN. Within two weeks, more than 80,000 copies were sold. Then 100,000. Then 200,000. The printer struggled to keep up with the orders not only from within Britain but in Australia and other Commonwealth countries.

Today, *Lolita* is considered a modern classic. Ranked as the fourth-best novel of the twentieth century by the Modern Library, thirteenth best by *Time* magazine, fifty-fourth by the *Telegraph*, and sixty-ninth by the *Guardian*. Although curiously, when the BBC asked its viewers to nominate their favourite books for its 'Big Read' list in 2003, *Lolita* was not included in the top 100. *Lolita* is also a cultural touchstone that is frequently referred to. In the song, 'Don't Stand So Close to Me', Sting warbles 'Just like the old man in that book by Nabokov'. Similarly, in the film *Manhattan*, Diane Keaton's character Tracy says, 'Somewhere Nabokov is smiling' when she discovers that Woody Allen's character Isaac is dating a seventeen-year-old. Meanwhile, the word 'Lolita' has even entered the English language as a noun: 'a precociously seductive girl', according to Merriam-Webster.

Opinion about the book, however, remains divided. While many argue that the main characters are compelling, the writing style brilliant, and the colourful descriptions of the American Midwest captivating, others vehemently disagree. They point out that Lolita was just twelve years old when she was kidnapped and raped multiple times by Humbert Humbert, and that the author does not sufficiently signpost this as a problem, making the book immoral. This extreme divergence in viewpoint has created a cultural flashpoint around the book, raising a number of larger questions about literature and the responsibilities of a publisher: is it possible to separate the morals of the fictional, albeit unreliable, narrator from the author who created them? And if not, can a book be too morally repugnant to be published?

'It was a triumph for George,' Nigel Nicolson later wrote. 'His nerve had held in face of much discouragement including my own.' As for the publisher himself, he was euphoric. '*Lolita* was a breakthrough in the liberalisation of the British obscenity laws,' George later said. The following year, Penguin Books used the same argument as had been deployed for *Lolita* – literary merit – to persuade a judge that they could publish an unexpurgated version of *Lady Chatterley's Lover* in Britain. It would take another decade for English courts to allow works that were considered obscene but without literary merit to be published, starting with *Oz* magazine in 1971. In the United States, a similar course was charted. Publishers and editors fought in the courts for the right to release *Lady Chatterley's Lover.* This was followed by Henry Miller's more sexually explicit *Tropic of Capricorn* and then William Burroughs's *Naked Lunch.*

The commercial success of *Lolita* also provided, George noted happily, a breakthrough in the fortunes of his publishing house: Weidenfeld & Nicolson. For now, at least, they were financially secure.

CHAPTER 6

The Group

1963

*In the creative process of publishing, the publisher may
not have the parent's pride of place – he is rather the
midwife in the creative, or shall I say procreative process
of launching a new literary being: a book.' – GW*

The success of *Lolita* brought George Weidenfeld many gifts. The
coffers of Weidenfeld & Nicolson were filled. His esteemed author,
Vladimir Nabokov, recommitted to having his books published by
the firm. Perhaps most important of all, George Weidenfeld's reputation as a leading publisher was greatly enhanced. Weidenfeld &
Nicolson was now *the* place where authors wanted to be published.

One of those to join the list was the American author, Mary
McCarthy. In her early fifties, McCarthy was best known for being
a satirist and critic, though by this time she had also published
eight books. 'Mary was handsome and flirtatious,' George recalled.
'She had an insatiable appetite for high gossip and a gift for turning social chatter into brilliant literary improvisation spiked with
sarcasm.' McCarthy's previous novel, *A Charmed Life*, had been
rejected by her British publisher Heinemann because of potential
obscenity. She had then been introduced to George by Sonia Orwell,
and the book was published by Weidenfeld & Nicolson. Despite the
success of this novel, McCarthy was not yet a 'Weidenfeld author'.
So when, at the end of 1962, she completed her next work of fiction,
The Group, she first offered it to the British publisher Hart Davis,
which was owned by her American publisher Harcourt Brace. The

novel told the story of a group of eight college girlfriends who met at Vassar College in New York and their colourful and entwined lives that followed, providing a gripping portrait of America's social and political climate in the 1930s. But Hart Davis took exception to some of its racier passages and rejected the manuscript. So McCarthy came back to George Weidenfeld. Before making a decision, he asked for an opinion from Barley Alison.

Barley was in her forties. By this point, she had been with the firm for more than a decade and was now head of fiction and a company director. One of her claims to fame was finding the typescript of Margaret Drabble's first novel in the 'slush pile' (book submissions that came direct from the author and not via a literary agent or an American or translation publisher). She read it, loved it, and insisted that it be published. When it was released as *A Summer Bird-Cage* the novel received tremendous acclaim. A former journalist and diplomat, Barley was petite, with a small face and bobbed hair. She was energetic, well-dressed and spoke with a deep, raspy Australian accent. Her Antipodean origins were frequently commented upon, as was her enjoyment of alcohol (a gin and tonic was her drink of choice) and the reasons she remained unmarried. A cigarette was rarely far from her lips and she had an infectious, happy laugh. She had her own office, a floor below George's, which was filled with manuscripts, on the desk, on the shelves, on the floor. Barley's task now was to provide a reader's report on *The Group*.

Weidenfeld & Nicolson, as with other publishers of this time, frequently relied on readers' reports to assess books submitted to the firm. This was particularly true of fiction titles whose potential readership was more difficult to ascertain than non-fiction. Books arrived in one of three ways. The easiest to deal with were those supplied by an established author or agent. The second were unsolicited manuscripts. These arrived every day, delivered by the postman, and were each logged in a large, red-covered volume by a junior assistant. Within its lined columns were added the date that the pages arrived at the office, the title, the author's last name, the format (manuscript or book), the agent's name (where applicable), and the verdict. This last varied from 'rejected', 'returned' and, in a very few cases (less than one per cent) 'accepted'. The final way in which manuscripts or books arrived at the office, or to be more accurate book ideas, was via the publisher. Hardly a day went by when George didn't inform his colleagues that he had met a person, typically famous or well connected, and he had suggested they write a book for him.

A few days later, Barley was ready to give her views on McCarthy's new book. This would normally be a formal written report but, in her excitement, Barley wished to deliver her summary verbally. She therefore headed upstairs, walked into George's office, and delivered her opinion in person. 'It is highly readable, extremely intelligent, and very funny,' she later recalled saying. 'It is, to my mind, the first one of her novels to be completely successful in that her characters are far more clearly drawn than in any of the earlier works and it seems to me to have more "heart". It is also extremely sexy, which is likely to sell more copies. I liked it very much indeed.'

Yet, Barley added a note of caution. The second chapter was potentially obscene. In one of its steamier passages, McCarthy described Dottie Renfrew having sex with a man she had just met, Dick Brown, in a hotel room:

Then, while she was still praying for it to be over, surprise of surprises, she started to like it a little. She got the idea and her body began to move too in answer, as he pressed *that* home in her slowly, over and over, and slowly drew it back, as if repeating a question. Her breath became quicker. Each lingering stroke, like a violin bow, made her palpitate for the next. Then, all of a sudden, she seemed to explode in a series of long, uncontrollable contractions that embarrassed her, like the hiccups.

George was not worried. Three years had passed since the release of *Lolita*. He was a great believer, as he would tell anyone who asked, that authors should be allowed to say what they wanted. Freedom of thought and freedom of publishing. *Lolita* had been an enormous success, why not this? George liked what he heard from his fiction editor and wrote to McCarthy's agent at A. M. Heath & Company in London with the good news: they would be delighted and honoured to publish *The Group*.

Over the next few months, Weidenfeld & Nicolson prepared for publication. The manuscript was copy-edited and proof-read. The cover art was chosen: a cream-white jacket on which, towards the top, was stamped the author's name, all uppercase and underlined, below which floated a large, brown square stamped with the title of the book *The Group* (in thin, black, irregular letters) sprinkled with eight attractive daisies. The text was laid out. High-quality paper stock was chosen (the same as had been used for *Lolita*), and a generous line and margin spacing was given, making it more pleasurable to read, though more expensive to print.

Mary McCarthy

In May 1963, Mary McCarthy wrote to George from Paris asking if he liked the copy she had provided for the back of the book. 'I hope this blurb is blurbish enough, mine usually aren't,' she wrote. 'My temptation is always to write a critical review instead of an advertisement.' She asked if he would be coming to visit her in Paris soon and said that she had just met with the American publisher Max Schuster, and they had talked about George. 'All very favourable,' she added reassuringly.

They still had to secure a printer. George had learned from the experience of *Lolita* that finding a company willing to take on a controversial title could prove difficult. On 2 July, Nicholas Thompson, editorial director of Weidenfeld & Nicolson, wrote to Western Printing Services in Bristol. 'As expected George is happy we should give an undertaking to pay any fine you might get at the Old Bailey for *The Group*.' He then added, soberly, 'I don't think we can give you a formal legally binding undertaking as this would be compounding a felony and that would probably land us in jail!'

Given that the book was that autumn's lead title, Barley Alison now focused on promotion. One of her jobs was to gather pre-publication quotes from renowned authors. These would be included in mail-outs to critics and reviewers in an effort to push the new title to the top of the pile. On 12 September 1963, for instance, Barley wrote to Cyril Connolly (by this time he had divorced Barbara Skelton and married Deirdre Craven). She said that McCarthy's American publishers had provided a list of possible 'leaders of opinions' but, with the exception of Connolly, they were all 'totally inappropriate'. She then continued, 'If you either hate doing this or hate the book, which I enclose herewith, don't hesitate to say so, since I shall simply write back to America, say that this is against our normal practice (as indeed it is) and shall never tell anyone at all that you were approached. Needless to say, however, if you were a friend of Miss McCarthy and did like the book, nothing would give us greater pleasure or help us more than to have a couple of words from you which we can quote.'

Barley also wrote to Iris Murdoch, author of *Under the Net, The Sandcastle* and most recently, *The Unicorn*. Using similar language to that in her letter to Connolly, the editor then added chummily that 'I am having my flat redecorated which is a nightmare' and 'Thereafter I think it will be very nice and hope you and John [the literary critic John Bayley, Iris's husband] will come and look at it.' Two days later, Murdoch responded, 'Thanks awfully for your letter and for sending the book. Sorry, I just can't, please forgive me. I don't want to give time to reading the book just now and if I did I would take a long time thereafter composing my sentence [...] I am so sorry, I'm sure the book is splendid.'

The Group was published in Britain in early November 1963 for 18 shillings, the same week as two non-Weidenfeld titles, Jules Feiffer's *Harry, The Rat with Women* (16s) and Len Deighton's *Horse Under Water* (16s). Typical of the press coverage was *The Times*, which lauded the 'superb set-pieces' and described some passages as 'scandalously ironic'. They also echoed Barley's reader's report: *The Group* 'is in some ways the most outrageously distorted of her novels, it is also perhaps her most enjoyable.' The other critics were no less euphoric. More than 20,000 copies were quickly printed. It looked like Weidenfeld & Nicolson had picked another winner.

Then, on 24 February 1964, a letter appeared in the *Edinburgh Evening News* from a Miss Margaret V. Paterson. The contributor wanted to 'congratulate' the county librarian of Midlothian for refusing to stock *The Group*, 'the theme of which is homosexuality'. This came as a big surprise to Barley and everyone else at the publishing house. She quickly searched through the book and found the cause of the issue. In chapter 2, seven pages after Dick and Dottie's sexual encounter, she located this briefest of references:

'Have you ever done it with a girl, Boston?' He tilted her face so he could scan it. Dottie reddened.

'Heavens, no.'

'You come like a house afire. How do you account for that?'

Dottie said nothing.

'Have you ever done it with yourself?'

Dottie shook her head violently; the suggestion wounded her.

'In your dreams?'

Dottie reluctantly nodded. 'A little. Not the whole thing.'

A further reference to a lesbian relationship occurred in the book's last chapter. In Barley's view, the letter to the Scottish paper was 'lunatic'. Surely, this was not going to be a problem. On 6 March, Barley responded to the paper. 'Either the County Librarian or Miss Paterson must be hopelessly confused,' she wrote, 'since Miss Mary McCarthy's novel could not be described by even the most imaginative of readers as a book "the theme of which is homosexuality".' If George Weidenfeld, Barley and the rest of the team hoped the issue would go away, they were wrong.

Seven days after Barley wrote her letter to the paper, the telephone rang in the offices of Weidenfeld & Nicolson. It was the managing director of Hutchinson, the company's distributors in Australia. Earlier that day, copies of *The Group* had been seized by the vice squad and the book was now banned in the state of Victoria. The state's Attorney-General, Arthur Ryiah, had publicly come out against the book. During a television interview, he had pronounced that *The Group* was 'the sort of book I'd rather not have in the hands of my teenage son or daughter'. As one newspaper pointed out, this last comment was confusing as his daughter was in her twenties and married.

A few days later more troubling news arrived from Australia. The book had also been banned in New South Wales and bookshops were cancelling their orders across the country. The question was what to do? If the company was to take action, should they adopt the same approach they had used with *Lolita* and fight the ban in the courts? Or perhaps a more hands-off approach might best serve the book and the campaign for literary freedom. Unsure of the best answer, George dithered, leading to angry pushback from Australian booksellers who felt abandoned. On 26 March he received a letter from a certain J. M. Lee in Canberra, admonishing him for timidity. 'Publishers have, on occasion, not merely the right to publish but a duty to stand by what they publish,' the letter-writer proclaimed, adding that 'If you and your agents believed that, by publishing *The Group* here, you did right, then you should have the moral fibre to stand by your belief.'

On 9 April, and with the book now widely unavailable, the *Australasian Post*, a weekly picture magazine read by millions of people, decided to let their readers know what they were missing. Under the headline THAT BOOK . . . WHAT IT'S ALL ABOUT, the magazine dedicated two pages of frothy coverage. They explained that in addition to the talk about lesbian fantasies, what may have influenced the ban was the 'step-by-step' description of Dottie and Dick having sex. 'By today's standards a man might have written about the same situation and few people would have been shocked,' reported the correspondent J. Stuart, whose first name was not given. 'The very fact that a woman has written these passages, obviously without reservations or embarrassment, and has vividly described the feelings of another woman, may be shocking to many people.'

On 20 April, George wrote to Professor D. H. Munro, president of the Freedom to Read Association, a freedom-of-speech advocacy group in Victoria. The publisher explained that he had been interested in backing a test case in the Australian courts as it would have 'served a useful purpose in focussing the attention of the public on the present unsatisfactory conflict' between national and state law. It would also have provided the chance to emphasise the 'literary qualities of *The Group*' and draw attention to the fact that Mary McCarthy is a 'serious, scholarly and highly respected writer'. The problem, however, was that the Attorney-General had ruled that the case would be adjudicated under Section 166 of the Victoria state code, which would mean it would take place before a magistrate, prohibiting the discussion of the book's literary merits and precluding the argument that the book should be considered as a whole. The lawyers had all told him that they would lose under this Section 166 code. 'The only action for us to take,' he continued, 'is to refuse to take part in such a ridiculously unfair contest and to press for change in the law.' On the positive side, George concluded, 'Both we and Miss McCarthy are delighted and touched that our present dilemma should have aroused so much public interest and such widespread and distinguished support in Australia.'

"WE'LL SELL 'THE GROUP' IN STREETS"

Many people had made written offers to sell the banned American novel, "The Group," in the streets of Melbourne "and risk being gaoled," the director of Melbourne University's Department of Audio and Visual Aids, Mr Newman Rosenthal, said today.

Mr Rosenthal said the offers were made to him in his capacity as provisional honorary secretary of the proposed Freedom To Read Committee to be formed next Tuesday.

Both Mr Rosenthal and the provisional chairman of the committee, Professor Hector Munro, of Monash University, said they had received a large number of letters from people offering support to challenge the present system of literary censorship in Victoria.

Many of the letters en-

To Read Committee their support.

Mr Rosenthal said he could not name the senders of two cheques for £50 until next Tuesday's meeting.

The meeting would not be a public meeting.

"At present it is being confined only to academics, writers, journalists, broadcasters, legal representatives, booksellers, pub-

'Action-by complaint'

Police investigated allegedly obscene novels and paperbacks in Victoria only after people had complained about them, the Chief Secretary, Mr Rylah, said today.

"Police do not go looking for this type of literature and I do not direct them to search for it," he said.

Mr Rylah is expecting a report soon from the Solicitor-General

Melbourne Herald, *20 March 1964*

The press coverage had been extensive in Australia. Storm gathers pace over 'The Group' proclaimed the lead article of Victoria's *Ballarat Courier*, while the *Age* announced Labour claims literary dictatorship and the *Melbourne Herald* declared we'll sell 'The Group' in street, giving the example of the director of Melbourne University's Department of Audio and Visual Aids, a Mr Newman Rosenthal, who had told the paper that many people would 'risk being gaoled' over the banning. In the end, the book's cancellation and all the publicity it engendered helped sales.

Before the book's publication in Britain, George had bumped into Dwye Evans, the chairman of Heinemann, at a book conference. 'I hear you've taken Mary's book,' Evans had said. 'Great mistake, you know. It won't sell more than two thousand copies. Too American. Too dirty.' By the first week of September, *The Group* had become a bestseller in both Britain and Australia. It was, by all accounts, another huge success for Weidenfeld & Nicolson, and its publisher, George Weidenfeld.

By the summer of 1964, George Weidenfeld and Barley's focus was no longer on Mary McCarthy: it had moved on to another of their American authors. On 26 June of that year, Barley wrote to this author. 'George and I have definitely decided to resign from the [jury],' she said, 'if you do not win the Prix des Editeurs next year.' The Prix des Editeurs was one of the world's most prestigious literary prizes. The book in question was *Herzog* and the author's name was Saul Bellow.

CHAPTER 7

Herzog

1965

'A publisher in his outlook programme and sense
of duty should be an internationalist.' – GW

On 10 September 1960, four years before the publication of *The Group*, Barley Alison had sat down at her desk in her study at 5 Harley Gardens in Chelsea and written a letter to her most prized author. She had delayed for eight weeks, but she couldn't put it off any longer. She had to find a way to save the situation, to rectify the breakdown between the publisher George Weidenfeld and the American author Saul Bellow.

At the time, Bellow was considered to be, if not the greatest, then one of the greatest living authors. His books regularly topped the bestseller lists in America, Britain and around the world. His publications brought in enormous income for himself, but also to the agents who supported him and the firms that published him. Many believed that Bellow, just forty-five years old, was at the height of his literary powers. Born in Lachine, Quebec, to Lithuanian-Jewish parents, Bellow had lived an itinerant life, including periods in Chicago, New York, Puerto Rico, Europe and Minnesota. Short, with dark wavy hair parted to one side, he was considered by many to be attractive and seductive. In America he was published by Viking Press, which also published Jack Kerouac's *On the Road* as well as books by Lillian Hellman and Arthur Miller.

George had known Saul Bellow for almost a decade after being introduced to him by Sonia Orwell. The first of Bellow's books he had published was *The Adventures of Augie March* in 1954. Since then, Weidenfeld & Nicolson had released more of Bellow's back catalogue, including *Seize the Day* and *Henderson the Rain King*. Next would come *The Dangling Man*, to be followed by *The Victim* soon after. George's dealings with Bellow went beyond the normal publisher–author relationship. When he was in London, Saul Bellow would call the publisher to his hotel and together they would 'kvetch' about 'pretty girls'. At the end of a European book tour organised by the State Department in 1960, George threw a party for Bellow at his house at 53 Eaton Square, a gathering attended by Stephen Spender, J. B. Priestley and other cultural luminaries. George also organised intimate private dinner parties for Bellow, before which, according to his biographer, the author would 'screen the female guest list for availability'. Sometimes the author would get up from the table and place a telephone call to one of the young women he had met during his visits to the publishing house and invite them to 'come round'.

Despite all this extracurricular attention, Bellow grumbled about the British publisher's failures and threatened to leave the firm. George didn't protect him from press attention. George didn't consult with him about the packaging of the books. George let his books go out of print. George didn't sell enough copies. And so, Barley, head of fiction at Weidenfeld & Nicolson, was attempting to repair the fissure by writing a letter to Bellow. 'Dearest Saul,' she began, 'my feelings of guilt about not having answered your various letters about your differences with George have now become so much part of the background to my life that I doubt whether writing will assuage them in any way.' Her first instinct, she said, had been to write to him and say, 'Please don't leave I couldn't bear it (which I really could not).' She then gave reasons why the author should remain with Weidenfeld & Nicolson: 'You are one of our most distinguished literary figures and so can bully us as you see fit. Also, George is personally very épaulé [supported] by you.'

Next, she turned to herself. 'Also, you know George goes through periods of thinking that I'm third rate [...] you must help me in this battle eventually.' She continued that in May and June she had entered an 'acute phase', she had become 'nervous' and drank too much, leading George to think that she was an 'acute alcoholic'. Having apologised for the length of the letter, and having told Bellow that he was the 'best living writer' and a 'genius', she concluded by begging him, 'Don't leave us, partly because I honestly think we are improving, partly because the danger that you might has so alarmed everyone that your slightest whim will be treated as priority, partly because you can count on me to see that everything possible is done. Finally, and purely personally, because I like to think that for the next twenty years I shall be sure of seeing you if you are in London or if I am in New York.' Barley's tidy handwriting had filled twenty pages. But that was not enough. She added a postscript. 'PS Do please write to me here and tell me whether you are going to leave us or not. I won't tell George as it is good for him to be anxious and uncertain, but it is not good for me. Love B.'

The letter seemed to do the trick. Soon, Bellow was telling everyone that he was back in the Weidenfeld & Nicolson fold. In the autumn of 1961 the first chapter of his new book, which he was provisionally calling *Herzog*, was published in the American magazine *Esquire*. On reading it, Barley immediately wrote to the author in Tivoli, New York. 'Needless to say I find it most exciting,' she wrote. She wondered when he might complete the manuscript, adding that apart from Henry Miller, he was the only American 'to be seriously considered' at the previous year's Prix Formentor.

She hoped that he could submit book proofs for the upcoming Formentor meeting in March. She was sure that he would find the prize money of $10,000 would 'come in handy'.

A few weeks later, a letter dated 10 November arrived at the offices of Weidenfeld & Nicolson. Saul Bellow wrote that he would not be ready for that year's prize, what he called the 'Prix Tormentor'. The good news, he said, was that he was now two-thirds of the way through the novel, so he should be ready for the following year's entry. Barley informed George about the contents of the letter. He was relieved to hear the positive news and excited that they would soon be receiving the manuscript from the famous American author.

Saul Bellow

The British publishing landscape had changed dramatically since George had launched Weidenfeld & Nicolson in the late 1940s. In addition to the executives who ran the well-established firms – John Murray, Heinemann, Collins, Macmillan, Duckworth and Penguin – there was now a new generation of publishers, many of whom were Jewish refugees who had fled Nazi persecution and brought an interest in European literature and culture to Britain. These included Tom Maschler (Jonathan Cape), André Deutsch (André Deutsch), Paul Hamlyn (Hamlyn), Max Reinhardt (Bodley Head), Robert Maxwell (Pergamon Press) and Ernest Hecht (Souvenir Press). All of these publishing houses had retained their independence except for Heinemann which, in 1961, had been purchased by the bus operator Thomas Tilling. This loss of independence had outraged many in the industry, prompting more than a dozen authors, including Graham Greene, to leave Heinemann and join Bodley Head. It was a sign of things to come.

Like Weidenfeld & Nicolson, who now had their offices on Bond Street near Oxford Circus, most of the major English publishing houses had their headquarters in central London (many in Bloomsbury and Covent Garden). These buildings were typically from the Georgian and Regency periods, comprising three or four storeys of shabby, cramped offices, bestowed with marble mantelpieces, floors made of pine and oak, and arrayed with ill-matching Victorian furniture. A long way from the steel-and-glass, corporate open-plan offices of today.

Like George, the vast majority of those running the firms were middle-aged white men. Many of the junior and middle-level staff were women, often unmarried and underpaid. Again, similar to George, most of the executives belonged to a club, typically the Garrick or Savile (George belonged to both), where they met authors, journalists, booksellers and others keen to ply their trade. Lunches were long and alcohol-fuelled, expense budgets were generous and little troubled by accountants. There were, however, differences. Where many of his peers still wore tweed jackets, George was always nattily dressed in well-cut tailored suits. Similarly, while booze was rife in the publishing industry, George (as already noted) didn't drink alcohol, choosing a glass of milk, apple juice or cup of tea in place of wine, beer or brandy. And even though other publishers attracted the attention of columnists, diarists and cartoonists, none did so as much as George, who went out of his way to court their fascination.

It was its book list, however, that made George's company truly stand out. Of the fifty-two titles that Weidenfeld & Nicolson had released in 1959, three-quarters were non-fiction and more than 60 per cent were penned by non-British authors, whereas the other publishing firms overwhelmingly released books by domestic writers and had an even balance between fiction and non-fiction. Also of note, for this same year, just 13 per cent of George's list was written by female authors, a tally similar to André Deutsch (11 per cent of thirty-eight books), again for the same year, but notably less than the more established firms: John Murray (19 per cent of forty-three books), Jonathan Cape (20 per cent of forty-six books) and Collins (21 per cent of 135 books).

Many years later, George would be asked by a German journalist how it was possible that he, an Austrian refugee arriving in England without any funds, had established a big publishing house in the post-war era. 'We followed a simple principle,' George would reply. 'I realised very quickly that the English publishers were jealous. I knew that the literary agents would not give their big authors to a small publishing house. But I had one advantage: I had studied the war, I knew politics, I had several languages. Thus I got to the German and Italian publishers who immediately recognised me as a partner.' Then, he had approached academics in the top British universities. 'Word got around,' he said. 'That is the young publisher who pays better than Oxford University Press.'

In 1961, two years before the publication of Mary McCarthy's *The Group*, the release of a novel by an American writer, therefore, was still a relatively rare event for Weidenfeld & Nicolson. The last big one they had published had been *Lolita*. Expectations and hopes for what might happen to their next Bellow novel were running high.

*

For the remainder of 1961 and into early 1962, there was silence from Saul Bellow. Weidenfeld & Nicolson had to plan the release of *Herzog* but they had no idea when this might be. Should they place it in the autumn catalogue? Should they pitch it to booksellers? Should they brief literary journalists and critics? Should they assign part of their promotional budget to *Herzog* (or *Mr Herzog* as Bellow sometimes called it), or could they use it for other books? On his next trip to New York, George attempted to call Bellow numerous times at the University of Chicago, but without success. The publisher was infuriated by the unreliability of the American author. George would later tell Bellow's biographer that while the author was 'mordantly witty when he wanted to be, he could also be self-pitying and irascible, particularly towards those who hurt his vanity', adding that Bellow could be both 'manifestly charming' and 'self-absorbed'.

Finally, at the end of May 1962, George had had enough. He asked his head of fiction to write to the author's agent to find out what was going on. 'What on earth has happened to Saul Bellow?' Barley asked Mark Hamilton from A. M. Heath on 30 May. 'Rumours reach me that he has remarried, disappeared in Chicago, where he apparently teaches and answers no letters, but no hint of a rumour have I had about when MR. HERZOG is likely to reach us. Do be kind and try and find out for me.'

The following day, a letter arrived from the author himself. Given that it had been sent from New York, it must have been written before Barley's missive to the agent. Bellow had great news. *Herzog* would be ready in a month. He had rewritten the manuscript 'innumerable times,' he said, 'it gives me no more pleasure and I am prepared to relinquish it early this summer'. He reported that at only 300 pages it was 'quite a short book' and that he felt 'silly about the time I've put into it'. At the letter's end, he said that 'one of these years I may even win the Fornicator Prize [*sic*]'.

A full year later and the book was still not ready. On 20 June 1963, Bellow's agents now informed Weidenfeld & Nicolson that *Herzog* was 'supposed to be finished during the summer'. 'Can this be true?' Barley wrote breathlessly to Bellow. 'It would be too marvellous if it were as I do <u>long</u> to read it quite apart from publishing it.' Two months later, a letter arrived at Weidenfeld & Nicolson's office from Tony Tanner, a scholar of American literature and fellow of King's College, Cambridge. He had just seen Saul Bellow in New York, he reported, and the author had asked that he pass on the news to his British publisher that he expected to 'have the novel ready this fall'.

Hoping to motivate Saul Bellow, Barley wrote to him on 1 October, reporting that both Weidenfeld & Nicolson and the French publisher Gallimard were 'determined to make a major effort' for him to win the Formentor's $10,000 prize. The American representative, Grove Press, was already 'interested' in *Herzog*, she reported, while the French contingent believed they could 'convert' the Scandinavians and Germans 'if *Herzog* was half as good as *Henderson*'. George Weidenfeld, she continued, was 'no mean backstairs intriguer and one way or another the omens are good'. There was a catch, however, if Bellow wanted to be considered for this year's prize. The book had to be published in at least one country before 1 May 1964. She therefore urged speedy completion of the manuscript by October. 'Any delays beyond this might be disastrous.'

When Christmas 1963 came and went and no manuscript had arrived, George Weidenfeld was struggling to keep his composure. Where was the book? They still weren't sure if the title was *Mr Herzog* or *Herzog*. The important trade rag *Publishers Weekly* had listed the book as coming out the following March in America, but no official confirmation had been given by the author or his agents. This time, Barley wrote to Thomas Guinzburg, the head of Viking Press, Bellow's American publisher. She pressed for an update on the book. On 28 January 1964, Guinzburg responded. 'It is nice of you to inquire about the progress of *Herzog*,' he responded politely. 'Mr Bellow is working on the final pages to give us a final manuscript within a month.' He then added, unhelpfully, 'There is of course no guarantee of this last.'

A week later, George was in New York again. At the end of one letter back to London, in which he listed the books he had sold to American imprints and which of their titles he had acquired, the publisher added a 'PS': *Herzog* had once again been delayed. Word on the street was that Bellow had embarked on a total rewrite of his new novel. A different story came from the author himself. At the start of February, Barley received a letter from Bellow informing her that he had just 'sent the last pages of *Herzog*' to his American publisher. He added that 'they tell me George is in NYC. I may or may not see him when I go there next week.' The plan was now to publish the book in the United States in August. Bellow would leave the country shortly before publication to 'avoid the noise and the idiocy of reviews, round-table discussions and some of the pain of dissection'.

Finally, book galleys of *Herzog* arrived at the London office at the end of May. They were quickly devoured by Barley. On 5 June she wrote a reader's report for George. 'This is a superb and very highly polished book,' she gushed, 'and, as a work of art fully justifies the years of effort and endless rewritings it has undergone. I should be very surprised indeed if it did not get acclaimed widely as the "Great American novel" at last and feel that no one will ever accuse Saul of being a middle brow popular author again [...] I am quite confident that people will still be writing about the book a hundred years from now.' Separately, Barley wrote to Bellow to say that she 'adored' the book and that it brought him 'particularly vividly to mind', despite the years since they had last seen each other. Barley then said that she and George would resign if the book did not win the following year's Prix Formentor.

With the excitement surrounding the publication of *Herzog* gathering, George dictated a memo under the title SAUL BELLOW and circulated it among senior staff. 'We are of course all aware of the necessity of building and selling *Herzog* at all costs for the dangers of losing Bellow through inadequate promotion are great, as both his agent and he are somewhat on the alert.' He proposed that they rush publication so it came out before Christmas, which would 'certainly help our turnover and save us locking up quite a lot of money through production commitments'. The staff agreed to hurry publication, but when the country's largest book club said they would only take the title on as their main selection of the month if the release date could be pushed to the following February 1965, the book was delayed still further. Then, to George's immense disappointment, the book club withdrew their offer, citing concerns about saleability. It was now too late to publish in 1964.

On 14 December 1964, Barley wrote to Saul Bellow about his upcoming visit to England. She said that she would 'severely restrict George's tendencies towards bizarre or violent entertainments', and that she had spoken with the company's publicity manager who was preparing for his visit. A week later, Barley received the author's reply. He said that he didn't want to be bothered by television and print journalists. 'Restful anonymity is what I mostly need,' he said. 'I've fought free of the American mass media. Why should I go abroad only to succumb to them? Is it loyalty to W&N that makes you betray me to your publicity director?' He then asked, rhetorically, 'Why do these fellows write books and then shun publicity?' It was contradictory, he conceded, but 'being lionized makes me unfiguratively sick'.

Several days later, George sent his own letter to Saul Bellow. 'I have been meaning to write to you for a very long time,' he wrote, 'but each week a new triumph for your book renders the letter drafted in my mind obsolete, for I wanted to congratulate you on your most marvellous and wonderful novel and to tell you how happy and proud we are to be the publishers of it in this country.' George then added that he would soon be in New York for all of February and most of March, where he hoped to see the author. 'I shall seek you out, wherever you are,' he said, then added that he could be reached c/o Mrs Fonda at 565 Park Avenue.

In the end, *Herzog* was published in September 1964 in America and in February 1965 in England – the British postponement irritated the author, as communicated through Viking, who called it 'a pity'. The *New York Times* declared the book to be both a 'masterpiece' and a 'classic', while the *Herald Tribune* said Bellow was 'the finest stylist at present writing fiction in America'. In contrast, all that the London *Times* could say positively about the book was that it was written with 'firefly wit'. *Tatler* was even less effusive. 'I recognise considerable talent in this book,' the review stated condescendingly, 'but the essence of *Herzog* himself does not seem worth the trouble that Bellow has taken to portray him.' Despite the lukewarm reception, *Herzog* went on to claim the number one spot on the bestseller list in both Britain and the United States. It also won the National Book Award in America.

Just after the publication of *Herzog* in England, George Weidenfeld arrived in New York for an extended stay. On this trip, George met with Saul Bellow several times. At the publisher's hotel. For long lunches near Central Park. For dinner and after-dinner entertainments. Time and again, the much-lauded author told George that he was unhappy with the British release of *Herzog*. He disliked the binding which he called 'couleur de merde'. He described the cover script as 'Jewy-looking'. He thought his author photo 'less than dreamy'. Worst of all, he detested the book's cover which he considered 'pokey' and 'dowdy'. To such complaints, George gave a 'huge look of bafflement and wounded innocence', Bellow reported to Barley. The publisher then 'tried very hard to make it up' to the author by running him about 'with glamorous maidens, some of them so tall you couldn't reach anything without a scaling-ladder. I thought they were all very amusing and good-natured and none of them could fathom George's designs.' A détente of sorts was secured. George promised to do better. Bellow would stick with Weidenfeld & Nicolson. The question remained, would the book win the Formentor Prize as Barley had so long promised?

Founded in 1960 by Europe and North America's most successful literary publishers, including Grove Press (USA), Gallimard (France), Rowohlt (Germany), Giulio Einaudi editore (Italy) and Weidenfeld & Nicolson, the Formentor's objective was to celebrate high-brow literature. There were two prizes, the Prix des Editeurs awarded by publishers and the Prix International by writers and critics. All decisions were made by secret ballot. The prize had attracted enormous attention when in its first year, 1961, it had crowned two winners: Samuel Beckett and Jorge Luis Borges.

Now, four years later, in April 1965, more than forty editors, writers and publishers gathered to discuss that year's entries for the Formentor Prize. In a letter to Saul Bellow, Barley provided a blow-by-blow report of what happened. 'The English press always accuse Formentor of being a publishers' racket,' she wrote, 'and this year they were right.' She and George had 'hand-picked' the jury members, including Mary McCarthy, John Gross and Francis Wyndham, all of whom were fans of *Herzog*. As planned, McCarthy started by supporting Ivy Compton-Burnett's novel and then switched later to Bellow's. The Germans were backing the latest book by the Polish writer Witold Marian Gombrowicz, while the French and American delegations were excited about the Japanese author Yushio Mishima. In the first round of voting, *Herzog* only received four out of twenty-one potential votes. To persuade the other jury members, Barley then embarked on a campaign of vigorous lobbying – something she had never done before and which was certainly forbidden by the rules. Just before the final vote, a member of the Italian delegation declared that reading *Herzog* had made him 'in some undefined way a better man'. This caused a stir. A final vote was taken, and the winner was declared: Saul Bellow and *Herzog*. They'd done it. After all the delays and hand-wringing, Weidenfeld & Nicolson's author had won one of the world's greatest literary prizes.

The feelings of bonhomie were not to last very long. By the autumn of 1966, just eighteen months since Weidenfeld & Nicolson had wrangled the Formentor Prize and its $10,000 winner's check, relations between the publisher and the author were at an all-time low. Through his London agents A. M. Heath & Company, Bellow communicated that he was 'personally disappointed' with the relatively small number of copies of *Herzog* that had sold in Britain and that he should have been consulted about the Penguin paperback cover which had left him 'badly upset'. In those days, paperback and hardback companies were separate from one another, with fierce competition between the firms. It would not be until the vertical integration of the early 1980s that it became common for both hardback and paperback editions to be published by the same company. The case of *Herzog*, therefore, was unusual, as Weidenfeld & Nicolson had made the arrangements with Penguin. This was why Saul Bellow held George responsible for the mistakes. The agent now announced that they were giving formal notice that the author was leaving Weidenfeld & Nicolson. A few days later, George learned that Mary McCarthy might also be planning to part ways with the company.

Losing one bestselling author was hugely problematic for George Weidenfeld; losing two was potentially catastrophic. On 30 September, George received a letter from Mary McCarthy which put him greatly at ease. She said that 'there's not a <u>word</u> of truth' in the rumours that she was leaving. She had, however, spoken with Saul Bellow the previous Christmas, during which he had told her that he was dissatisfied with how his books were being managed in England. At the time, she said, she did not pay this much attention 'given Saul's persecution complex'. As far as she was concerned, she had 'no cause for complaint' with either George or his publishing company. She added that various rumours about her were also circulating by this time, one of which was that Simone de Beauvoir didn't like her because allegedly she had had an affair with Jean-Paul Sartre. Of course, this was ludicrous, she wrote, as she had never met Sartre.

George Weidenfeld, 1960s

On 18 October 1966, George wrote a typewritten letter to Saul Bellow. 'Needless to say I am extremely upset by the fact you feel we have ceased to be the right publishers.' George now stressed that his firm had 'put a great deal of enthusiasm, commensurate with our respect and esteem for this book, into its promotion'. The publisher, ever the canny salesman, then assured Bellow that he would never insist on making the author remain with the firm even if he was obliged to by various legal agreements, but could he ask one thing? Could they delay any decision and meet in person, wherever suited Bellow, so they could discuss future plans? He then added a farewell handwritten in blue ink, 'Your dejected and depressed friend and fan, George'.

A month later, Bellow responded. He enumerated his by now familiar complaints. The bad communication. The bad book cover. The bad sales. He then apologised for mentioning to a rival publisher that Mary McCarthy was unhappy with Weidenfeld & Nicolson, 'that was stupid of me,' he admitted. Unable to leave it at that, he then turned on McCarthy, telling George that 'Mary has made an indecent fuss about it, like a woman at whom some man has made a pass raising a cry of rape. Apparently, no one has made passes in quite a long time and she wants the world to know how desirable she is, and how perfectly awful the man.'

By this point, rumours that the American bestselling author was leaving Weidenfeld & Nicolson had crossed the Atlantic and journalists were pestering Bellow for comment. This made him grumpier still. To make matters more complicated, George's head of fiction and company director, Barley Alison, now also secretly encouraged Bellow to leave the firm. 'I am so sorry to involve you in this conspiratorial correspondence,' Barley wrote to Bellow on 10 December 1966 at his home on South Shore Drive in Chicago, 'I must warn you that this is the most shameless "begging letter" you are ever likely to receive.' The editor laid out her plan: she would give formal notice to leave Weidenfeld & Nicolson (she craved independence). George would purchase her shares in the company. She would then use these funds to establish her own literary firm, Alison Press. Key to the success of this new venture would be building up a 'good small list', including, she hoped, Saul Bellow.

Now came the crucial part of Barley's scheme. George was planning to meet Bellow in New York in ten days' time and would try and persuade the author to remain at his publishing firm by offering Barley as his editor on loan from her new firm. If this did not work, Barley continued, George would then pull out a letter from his pocket from herself, inviting Bellow to move to Alison Press. She now pleaded with Bellow to refuse George's initial offer (to remain at Weidenfeld & Nicolson), but not to let on that he had been forewarned, otherwise she would be revealed as the 'monstrously disloyal and Machiavellian plotter I really am'.

Just before he was due to depart for America, George received a letter from Saul Bellow's agent. He wanted to make it crystal clear so that there were no misunderstandings or false expectations in the run-up to the meeting in New York: his client had decided 'finally to close the door' on his relationship with Weidenfeld & Nicolson. Saul Bellow would definitely be leaving. A week later, on 20 December 1966, George met Saul Bellow at the resplendent Carlyle Hotel in New York – for many years, the publisher's home-from-home. They sat around a small table in the lobby, George sipping on a glass of apple juice, Bellow enjoying a series of alcoholic beverages. After catching up on each other's family news and discussing how each planned to spend Christmas, they got down to business. The publisher had prepared well. George first handed the author a memorandum that showed impressive historic hardback sales. Once Bellow had read the figures, George passed him another sheet displaying equally remarkable paperback sales. Next, the publisher handed over a thick stack of fan letters from the Book Society and other book clubs. Bellow was suitably flattered.

With the warm-up act now complete, George cut to the chase. Leaning forward a little, a steeliness now entering his eyes, the publisher said that even if the author wanted to leave, he couldn't. Weidenfeld & Nicolson retained the option to publish Bellow's next book. That was the stick. Now came the carrot. With his voice softening, a slight opening up of his body position, all the time supported by a warm smile and a sparkle in his eye, George now made the offer. His firm would guarantee to print a minimum of 40,000 copies of Bellow's next novel. This would be supported by considerable advertising and promotional support. More than this, they would reprint all of Bellow's books as a uniform edition. All cover art would be submitted to the author ahead of time in rough draft. Finally, Weidenfeld & Nicolson would renounce its option on further works. It would have been 'insane to turn down George's proposal,' Bellow later told the British publisher Tom Maschler, who had tried to poach him.

In the end, Saul Bellow remained with George throughout the late 1960s and into the next decade. During this time, George published *Mr Sammler's Planet* (1970), another critical and commercial success, which went on to win Bellow his second National Book Award. The book was built around two days in the life of Mr Sammler, a survivor of the Holocaust, told in stream of consciousness punctuated by a handful of set pieces.

In the novel, Bellow's portrayal of an African-American pickpocket is striking. Three times Bellow uses the word 'animal' to describe this man. He also compares him to an elephant and a puma and calls him a 'black beast'. He later calls this character's penis 'a snake'. At the time of the book's publication, the critic Joseph Epstein wrote that Bellow had intended 'to offend whole categories of the reading public as well as most of the people who write about books'. Later, Bellow's biographer James Atlas said of the pickpocket passages that 'a more overtly racist cluster of images is hard to imagine'. Given such concerns and the change in publishing tastes, it is an open question whether *Mr Sammler's Planet* would have been published today, let alone won the National Book Award in 1971.

*

Around the time that *Mr Sammler's Planet* was published, Weidenfeld & Nicolson – like most of the British and American publishing industry (including booksellers, wholesalers, printers and reviewers) – was almost entirely made up of white employees. This was also true for its shareholders and directors. Few of the company's titles up to this point had been written by ethnically diverse authors. Indeed, of the almost 1,500 books that they had published by the early 1970s, only a handful were written by people of colour.

There were, however, exceptions. Recent examples included the Ghanaian philosopher William Emmanuel Abraham's *Mind of Africa* in 1962, the Japanese playwright Kōbō Abe's *The Face of Another* in 1964, the Kenyan-born American academic Ali Al'amin Mazrui's *Towards a Pax Africana* in 1967, and Cyril Hamshere's *The British in the Caribbean* in 1972.

In July 1968, Weidenfeld & Nicolson also published Enoch Powell's *The House of Lords in the Middle Ages*. The book was released just three months after the Conservative politician delivered his infamous 'Rivers of Blood' speech calling for the expulsion of newly arrived black immigrants from Britain. Some might argue that this illustrates the company's lack of sensitivity towards issues of race. Others might say that this is another example of George's commitment to publish fictional books whose characters he found repulsive (as with *Lolita*), or non-fiction books whose contents he did not agree with (as with the books by Hitler, Bormann or Hoess). Whichever is true, it remains noteworthy that *Mr Sammler's Planet*, with its 'overtly racist cluster of images', was published by Weidenfeld & Nicolson.

By the mid-1970s, Bellow's reputation as a difficult author was, according to one of his biographers, 'well established'. To his American agents he was known as 'God', in a bad way. George Weidenfeld, therefore, was not the only one to be the recipient of Bellow's wrath. In truth, the author had complicated feelings towards the publisher. At one point, Bellow told his agent Mark Hamilton that he was 'very fond' of George Weidenfeld and his team but that they had never taken him very seriously. 'I have repeatedly tried to discuss matters with them,' he confided, 'but they elude me with a drink or a pleasant chat.'

For her part, Barley Alison decided against starting up her own firm, and instead she set up a successful list within the publishing house Secker & Warburg. In early January 1975, Saul Bellow told George that he was finally leaving Weidenfeld & Nicolson. This time it was for real. Gallingly, Bellow would be taking his latest work with him, a novel that was almost complete: *Humboldt's Gift*. This book would be seen by many as Bellow's finest work. It would go on to win him the Pulitzer Prize for Fiction.

On hearing the news that Bellow was joining Barley's list, George wrote to his protégé. 'Dear Barley, I had of course no inkling of his decision when I spoke to you on the telephone.' He then added graciously, 'I wish you the best of luck for your future working relationship with him.' Four days later, Barley wrote back to George. 'It would be disingenuous to pretend that I am not wildly excited and overjoyed to have been offered so distinguished an author to my modest list, but it is true to say that I would have been happier still had Saul been leaving any publisher other than W&N.' She then added, 'After all I had not only met Saul through you but would never have become a publisher at all except at your instance and certainly would not have made a success of it without twelve years of thoroughly sound professional training in your organisation. Love as always, Barley.' No mention was made of her being 'monstrously disloyal' or a 'Machiavellian plotter'. It is unlikely George ever learned of the extent of her betrayal.

In the end, Saul Bellow had found a way to leave George Weidenfeld. Remarkably, his departure took place more than nine years after it had been first announced. Somehow, against all expectations and quite Houdini-like, George Weidenfeld had wriggled out of his predicament time and again. Despite all the complaints and nagging, the publisher had convinced America's bestselling author to remain with his firm. Like the great entre- preneur that he was, George had succeeded in saving the deal far longer than most other people thought possible.

This view of George as a world-class persuader is affirmed by Jonathan Lourie. Lourie knows a thing or two about business; through his company Cheyne Capital he manages assets of around $10 billion and is one of the most successful fund managers in Europe. He is also George's godson. Lourie puts it simply: 'George Weidenfeld was the best salesman I ever met.'

CHAPTER 8

███████

1967

'If the British publisher before [WW2] was the primus inter pares in the world order, in the forties and fifties right up to the mid-sixties, he turned into a sort of Greek in the Roman empire of the American publishing orbit.' – GW

By the mid-1960s, George's company was once again in financial trouble. Despite the successes with Mary McCarthy, Saul Bellow and Nabokov, not to mention Claude Lévi-Strauss's *The Savage Mind*, Henry Miller's *Plexus* and *Nexus*, and Eric Hobsbawm's *The Age of Revolution*, Weidenfeld & Nicolson was struggling to pay its bills.

George's firm was not alone in feeling the pinch. Across the publishing world, literary agents were pushing advances higher and higher, the price of paper was ever increasing, as were wages and other fixed costs, while the general public was less eager to reach into their pockets for high-priced books. Yet, there were also issues particular to Weidenfeld & Nicolson. One of the reasons for the company's poor financial situation was the excessive spending habits of its publisher. George liked to travel frequently, to New York, to Paris, to Vienna, to Frankfurt, always first class and always in style. He liked to entertain at the priciest of restaurants and throw the most extravagant of parties. These last took place almost every week. Sometimes more than once a day. Lunches held for a visiting author and a dozen well-known personalities. Dinners for twenty in honour of a journalist, politician or other celebrity, followed by a party for a hundred more. And all the time, George not only looked for new authors but worked hard to promote his existing titles. These gatherings were the talk of the town, attracting those from pop culture as well as from George's inner circle. According to *The Times*, these parties rivalled 'Anne Fleming's and Lady Pamela Berry's as the best functions in London'.

'He loved getting people together,' remembers the interior designer Diana Phipps Sternberg, who first met George Weidenfeld in the 1960s, becoming one of his closest confidantes. He invited a wide range of people; the guests were 'incongruent', selected according to both the quality of their personality and their achievements. He wanted to see what happened if he put them together. That is why the gatherings were so successful, Diana says: you never knew who you were going to meet, what kind of experience you were likely to have. This was one of his gifts. 'I don't think anyone knew who he was, he could be almost anything to anyone,' she continues. 'He was so wonderfully educated. He was certainly the most interesting person I met in my life.'

To solve the financial pressures that he was facing in the mid-1960s, George pursued three strategies. One personal and two business. All three would provide positive results, yet all three would, before long, falter.

The first stratagem was announced on 14 July 1966 in the *New York Times:* George Weidenfeld, British publisher, would soon be marrying the American heiress, Sandra Payson Meyer. Aged thirty-eight, Sandra was eight years George's junior with three teenage children of her own. Her mother, Joan Whitney Payson, was an art collector, majority owner of the New York Mets baseball team, and sister to John Hay Whitney, former ambassador to Great Britain. Soon after arriving in London, Sandra had met George at the house of their mutual friend, Diana Phipps. Sandra was 'a tall, imperious blonde with a Vanderbilt face and marvellous cheekbones,' the publisher later told Gina Thomas, a journalist and close friend. Sandra also came from a world, George added, that was deeply anti-Semitic. And it was full of secrets. Sandra was an alcoholic, for which she had sought treatment. She had left rehab shortly before meeting George. Two weeks after their wedding was announced in the papers, Sandra and George married on 31 July 1966. The party was held at the American Embassy, hosted by the ambassador David Bruce and his wife Evangeline.

It would be wrong, however, to cast the union as simply trans-actional. According to those present, George and Sandra made a sweet couple. He doted on her. She returned the affection. She also thought kindly of his parents, Max and Rosa. The day after the wedding, she wrote them a letter:

Dear Mr and Mrs Weidenfeld
   I pray that I will be able to be the very best of wives to your treasured son. Wasn't that a wonderful wedding and reception and everything and aren't we going to have a splendid and meaningful life together. I'm so sorry not to have seen you to say a proper good-bye but do know I send you my very warmest good wishes.
   Fondly, Sandra.

Sandra and George just after their wedding, Laura (left),
Sandra's daughter Averil (right)

Soon after the wedding celebrations, George and Sandra moved into Cleeve Lodge, at 42 Hyde Park Gate, a few steps from number 28 where Winston Churchill had lived until the year before. One of the finest mansions in London, according to *Vanity Fair*, the two-storey, 4,500-square foot, white-painted Georgian house was purchased as a wedding present by Sandra's family. They were not alone in the house. There was Doug Phipps the driver, who was prone to drink. The cooking was done by Little George. Elario the butler lived with his wife Irma in the basement (her duties included house cleaning, shopping and laundry). Sandra had her own car, a Mercedes 250 SE, which was parked on the quiet cul-de-sac.

Sandra often travelled with George when he went away for work. They had dinner with Véra and Vladimir Nabokov in New York. They met Mary McCarthy in Paris. And they journeyed to Austin, Texas, to stay with former president Lyndon B. Johnson and his wife Lady Bird. 'Thank you for your warm and gracious note following your visit to the Ranch,' wrote LBJ to George. 'I should tell you, however, that the real pleasure was ours – and the only thing that could have added to that pleasure would have been for you and Sandra to be here for the dedication of the Library.' When Lady Bird Johnson travelled to England to promote her new book, she was also dazzled by the Weidenfelds. 'Dear Sandra and George,' she wrote after a sumptuous dinner was thrown in her honour at Cleeve Lodge, 'This has been a glorious time for all of us in London town! The red carpet you rolled out was lined with sable and sparkled with champagne.' Sandra was socially insecure and found these overseas trips taxing, but she wanted to be close to her husband, so she persevered.

To celebrate George's fiftieth birthday in September 1969, Sandra decided to make him a book of remembrances. Although she didn't know many of his friends, and was intimidated by their intellect and cultural sophistication, she reached out to each individually and invited them to contribute a drawing, a poem or another literary effort. 'I'm trying to keep it a big secret,' she wrote, 'for that I need your help.' If she was anxious that few would respond, she need not have worried.

Soon artworks, poems, photographs and other tributes began arriving. A watercolour of a butterfly by Nabokov. 'For young George,' wrote the author, 'from old Vladimir'. A poem from Edna O'Brien, another from Stephen Spender. Two diary pages from Margaret Drabble. A colourful crayon portrait of George by Feliks Topolski. A pencil sketch of the publisher by Cecil Beaton. Prose from Mary McCarthy, the philanthropist Brooke Astor, the philosopher Isaiah Berlin and Teddy Kollek, who had just been elected for the first time as mayor of Jerusalem. There was also an affectionate note from George's mother Rosa, along with a heart-shaped letter of love, in Latin, from his sixteen-year-old daughter Laura.

Sandra had given her husband the one thing that she knew he desired: confirmation of his friends' and family's affection. Each one of these contributions was a sign of respect not only for George, but also for the project's orchestrator, Sandra.

Despite the travelling together, the social gatherings and the small acts of kindness, George and Sandra's marriage ran into problems. There were small issues. Sandra liked to have breakfast downstairs and eat off her Minton breakfast set with large cups. George preferred to take his breakfast in bed, and drink coffee from the small delicate cups he had brought back from Italy. And there were bigger issues. George worked long hours and was frequently away. Sandra's children had remained in America and they begged her to join them. She therefore spent much of her time in New York. There were 'good patches and bad patches,' George later remembered, 'and we tried hard to overcome the problem of rival pulls'. Torn between two lives, Sandra was hit by depression and, when George was away, began once more to drink.

'Sandra was out of her depth,' recalls the author David

Pryce-Jones, 'she was made to do things she had no interest in doing'. Unlike George, who enjoyed attending parties and going to the opera, Sandra preferred to stay at home. 'It's rather an awful thing to say,' Pryce-Jones adds, 'but she was probably not intelligent enough for George.' Five years after marrying him, Sandra moved out, returning to the United States and her children. George was once again living by himself.

George's second financial strategy was to find a new business partner. Going beyond his normal arrangement with other publishers, he was looking for someone who might share the ongoing risks of the industry. He found the ideal candidate in Fred Praeger. Like George, Praeger was born in Vienna and had fled the country after Hitler's tanks rolled into Austria during the *Anschluss* of 1938. He had also lost family members in the Holocaust and, while George set up a publishing company in London, Praeger had established his eponymous firm in New York. After a number of discussions, the two men agreed on a long-term commitment to publish each other's titles, even if they were not commercially viable.

In 1965, for instance, George acquired the following three books from Praeger: an autobiography by Heinz Barwich, a leading scientist in the Soviet Union's nuclear programme; *Road to Jerusalem* by the historian Barnet Litvinoff; and *Three Essays on Ideology and Development* by the French philosopher Raymond Aron. These appeared to have real commercial potential. In return, Praeger purchased *The First Hundred Days of Harold Wilson* by Anthony Shrimsley, *The Inorganic Raw Materials of Antiquity* by André Rosenfeld and *Structural Changes in the Economy of Ghana, 1891–1911* by Robert Szereszewski, none of which were likely to reach the bestseller list, but each was taken on by the American publisher. By the mid-1960s, Weidenfeld & Nicolson had published scores of Praeger books, many of which proved financially successful. What seemed perhaps strange was that Praeger was willing to accept a series of duds in return. With his keen eye for financial detail, it is likely that George wondered how Praeger would be able to cover his publishing costs.

Any doubts would have been answered when, on 24 February 1967, the *New York Times* revealed that Frederick A. Praeger Inc. had been receiving money from secret government sources for more than a decade. When questioned by journalists, Praeger confirmed that he had published '15 or 16 books' at the suggestion of the Central Intelligence Agency. Asked if the link with the CIA was continuing, he stated, 'I have no comment.'

In a subsequent *New York Times* article, Howard Hunt (Chief of Covert Action for the CIA's Domestic Operations Division, and later one of the Watergate burglars) was quoted as saying that 'We funded much of the activities of the Frederick D. Praeger Publishing Corporation in New York City.' If this was true, it is likely that many of the Praeger books published by Weidenfeld & Nicolson were funded, at least in part, by the CIA.

A closer look at the three books acquired by George from Praeger in 1965 provides an illustration. It emerged that Heinz Barwich, the scientist who had worked in the Soviet nuclear programme, had not only defected to the United States but had also worked as a CIA spy. Similarly, it was revealed that Raymond Aron was a co-founder of the Congress for the Freedom of Culture and contributor to *Evidence* magazine, both of which were funded by the CIA. As to the third book by Barnet Litvinoff, though he had Russian parents, there is no evidence he was connected to the American intelligence community.

Praeger was not George's only brush with the CIA. In May 1967 the *Saturday Evening Post* reported that *Encounter* magazine, the monthly American-British journal, was yet another organisation secretly funded by the CIA and MI6. They quoted Thomas W. Braden, who headed the CIA's division of International

Organizations in the 1950s, who said that *Encounter* had received money for more than ten years 'and few outside the CIA knew about it'. Soon after this news broke, the co-editor of *Encounter*, Stephen Spender, resigned. In the *New York Times*, Spender said that he had heard rumours for years, 'but I was not able to confirm anything until a month ago'. Spender was one of George's authors, his book *Learning Laughter* having been published in 1952, and he was currently working on *The Year of the Young Rebels*, which would be released in 1969. Other Weidenfeld & Nicolson authors published in *Encounter* included Edith Sitwell, Isaiah Berlin and Hugh Trevor-Roper among many others. Melvin Lasky, the intellectual anti-Communist – who was suspected of being a CIA agent – was another of George's authors. To say there was an overlap between the magazine and the publishing house would not be an exaggeration.

In early June 1967, George received a letter from Mary McCarthy. 'I gather that the Encounter excitement has somewhat abated in London. But I don't think Mel[vin Lasky] will be able to brazen it through; information here is that he was the CIA man ... If this is so, then Stephen [Spender] has grounds for a sense of injury.' She then added, 'You can't swear that your magazine has complete editorial freedom if one of the editors was secretly controlled.'

Was George Weidenfeld aware that Frederick Praeger received money from the CIA? It is not clear that he knew of this before the news broke in the mid-1960s, but given the extensive publicity and his propensity for gossip, it is highly likely he was aware after this point. Yet, knowing this information didn't seem to bother him, for he continued working with Praeger until the mid-1970s. And what about *Encounter*? He clearly knew about the story after receiving Mary McCarthy's letter. Was George aware that many of his authors contributed to a magazine funded by the CIA before the news broke in 1967? 'He likely would have known,' says journalist and close friend Hella Pick. 'It was widely suspected' that *Encounter* had connections with the intelligence services. Either way, he continued working with Spender, Lasky and many of the other contributors into the next decade and beyond. Did the publisher benefit financially from these intelligence connections? That is less clear. Certainly, there was some indirect benefit, in that books were made available to him that otherwise might not have been, and from which he made some profit. Equally, he was able to publish authors who had made their name in part by being associated with *Encounter*. Yet, any financial profit was limited. Instead, of his three new strategies, it was the third that would prove most consequential.

On 4 August 1968, less than a year since the *New York Times* had disclosed that 'much of its activities' had been funded by the CIA, Frederick A. Praeger Inc. purchased a 39 per cent stake in Weidenfeld Holdings Limited in return for an investment of $375,000. Although Frederick A. Praeger Inc. was no longer owned by its namesake, having been purchased by Encyclopedia Britannica two years before, it would be Fred Praeger himself who would sit on the Weidenfeld board along with a representative of Encyclopedia Britannica. As part of the deal, Frederick A. Praeger Inc (or its parent company Encyclopedia Britannica) also purchased a small portion of George's shares for an additional £61,260. They also agreed to purchase the rest of the publisher's shareholding whenever he desired. This so-called 'put' option was valued at $1.2 million.

Weidenfeld & Nicolson was now well capitalised. As for George, he was, at least on paper, a wealthy man.

CHAPTER 9

The Double Helix

1968

*'Publishing houses, whether in the realm of entertainment or
instruction, are still talent agencies or professional partnerships,
rather than streamlined professional entities.' – GW*

On 23 June 1966, Weidenfeld & Nicolson moved into their new
office at 5 Winsley Street, a few steps from Oxford Circus. The place
was a mess. Piles of books everywhere. Stacks of chairs that needed
to be placed behind desks. Framed pictures covered in brown paper
leaning against walls. Men in aprons coming in and out pushing
dolly carts full of boxes. Editors trying to read manuscripts, despite
it all. Secretaries tapping away at their typewriters. In one corner,
a small group of staff members were trying to get the new Xerox
machine to work. In another, a huddle of production staff discussed
deadlines and copy-editing schedules. A sense of frustration, yet
having to get things done, hung in the air.

Into this frenetic chaos walked a thirty-eight-year-old American
professor of biology named James Watson. He was tall and slender,
his dark hair formed into a widow's peak. In his hand he carried a
worn leather briefcase. He hadn't made an appointment. It would
have been hard to do so with the phones not yet working. He was
one of the first visitors to Weidenfeld & Nicolson's new premises.
Beaming a wide toothy smile and making best use of his soft
Midwest accent, he introduced himself at the reception on the
first floor and explained that he wished to pitch a book. He was
asked to wait in one of the few chairs that were turned right-side

up. Several moments later, he was ushered into a back office, to see the publisher. George rose to greet his visitor, and of course knew who he was. Just four years earlier, in 1962, Watson had won the Nobel Prize for Medicine or Physiology along with two of his colleagues, Francis Crick and Maurice Wilkins, for discovering the genetic structure of DNA at the Cavendish Laboratory, Cambridge University. The media attention had been enormous.

Watson jumped straight in. Would George be interested in a book about their research? It was not going to be a stuffy academic tract, Watson assured the publisher; instead it would focus on the personal stories of those involved. He added that there was an American publisher already in place, Harvard University Press. Thomas Wilson was the editor. They didn't have a contract yet, but the main terms had been agreed. Was George interested? James Watson wanted to know quickly because if it was a 'no', he would go to another publisher. He was on his way to Greece and only had a few days in London. He had already spoken to one of George's chief rivals, André Deutsch, but Watson's preference, given their recent publishing successes, was to go with Weidenfeld & Nicolson. George said that he was flattered and of course interested. He then asked if there was something he could read. To his surprise, the visitor pulled a ream of papers out of his briefcase and handed them to him. This was a complete manuscript. On its front cover was the title, *Base Pairs*.

After Watson left, George asked Nicholas Thompson to take a look at the book. Was it as good as James Watson claimed? Thompson read it over the weekend and reported back to the publisher first thing on Monday morning. The book was even better than expected. It was not only an inside account of one of the greatest scientific discoveries of all time, it also revealed the quest with enormous verve and excitement, capturing the infighting and petty jealousies of those involved, along with the very real obstacles they faced, the ups and downs of the chase. What life was really like at Cambridge University. The relationships between the scientists. Even their love lives. The writing was crisp and compelling. It was going to be a smash hit.

James Watson with a reproduction of DNA double helix

On Tuesday 5 July, George wrote to James Watson. 'May I say, first of all, how very excited I and my colleagues are at the possibility of our publishing for you in this country,' he began. 'We shall certainly consider it our major book for next spring and promote it with all our energy and enthusiasm to ensure the widest possible distribution.' He then turned to the editorial content, and said that though the subject fascinated him as a non-scientist, he was concerned that the material might prove 'difficult for the layman'. To solve this, he suggested generous use of illustrations of both the incorrect and correct final scientific models, as well as photographs of the principal figures working in the labs. He then asked Watson what he envisaged.

The American scientist was nothing if not confident. He believed that if the book managed to 'penetrate beyond the relatively limited circle of the Science establishment', then it should have 'enormous' – six-figure – sales, and he wished the contract terms to reflect this possibility. Having already made his calculations, George now offered an advance of $10,000, a significant sum at the time. He promised an unprecedented publicity and marketing campaign. In return, he wanted the rights not only to distribute the book in Great Britain and around the Commonwealth (including Canada), but also to sell the book to international publishers. The terms seemed attractive to Watson. He asked for a copy of the publishing house's standard contract so that he could read it while in Greece, and promised to make a decision upon his return in a couple of months. In a letter to Thomas Wilson at Harvard University Press written a few days later, George wrote that Watson 'gave the impression that he was well disposed to publishing with us'.

In September, discussions continued on the contract. First on the agenda was the title. *Base Pairs* was dull, everyone agreed. Watson suggested *Honest Jim*. Although both publishers believed that this not only smacked of arrogance but might be potentially inflammatory to his colleagues, this was the title used in the agreements. By the end of the month, Watson had signed contracts with both Weidenfeld & Nicolson and Harvard University Press. As he hoped, George had acquired the translation rights, though he would give a third of the proceeds to Harvard University Press in appreciation of their early manuscript efforts. In the meantime, another problem grabbed their attention. In October 1966, George received a letter from his libel lawyers in London.

Sharing a manuscript with lawyers, also known as a 'legal read', had long been an integral part of the publishing business. In addition to concerns about libel, attorneys checked for breaches of privacy and confidentiality, as well as copyright infringement. George had a long-standing relationship with the firm Oswald Hickson, Collier and Company, who were quick to review anything the publisher wished him to look at. The report on *Base Pairs* was detailed. The references to Watson's colleagues and fellow Nobel Prize winners, Crick and Wilkins, were defamatory. These should be toned down. Better still, they should be given a chance to review the manuscript and be asked for their approval. Far more problematic, the lawyer said, was the portrait of Watson's third colleague, the British chemist Rosalind Franklin. There were numerous negative comments about her, with the result that she came across as 'a dominating, bad tempered and unpleasant woman'. This would have to be corrected.

When Watson was shown a copy of the libel report, he let the publishers know that they need not worry about defaming Rosalind Franklin as she had died in 1958 and, according to British and American law, the dead could not be libelled. As to the others, Watson had shared a copy of the manuscript with both Crick and Wilkins and was waiting for them to give their approval. But they didn't. On 10 November, Watson informed his British publisher that Crick and Wilkins were refusing to sign waivers.

Then, two days before Christmas, on 23 December 1966, Crick wrote to Nathan Pusey, the president of Harvard University, the person ultimately in charge of Harvard University Press. 'It is quite unprecedented,' declared Crick, 'for a scientist to publish an account of joint work to which his collaborators object.' Apparently sympathetic to this argument, Pusey replied on 13 January that he was forwarding the matter to the Board of Syndics, a group of twelve academics who advised Harvard University Press. 'I'm about 90 per cent sure we're going ahead,' Joyce Lebowitz, the lead editor at Harvard University Press, said to James Watson. 'Relax.'

Four months later, on 13 April 1967, with the matter still pending, Crick wrote a six-page missive directly to James Watson with a line-by-line rebuttal of the book. At the letter's end, he summed up his argument as follows: 'My objection in short is to the widespread dissemination of a book which grossly invades my privacy and I have yet to hear an argument which adequately excused such a violation of friendship. If you publish your book in the teeth of my opposition history will condemn you.'

That same week, George wrote an internal memo to his editorial director, Nicholas Thompson. 'This is quite clearly developing into a cause celebre which, if we succeed in publishing the book, should help it enormously,' he wrote. 'It is, on the other hand, possible that it might quite easily never see the light of day.' He then added that 'It is now up to us to find out from our lawyers if, whatever the US situation, we can publish the book.'

Finally, in the last week of May, Harvard University Press made a decision. Immediately after, editor Joyce Lebowitz wrote to James Watson with the news:

> I think I want to say rather formally in writing how sorry I am that we're not being allowed to publish your book. It's a wretched decision, one we're sure to regret for a long time to come. Others can be generous and understanding about it – myself I just don't feel like accepting it with professional calm, jolly old sportsman-ship, and grown-up good grace.

Apparently, even though the Board of Syndics had voted unani-mously that Harvard University Press could publish, Nathan Pusey had made the final decision. He did not want Harvard to be entangled in an international controversy among scientists. The story did not go unnoticed. HARVARD VETOES NOBEL WINNERS' BOOK, screamed the headline of the London *Times*. Meanwhile, the *Harvard Crimson* wrote that Pusey is 'less interested in diversity of viewpoint than bland tranquillity'.

Worried that George might also pull out, Watson wrote to Weidenfeld & Nicolson in London. 'Crick and Wilkins have resorted to legal threats to stop publication,' he wrote, 'so we are now having the ms [manuscript] looked at by the best legal brains.' Then, having discussed further publication details, he added, 'In any case, let me assure that not for a moment have I considered abandoning the publication and I hope very much that Weidenfeld will want to see it through to the finish.' Wanting to comfort the American scientist, Nicholas Thompson wrote straight back. 'Please be assured that we are as keen as you to see the matter through to the finish and the book published in an unbowdlerised form.' The truth was slightly different. George Weidenfeld was still waiting for his lawyers to give the green light.

In the meantime, the book had been sent to Atheneum Books in New York (almost certainly by Thomas Wilson, the editor at Harvard University Press who would be moving there at the year's end). Recently established by three of the city's leading literary figures – Alfred A. Knopf, Hiram Haydn and Simon Michael Bessie – Atheneum Books was viewed as an up-and-coming publisher. On 26 April, Bessie wrote a letter to George in London. On the outside of the blue- and red-striped envelope was written in blue ink the word 'confidential'. He reported they were now considering the project. 'I've read it and found it fascinating,' Bessie wrote, 'I hope it works out and we shall be doing this together.' Once he had heard back from his lawyers, Bessie continued, he would let George know.

In July the American lawyers cleared the manuscript for printing. In Britain, where the people featured in the book lived and where the libel laws were more onerous for publishers, it was proving more difficult. Finally, on 20 September 1967, George sent his peer at Atheneum a cable:

DECIDED TO PUBLISH WATSON SORRY DELAY REGARDS GEORGE WEIDENFELD

In the end, what had given the British libel lawyers confidence was that one of their senior partners had shown the manuscript to a close friend who had known Crick for many years. Apparently, this friend had said that James Watson's portrait of Francis Crick was true to life. Proceeding, however, would not be without its risks.

It was around this time that Watson received a letter from John Maddox, the editor of *Nature*. 'Let me say again that I admire the book immensely and think that its publication will be a public service,' he said. 'I also think you will have to barricade yourself in for six months or so after it appears.'

The Double Helix, as it was now known, was all set to be published in April 1968. The press releases were ready. Interviews with journalists in London and New York were arranged. The text would be serialised in the *Atlantic*. All seemed to be going to plan, until the cover art for the British edition arrived on James Watson's desk. The back cover had lines such as 'Which eminent English biologist created a scandal at a costume party by dressing up as George Bernard Shaw and kissing all the girls behind the anonymity of a scraggy red beard?' and 'Who is the top Cambridge scientist who gossips over dinner about the private lives of women undergraduates?' Watson was outraged by the flippant tone. The inside flap was hardly better. 'The moment we edged through the door into the crush of half-drunken dancers we knew the evening would be a smashing success, since the attractive Cambridge au pair girls were there.'

The author immediately wrote to his American publisher. '*Double Helix* fly-jacket is disgraceful insult to Francis Crick, demand you withdraw all copies and replace with cover showing you are more than cheap scandalmongers. Reply immediately. If necessary I will bring immediate suit.' Thomas Wilson called George, who was staying at the Hotel Pierre in New York. When the publisher said that they had already agreed to change the cover, Wilson said he was worried that a few of the jackets might be 'being preserved in the wrong hands'. George said that he was already alive to this and promised to make certain that all covers would be 'found and destroyed'. He also said that he realised the danger of letting similar material creep into the advertising copy when the book was published. Reassured, Wilson said he would let Watson know.

This didn't stop the author from sending his own letter to London, saying that if their advertising included any 'hint of scandal or mischievous gossip', and as a result Crick sued, then Weidenfeld would pay the legal costs.

As their lead title for the spring, Weidenfeld & Nicolson had committed to a significant advertising campaign for *The Double Helix*. In addition to purchasing display advertisements in the book trade papers, they had also paid for space in the *Observer*, *Evening Standard* and *Sunday Times*. They had paid for a fifteen-second film teaser, which would be played for twenty-six consecutive weeks, from 1 July to the year's end, at four Classic Cinema venues, including Chelsea, Hampstead, Notting Hill Gate and Kensington. This was a highly unusual effort for any British publisher, let alone Weidenfeld & Nicolson.

The press conference for *The Double Helix* was held at 11 a.m. on Wednesday 15 May 1968 at the Savoy Hotel in London. With its light brown wall panelling and art deco decorations, the Mikado room was an elegant spot to hold a book launch. Dressed in a dark suit and tie, James Watson walked in first, followed by his proud publisher, George Weidenfeld. The place was packed. The room's official capacity was thirty-five people. More than fifty had squeezed in. A few lucky ones had seats, the rest were standing. There were literary editors from the main national and regional newspapers. There were correspondents from the glossy magazines and hacks from news agencies. There were science journalists and international correspondents. After being introduced, Watson gave a short ten-minute presentation. He explained why he wrote the book. He gave the story's central premise and shared what it was like to be an American in the English academic life of the fifties. Then came the questions, thick and fast. Flashbulbs popping. Arms raised high in the air. What was it like to find the secret of life? Could his discovery be used to cure cancer? When would scientists be able to clone humans? Never before had a scientist been treated like a pop star.

After the press event, George hosted a lunch for Watson and his wife Elizabeth at the Savoy. Joining them were Nicholas Thompson and the science writer Gerald Leech. After lunch, the author was driven to the BBC where he was interviewed for the *Twenty-Four Hours* show. From there, the publicity tour continued, relentlessly. Interviews with *The Times*. ITN *News at Ten*. *Late Night Line-Up* on BBC television. A Granada current affairs programme, as well as appearances on four radio shows, *World of Books*, *World at One*, the *10 o' Clock Show* and the BBC Overseas Service. It was a media blitz.

Over the following days and weeks, *The Double Helix* sold swiftly in Britain, the United States, France, Germany and more than a dozen other countries. A month later, an editorial executive prepared a memo for George Weidenfeld. 'The book is selling at a phenomenal rate,' he reported. He had ordered paper for an additional 10,000 copies. They would have to reprint soon after that. *The Double Helix* was a certified bestseller. George Weidenfeld was a success.

First edition book cover, The Double Helix.

Since its publication, *The Double Helix* has been recognised as one of the most important books of the twentieth century. In 1998 the book was listed by the Modern Library as seventh on its list of the 100 best non-fiction books. In 2011, *Time* magazine chose the book as seventy-fourth in its top 101 'All-time nonfiction books'. A year later, *The Double Helix* was named as one of the eighty-eight 'Books That Shaped America' by the Library of Congress. In 2015 the *Guardian* chose the book as fifteenth on its list 'The 100 best nonfiction books'.

Yet, *The Double Helix* has also received considerable and, perhaps, growing criticism over the years. Most of this has focused on James Watson's relentlessly negative portrayal of his former colleague Rosalind Franklin. And this was *after* the libel lawyers had encouraged him to tone down his language. One of those to challenge Watson was the writer Anne Sayre. In her book *Rosalind Franklin and DNA* published in 1975, Sayre pointed out that Watson called Franklin 'belligerent', 'unattractive', and said she had an 'acid smile'. He criticised her for not wearing lipstick and for not taking 'even a mild interest in clothes'. Later, when they disagreed about their work, he said she became 'positively aggressive', 'pugnaciously assertive', and 'increasingly annoyed'. At one point he reported that she 'had to go or be put in her place'. Sayre also quoted Watson as saying that the 'best home for a feminist [such as Rosy] was in another lab'.

Other observers said that James Watson not only demeaned Rosalind Franklin, but he failed to give credit for her contribution to the identification of the double helix. In her book *Rosalind Franklin: The Dark Lady of DNA*, for instance, published in 2003, the biographer Brenda Maddox argued that without Franklin's scientific discoveries, Watson, Crick and Wilkins would never have uncovered the secret to life, at least not when they did. In the eyes of Maddox, and many others, Franklin was robbed of the Nobel Prize.

In the years after her death, Rosalind Franklin's reputation has grown and with that, her accolades. The National Portrait Gallery in London hung her picture next to that of Crick and Watson. The European Space Agency named its ExoMars rover 'Rosalind Franklin'. The UK's Royal Mint announced a 50-pence coin to celebrate the hundredth anniversary of her birth. The University of Portsmouth changed the name 'James Watson Halls' to 'Rosalind Franklin Halls'. While the American National Cancer Institute created the Rosalind E. Franklin Award for women in cancer research.

'Whenever I'm asked to name one book that was an unexpected worldwide success,' George Weidenfeld later said, 'I think of J. D. Watson's *Double Helix.*' A year after the book's publication, he would have another big success on his hands, this time from a writer he had known for many years.

CHAPTER 10

Mary Queen of Scots

1969

'Napoleon once said that no one knows us as well as our valet.
It might be said by way of paraphrasing that no one knows an
author – his psyche, his temperament, his whims and quirks,
his qualities and feelings, his charismatic heights and depths
or pettiness and frailty – as well as his publisher.' – GW

'Nobody expected it to be a bestseller,' recalls Antonia Fraser (née Pakenham), talking about her book *Mary Queen of Scots*. There was no extravagant launch party at George's house. No speech declaring it would be a book of the year. No massive publicity campaign. 'It was a real surprise, including to George.'

On the staff of Weidenfeld & Nicolson back in the 1950s, Antonia had worked hard, but she was considered a junior employee. At a party, George had once described her as a *'Jeune fille en fleur'*. In addition to her duties as publicist and editorial assistant, she had written two books, one on King Arthur, the other on Robin Hood. She had left the publishing house in August 1956 intending to take up a publishing job in the United States. A month later, she had married the Conservative MP, Hugh Fraser, decided not to take the American position, and then gave birth to her first child, in May 1957. Since then, she had four more children and written two illustrated books: *Dolls* and *The History of Toys*. Both of these titles were published by George and for both she had been paid a flat fee instead of an advance and royalties. It was then that her mother, Elizabeth Longford, historian and author, announced that her agent wanted her to write a book about Mary Queen of Scots. 'You can't do that,' cried the daughter, in horror, 'She's my Mary Queen of Scots.' To which her mother said, cheerily, 'In that case I'll do Wellington.' It was with this background that Antonia Fraser went to see Graham Watson of Curtis Brown and told him about her plans for her new book. Excited, Watson signed her on as a client.

By this point in the mid-1960s, it was increasingly common for authors to be represented by an agent. The top agents in Britain included Greene & Heaton, Eric Glass, A. M. Heath, David Higham Associates and Curtis Brown. Typically, agents were paid 10 per cent of the author's income, covering advances, royalties and any other money received. Their task was to negotiate the contract and represent the author's interests in case of a dispute. Publishers grudgingly accepted the role of the agent, though many bemoaned their presence in the industry. They blamed the agents for pushing up book advances, for interfering with the precious publisher/author creative relationship, for encouraging their clients to act as demanding divas.

Which was why Antonia was nervous when she agreed to have lunch with her former boss, George Weidenfeld. She felt a little guilty. Would he be upset about her having an agent, about there being an intermediary standing between her and her publisher? They met at the Ritz. The meal was enjoyable, the conversation flowed easily. Towards the end, Antonia spoke about her new book, which delighted him. She then revealed that from this point forward she would be represented by Curtis Brown. George was unfazed by this announcement, remaining composed. 'I need not have worried,' she recalls. A contract was agreed on 4 June 1964. She would be paid an advance of £2,000, a significant sum at the time. The delivery date was set four years into the future, 30 March 1968, giving ample time for research, writing and editing.

Antonia Fraser threw herself into researching the rich history of

Mary Queen of Scots. She spent time in the archives poring over old documents. She visited the places important to her subject's biography – Stirling Castle her childhood home, Fotheringhay where she was executed, Westminster Abbey where she was buried. By the end of the third year, she had amassed stacks of research.

In the middle of her research, the now thirty-three-year-old Antonia Fraser flew to America to promote her book *The History of Toys*, which had just been published by Delacorte Press. An article written by Charles Monaghan for the *New York Times* gives a sense of how she was perceived by some people at this time. 'She looks for all the world like a willowy Julie Christie, blond locks escaping as they wish from a pulled-back hairdo. But a Julie Christie would never think of kissing her agent, specially on television,' it began. Then, at great length, the article provided details about her husband Hugh Fraser and father Frank Pakenham's careers, before commenting on the young woman's passion for parties, the opera and art galleries. 'I'd love my picture to be there some day,' the newspaper reported Antonia saying, 'with a plaque like there is under a marvellous man: wit, raconteur, author, dandy and balloonist... I'd like it to say "beauty" too.' The journalist then added, 'It undoubtedly will.'

With her ten-day book tour of America complete, Antonia Fraser flew back to England, returning to *Mary Queen of Scots*. Her research was halted, temporarily, when she gave birth to her sixth child in May 1967. Soon after, she began writing in earnest, tapping away at a small portable typewriter. During this period, she and George had no conversations about the book. For while they now considered each other to be friends, and met frequently on social occasions, they did not talk about her writing. He was entirely hands off. Indeed, while she was writing the book, she was not in touch with anyone at Weidenfeld & Nicolson.

Finally, in July 1968, Antonia Fraser completed the manuscript. The last words of the epilogue read, 'As Mary herself embroidered so long ago at Sheffield on the royal cloth of state which was destined to hang over the head of a captive queen: *In my end is my beginning*.' It was done. Antonia stacked the papers and delivered them to Graham Watson at Curtis Brown. The manuscript was then forwarded to Tony Godwin, the project's editor at Weidenfeld & Nicolson. Godwin had previously been at Penguin, where he had established their Penguin Modern Classics series. George had enticed him over to Weidenfeld & Nicolson three years earlier to freshen up the list. Which is exactly what he had done.

After being proof-read and laid out by the typesetter, the book ran to 555 pages. Antonia Fraser was not sure if George himself read the manuscript, but 'he was always very encouraging' she remembers. When it came to publication, the book was acquired by Delacorte Press in the United States. Just before its release, the American publisher wrote a letter informing the author that they were reducing their first print run from 5,000 to 3,000 copies, explaining their decision that the book was dry and scholarly and would be of little interest to American readers.

Mary Queen of Scots was published on 15 May 1969, priced 18 shillings. The book received wide and overwhelmingly positive attention. The *Sunday Mirror* announced the book's arrival on its front page next to a revealing picture of Raquel Welch dressed as a 'slave girl', taken from an upcoming film with Ringo Starr. The *Birmingham Post* concluded that Antonia Fraser had portrayed the queen 'readably and romantically'. The *Times* commended the author on being 'clear headed' and that 'perhaps her most useful asset is her commonsense sympathy of one woman to another'. The *New York Times*, which had written so condescendingly about her three years before, reported that Fraser's book was a 'careful and sympathetic biography' and 'full of interesting detail and so rich in human interest'. Finally, the *Illustrated London News* compared her favourably with her biographer mother, Elizabeth Longford, and congratulated her on her 'first-class piece of work' and her 'clear political brain'.

'*Mary Queen of Scots* went on to be an astonishing success,' Fraser later wrote in her memoir, 'that is to say it astonished my publishers and it astonished me.' The book remained on the bestseller list for eight months. In their round-up of the year's most successful books, *The Times* mentioned both *Mary Queen of Scots* and the biography by Antonia's mother, Elizabeth Longford, entitled *Wellington*. Both of course were published by George Weidenfeld. 'His involvement was enthusiasm at the beginning, giving me a contract,' Antonia Fraser remembers, 'and then being very encouraging when it came out.'

Over the next fifty years, Antonia Fraser went on to publish a series of bestsellers, all with Weidenfeld & Nicolson. These included *Marie Antoinette, Love and Louis XIV* and *The Six Wives of Henry VIII*. George was supremely appreciative of Antonia's contribution to Weidenfeld & Nicolson. In a speech given many years later, he would say that if someone held a gun to his head to pick one out of all his thousands of authors, he would unhesitatingly yell the name 'Antonia'.

Antonia Fraser (right), George Weidenfeld and Antonia's mother Elizabeth Longford (left)

'He was deeply respectful,' recalls Antonia Fraser, talking about George Weidenfeld's treatment of women, 'in every way George was a gentleman.'

Whenever stories were written about the publisher in the press, it was common for a journalist to comment on George's relationship with women. Most referred to his many marriages. His romances with celebrities. His courtship of the young and the beautiful (George had a rule that they could not be younger than his daughter Laura). When talking in private, however, the responses of women varied.

First, there is the group who say that the publisher 'enjoyed the company of women', but didn't believe his behaviour to have been objectionable or immoral. Hella Pick, the journalist and author who worked with George for many years, is among these. She first met George in the 1960s and has written a number of books for Weidenfeld & Nicolson, including *Simon Wiesenthal: A Life in Search of Justice* and *Invisible Walls*. She says that he pursued her for a while, but she did not encourage him, and for the rest of his life they remained close friends.

Another woman with fond memories is the former model Aldine Honey, who had a romantic relationship with George for several years in the late 1970s. 'He could practically have anybody he wanted,' she says. 'Not that he was an attractive man, but his personality and his intellect and his charm were brilliant.' In her experience, she continues, 'He treated women with respect,' adding that, 'George was the most fascinating person I ever met. He had a phenomenal brain and intellect.' Aldine says that she and George had a 'special relationship' and that he had suggested he and Aldine marry 'several times'. She declined, she adds, concerned that 'intellectually she would not be able to hold his attention'.

Connie Sayers, who worked with George in New York in the 1980s, says that she had never seen him behave in an inappropriate way, either to herself or others. Instead, she remembers that 'women were utterly charmed by him'. Gila Falkus, who worked in the Weidenfeld & Nicolson editorial department in the 1980s, notes, 'We all knew he was a womaniser, but we thought he liked rich blond American millionaires.' She adds that the womanising 'mostly' took place outside the office.

Then there is a second group of women who say that both their and George's behaviour was transgressive. Perhaps the best example of this is Barbara Amiel. In 1985 she was a successful newspaper columnist and, while married, had an affair with George. Another example was Barbara Skelton who, as already mentioned, had an affair with the publisher while she was married to Cyril Connelly. Apparently, there were many, many more marital affairs. For instance, George stated that in the 1950s he had had an affair with Princess Herzeleide von Preussen, granddaughter of the Kaiser, when she was married to Prince Karl Biron von Curland. Adultery was 'acceptable among George's circle,' says Diana Phipps Sternberg, another close friend of the publisher, 'so long as you were discreet and you didn't create any jealousy.' 'There was safety in this,' she adds, 'in that it was unlikely to lead to commitment. And, remember, it was just as much the woman's choice as George's.'

And then there is a third group of women who view George within the context of male behaviour at the time. Pat Kinsman started working as George's secretary in the 1970s at the age of twenty-seven. After taking a short break in the early 1980s, she remained working for him till he died in 2016. By many accounts, she was one of the people who knew George the best. Pat says that when she first arrived at the Weidenfeld & Nicolson office she was told by his older secretary, Mary, that it was rumoured George slept with all his secretaries. Pat remembers, 'It was a very friendly and relaxed place then. George was not a groper. His way was vocal – extravagant flattery – and there was no "one point" to be rebuffed. It was sort of habitual (as in, more of a habit) with all the women he liked. It didn't make me uncomfortable.' She continues, 'He was by no means the only man to behave in this way towards women – although probably far more entertainingly than most. It was a different time. What now seems reprehensible back then was fairly routine.'

Finally, there is a fourth group: women who found the publisher's behaviour unacceptable at the time it took place. The year was 1984, the occasion the launch of Victoria Glendinning's book *The Life of Vita Sackville-West*. George was at the centre of things as usual. 'He was completely over the top with the young women,' remembers Vanessa Nicolson, who had just left university and was Vita Sackville-West's granddaughter. 'He was all over me at one point,' she says. He then summoned another woman and told her they had to get a job for Vanessa. She recalls that she had experienced this kind of behaviour from other men, that it was prevalent at the time. 'There were these older men who were in positions of power,' she remembers. 'You just had this feeling, it wasn't even articulated. Somehow. It was just the sense of this guy is a bit too close to me... He seems big and looming, you know? And invading your space a bit. There's a word that keeps coming into my head. It's "creepy".' Vanessa Nicolson thinks about this a little more, then adds, 'I don't know if he was like this to a lot of young women. He was just someone you wanted to run a mile from.'

Another person who found George's attitude towards women challenging was Alexandra MacCormick, who worked with him in the 1980s. Most of the office staff were women, except the directors who were, with one exception, all men. She was paid so little for her role as a senior commissioning editor that she had to take on a second job at a wine bar in Battersea. She became so fed up with her long working hours for such a low wage that she asked George for a raise. 'Oh, can't your father let you have a bit more, increase your allowance?' asked George. When MacCormick said her father had died when she was a teenager, the publisher replied, 'Oh dear.'

He then asked, 'You're not married are you?' When she said she wasn't, he replied, brightly, 'Don't you have a boyfriend who can sub you a bit?' She was shocked. 'Are you suggesting I take money from my boyfriend?' To which George said, 'Yes, but I will think about making you a director.' He never did.

CHAPTER 11

The Governance of Britain

1976

*'It is the pride of any self-respecting publisher to
have deliberately in each list "loss-leaders", works of
scholarship and literary experimentation.' – GW*

Early in the morning of 27 May 1976 there was a knock on the door
of the guest bedroom of Aberuchill Castle in Perthshire, Scotland.
From under the covers of the huge bed, George Weidenfeld
instructed the attendant to enter. The room was so large that it
took the attendant a few seconds to arrive at the bedside, where he
gently placed the tray on the covers. Next he padded over to the
curtains, which he pulled back, letting in the light.

With some effort, George sat up. He was in his pyjamas and
alone, his divorce to Sandra having been finalised a few weeks
before. Next to the cup of tea was a rack of toast, along with a
small pot of jam, a patty of butter, a plate and a knife. Also on the
tray was a range of the day's newspapers. Sitting up in bed, a stack
of pillows arranged behind him, George turned to the papers. The
front page of *The Times* featured a large photograph of the leader
of the Conservative opposition, Margaret Thatcher. The story in
the top right corner was of more interest. This article contained
the names of forty-two people who had been given honours by the
retiring Labour prime minister, Harold Wilson. Included among
these were life peerages for Sir Lew Grade, Sir Bernard Delfont
and Sir Joseph Kagan. There was another name listed: George
Weidenfeld.

The publisher was used to reading about himself in the press, and while he had been expecting this announcement, to see his name so acclaimed was deeply moving. This was significant public confirmation of his efforts. Seven years earlier, he had received a knighthood. Following that announcement, he had been sent hundreds of congratulatory letters and cables. The vast majority were clearly sincere in their happiness for him. But not all of them. The president of the Publishers Association had written to him, for instance, commending him on the 'hard work which you have put in to attain your Knighthood'. According to the author David Pryce-Jones, this letter had made George 'very upset'.

With the new accolade, George would become a baron. A life peer, able to give speeches in the House of Lords and comment on the government's business. From this point forward, people would use the honorific 'Lord' when addressing him. Forty years after arriving in London as an Austrian-Jewish refugee, barely able to speak English, with few friends or contacts, he was part of the British Establishment. He had officially arrived.

If George had been expecting jubilation, even praise, instead what he found in the article he was reading was outrage. At who was on the list. At how the names had been selected. Sydney Bidwell, Labour MP for Ealing, described the announcement as 'messy' and 'nothing to do' with the Labour government's mission. Another Labour MP, this time representing Perry Barr in Birmingham, said 'I have 50 people in my local party who have done more as individuals than this lot put together.' While Conservative MP Teddy Taylor said that the list tended to 'cheapen the whole principle of honours', which should not have been given to 'cronies and associates'. Then there was Neil Macfarlane, Conservative MP for Sutton and Cheam, who proclaimed that the list was symptomatic of the way the country had been 'demeaned and debased' during the premiership of Harold Wilson.

The implication was that those on the list had been chosen not for their talents or hard work, but for their connections. And with this came a snide, snickering, mocking tone. So, while George Weidenfeld had 'made it', in many ways he had clearly not.

George had first encountered Harold Wilson just after the war in late 1945, when the future prime minister was an academic and George and Contact Books Limited had published his book, *New Deal for Coal*. Unsurprisingly, it sold few copies, but through its release the publisher had become acquainted with the author. Over the next decade, George and Harold Wilson had little contact, occasionally meeting at parties or other literary events. Nevertheless, from afar, George watched with interest as Wilson distinguished himself in government. He had been appointed at the war's end to be parliamentary secretary to the Minister of Works and then, aged thirty-one, president of the Board of Trade, the youngest cabinet member in more than forty years. Next, Wilson was appointed Shadow Chancellor of the Exchequer and then Shadow Foreign Secretary. George's interest went beyond admiration for the man's mastery of policy briefs, political acumen and organisational skills. For the publisher was also a Labour supporter. Soon after arriving in the United Kingdom, the Austrian refugee had made a decision on which party suited his values and ambitions. 'A foreigner coming to England tended to favour the Labour Party over the Tories,' he later told Gina Thomas, 'because the mood and those of the Left seemed much more welcoming and sympathetic'. He also noted that, in the years following the Second World War, members of the Conservative Party tended to be more anti-Semitic and less supportive of the state of Israel than those in the Labour Party.

Then, in 1963, after Wilson had won Labour's leadership battle, and aware that Weidenfeld & Nicolson had published *New Deal for Coal*, two party members approached George to see if he might be interested in a few books by Labour politicians. The publisher said he was indeed interested. In the end, Wilson was the only one of them to deliver a publishable manuscript. First came *Purpose in Politics*, followed by *The Relevance of British Socialism*. His next book was *The First Hundred Days*, released in October 1964, a few months after Wilson was elected prime minister. Then came *Purpose in Power*, a collection of his notable speeches. All these books were released by Weidenfeld & Nicolson.

George's interactions with Harold Wilson were not limited to the world of publishing. Perhaps nowhere was this more apparent than in the debate over whether Britain should join the European Economic Community (EEC). Following a request from the Wilson government, George convened an informal group of business leaders, lawyers and academics to help win the argument about joining the EEC. He set up a dinner between Wilson and the proprietor and editor of *Der Spiegel* magazine, Rudolf Augstein. He arranged an interview for the prime minister with *Le Monde* newspaper in France. He organised a panel of British experts to appear on West German television and he wrote a pro-European letter to the newspapers and persuaded an impressive range of celebrities to sign it, including the artist Henry Moore, the novelists Edna O'Brien and C. P. Snow, the poet Stephen Spender, along with the philosophers Bernard Williams and A. J. Ayer. George also passed intelligence along to the government that he picked up during his travels around Europe. On 10 February 1967, for instance, he wrote to Richard Crossman, the leader of the House of Commons, saying that he had received 'an interesting brief' from the *Washington Post* German correspondent who, in his opinion, was 'one of the best-informed foreign observers in Bonn'. He also happened to be Melvin Lasky's brother-in-law, the same Melvin Lasky who was co-editor of *Encounter* magazine.

Meanwhile, George's relationship with Harold Wilson and his inner circle strengthened. In 1971 he published the former prime minister's memoirs about his time in office, *The Labour Government: A Personal Record*. One year later, Weidenfeld & Nicolson published

Inside Number 10 by Marcia Williams, Harold Wilson's private secretary and head of his political office. When Wilson won re-election in February 1974, George was a frequent guest in Downing Street. He was a great supporter of Wilson's decision to hold a referendum to obtain the public's consent to Britain's entry into the EEC, and when the referendum was successful, on 5 June 1975, the publisher shared the prime minister's satisfaction.

Harold Wilson and Marcia Williams (Lady Falkender)

In February 1976, George received a call from Downing Street. He was told to go immediately to the House of Commons and wait for the prime minister in his private office. At this time, rumours and innuendo were rife among the hacks of Fleet Street that the Soviets had an undue influence on the prime minister – a so-called 'Russian connection'. At 10.30 p.m. Wilson walked in and asked George to find out if the CIA was behind the smears. 'I can't get any sense out of our own people,' he said. 'I want to know if the Americans are involved.' A few days later, the publisher flew to Washington DC. There he met with Frank Church, the head of the Senate's intelligence committee. Church said he would look into the matter. Next, George travelled up the coast to New York to see George

H. W. Bush, who was a friend of his ex-wife Sandra and at the time ran the CIA. They met at the Waldorf Towers. It wasn't long before George heard back from the Americans: the United States was not attempting to undermine the British government, he was told, though they could not account for 'hired hands' who might be working at a lower level. By phone, George reported back to the prime minister's secretary, Marcia Williams, who was now known as Lady Falkender having been elevated to a peerage in 1974. They spoke in code: Bush was 'Gary Cooper', Wilson was 'The Producer'. 'Gary Cooper would like to see The Producer again,' George said, speaking loudly down the line. When a date was suggested, Lady Falkender replied, 'It's got to be before that.' George had no idea what she meant, but he would find out, as would the rest of the world, two weeks later.

On 16 March, Wilson told the House of Commons of his decision to step down as prime minister. He said that he had always planned to retire at sixty (his birthday was five days before) and that he was exhausted. The real reason may have been that he knew he had dementia. Wilson said that he would stay on for three weeks and then hand over to whoever was elected by Labour to become the next party leader.

That night, George hosted the prime minister and Lady Falkender for dinner. It was just the three of them; the meal was prepared by the publisher's cook, Little George. They gathered around a small table in George's flat. For months, George and Lady Falkender had known that Wilson might resign. They had tried numerous times to persuade the prime minister to stay on till the end of his term. Yet, when Wilson had made the announcement earlier that day, George had been caught unawares. Harold Wilson was 'tense', Lady Falkender later recalled, 'and in a bad mood'. She criticised him for not thinking about the people who worked for him, presumably meaning her. He tried to change the subject, at which point she walked out, slamming the door behind her. Without saying a word, Wilson ran after her into the night. Later, Wilson's driver would return to collect the prime minister's pipe which he had left on George's table.

It was within this febrile atmosphere, during his last days in office, that Harold Wilson considered to whom he might give honours: a peerage, a knighthood, an MBE. And it was this list, announced on 27 May, six weeks after Wilson's departure, that George had read while staying on a Scottish estate.

In the weeks and months that followed the publication of the honours list, the press reported one revelation after another. Joe Haines, the prime minister's press secretary, disclosed that it had been Lady Falkender who had drawn up the original list, not Harold Wilson. It was also reported that the paper she had used was pink or mauve in colour. From this point on, therefore, it was known as the 'Lavender List'. The *Liverpool Echo*, having pointed out that one of those who received a knighthood, James Goldsmith, had contributed money to Conservative Party funds, then asked: 'What conceivable reason would he receive an honour apart from the fact that he is a friend of Lady Falkender?' Paper after paper poked fun at a self-described socialist prime minster honouring 'show biz kings' like Lew Grade and Bernard Delfont. Another outlet revealed that Miss Peggy Field, who had been awarded an MBE, was also the sister of Lady Falkender.

There were many, however, who were happy for George and his elevation to a peerage. One of these was his old partner, Nigel Nicolson. 'It moves me very much, when I look back at the struggles you have endured, to see you enter a sort of harbour,' he wrote on the same day the peerage was announced, continuing:

A harbour from which you will sail out often again on a new
voyage of exploration, but a harbour always to return to, where
you feel welcomed, secure, honoured and loved. Dear George,
you have deserved this more than any of your fellow-honorands,
for you started with the least advantage and by courage, hard

work, intelligence and enterprise, you have created something
of enduring value. Besides that you have given the world a lot
of pleasure, and extracted much from it, and if that is not the
purpose of life, I do not know what is. Today I feel the happiness
which you must feel, and send you not only my congratulations
but my thanks.

Swamped by letters of congratulation, George took some time to
respond to Nigel Nicolson. He did so on 14 June. 'Among a large
assortment of letters, many painfully kind, some even touching,
there is no other message I have read with such pleasure, and for
which I am so grateful, as yours', he wrote, adding that he had
re-read some of their old correspondence during crucial moments
of their friendship and 'found myself on each occasion realising and
appreciating the enormous part you have played in my life'. After
repeating his affection for Nigel Nicolson, he said, 'You have been
one of the closest friends and perhaps the most generous and loyal
of them all.' He then added, 'May our strong friendship continue
for many years.'

In October 1976, just five months after resigning as prime minister, Wilson published another book, once again with Weidenfeld
& Nicolson, though this time in partnership with the publisher
Michael Joseph; the former took responsibility for the editorial
content of the book while the latter was in charge of production,
marketing and distribution. Titled *The Governance of Britain*, the
book detailed Wilson's time in power and explored various policy
proposals.

'Not a word of this book was written until 7 April 1976, two
days after I left office', Wilson explained in his preface. 'No prime
minister in the 1970s would have the time to do that or keep a
diary.' His writing on national security was hardly illuminating,
running to fewer than two hundred words and ending with the

explanation: 'There is no further information that can usefully or properly be added before bringing this Chapter to an end.' Of more interest was Wilson's description of how his time as prime minister had been spent. Looking back at the last three months of 1975, he found that he had eight audiences with the Queen, met the cabinet and other ministers seventy-eight times, had one state visit, and had taken part in eight TV or radio interviews. Apart from Christmas, he had no private or social engagements. As to what made a successful prime minister, he said that in addition to the need for communication and vigilance, there were two factors: 'sleep, and a sense of history'. He then added, 'I have never had a sleeping pill in Number Ten. Have never needed one.'

Upon its release, the newspapers marvelled – perhaps tongue-in-cheek – at how quickly Wilson had written the book. One stated that the former prime minister had written 60,000 words in a week. The *Sunday People* said the book was 'more readable than the title suggests', while the *Birmingham Post* reported that the book 'starts in an unpromising manner but in the end delivers quite handsomely'. They then invited their readers to join Wilson for what they called a 'Literary Luncheon' at the Albany Hotel. In return for paying £5.50, a not inconsiderable sum, they would be provided lunch, after which they would have the opportunity to hear the former prime minster share his thoughts and then, after that, be able to meet him as he signed copies of *The Governance of Britain*.

In its review of the book, *Private Eye* reported that George had paid Wilson £250,000 for his memoirs in the hope of securing a peerage and that, when published, the memoirs were a financial disaster. After George complained that this story was untrue, the magazine issued an apology. They said that the advance was a tenth of what had previously been reported and the venture 'showed a satisfactory profit'. What they didn't amend, because they didn't feel they had to, was the allegation that George's peerage was connected with the publication of Harold Wilson's various books.

In response to the complaints about the Lavender List, Harold Wilson attacked the 'misrepresentations', calling them 'a campaign of innuendo' and an 'orchestrated [...] vendetta'. Later, he stated that anti-Semitism was probably behind much of the criticism (of the nine life peerages given out by Wilson – and it was the life peerages that people most reacted to – four were for Jewish men). For her part, Lady Falkender believed George deserved his honour. After all, she maintained, he was a 'leading member of the Jewish establishment in Britain' and was one of 'Harold Wilson's oldest friends'. As such, she continued, George had played a major role in the events 'near the resignation and afterwards'.

In the years following the Lavender List, George grew increasingly concerned about Harold Wilson's and Lady Falkender's finances. Wilson had a state pension, but this would be around £3,500 per year (set at 37.5 per cent of his previous prime-ministerial salary). Falkender's position was even worse. At one point, George wrote to his libel lawyer and friend, Peter Carter-Ruck, describing a 'disturbing conversation with Lady Falkender and her sister [...] regarding Sir Harold's and their financial situation and they asked me to get in touch with you to discuss in some detail the question of whether some way could be found to establish a research foundation (or some other formula) that would immediately benefit Sir Harold and, indirectly, them'. Other former prime ministers had received considerable financial support from private sources after they left office, he continued, including Ted Heath, who was provided with 'a secretariat, travel and research grants and other prerequisites'. In the end, however, no funds were forthcoming and George was forced to provide the assistance himself. He did so in the best way that he knew how: he offered to publish more books by Harold Wilson. These contracts, he wrote, would 'aggregate to large sums of money'.

George also provided Lady Falkender with a series of well-paid book contracts. He worked tirelessly to help her son Tim get a job and even supported her submission to Lloyds Bank for an

American Express credit card. Even this was not enough. At one point Lady Falkender wrote to him complaining of his inattention, adding 'George, our understanding was clear.' The exact nature of this 'understanding' remains unknown.

Looking back on the Lavender List, George later called the affair 'unfortunate' and 'unorthodox'. Furthermore, he confessed that he found the media coverage of himself in the gossip columns 'gruelling'. The announcement was not, however, without its small pleasures. When speaking about this period, he told one listener that 'it rankled the publishing fraternity that I should have been singled out', before adding, with some glee, that the chairman of Heinemann 'spilt his sherry on hearing the news at the Savile Club'.

In mid-June 1976, George Weidenfeld was driven to Westminster to be introduced at the House of Lords. In a small anteroom his attire was prepared. On top of his dark suit was draped a robe of full-length scarlet wool topped with a collar of white miniver fur. At the front, it was closed with black silk satin ribbon. On the right side of the robe were dashed two wide bars of miniver (edged with gold oak-leaf lace) indicating his rank as baron. On his head was placed a bicorn hat. After a brief, excited pause, he was called into the chamber. There was a procession. First came the Gentleman Usher of the Black Rod, followed by the Garter Principal King of Arms and then George's Senior Supporter, Lord Melchett. Fourth in line was the publisher himself, and finally Lord Longford (Antonia Fraser's father), the Junior Supporter. The group walked sombrely towards the Lord Chancellor, who stood on the far side of the chamber wearing court dress with a tricorn hat on his head. As they approached, they stopped three times and bowed towards the Cloth of Estate, the canopy which hung above the throne. Then, at a signal from one of his proposers, George knelt on the cold stone floor before the Lord Chancellor and handed over the Writ of Summons, which was a command from the Queen to attend Parliament. George then swore an oath of allegiance and signed an undertaking to abide by the House of Lords Code of Conduct. 'I welcome you to the House,' the Lord Chancellor now boomed. 'Hear! Hear!' called those in the chamber. After shaking hands with the Lord Chancellor, George was then led out of the chamber to celebrate.

For the new Baron Weidenfeld of Chelsea, it was a joyous and deeply satisfying occasion. The one regret he felt was that his father, Max, had been unable to witness the accolade, having died nine years earlier. George was deeply sad that his father could not be present when his son was welcomed into the heart of the Establishment.

Baron Weidenfeld of Chelsea

CHAPTER 12

Unity Mitford: A Quest

1976

'Literary fashions are very often influenced
by great historical events.' – GW

There were four of them sitting in George's study. It was a tense, legal stand-off. The official address was Flat 23, Turner's Reach House, 8–10, London SW3. To George and his friends, however, the flat was known as 'Chelsea Embankment'.

From the outside, the four-storey building was unremarkable, except for its location next to the River Thames and the small round black-and-white clock that hung from its red-brick exterior. But it was the interior that shone: the grand entrance hall brimming with sketches of naked women by Gustav Klimt; the drawing room painted in vivid red and easily convertible to a dining space for more than fifty guests; an alcove draped with tapestries and filled with a table and gilt chairs for more intimate meals; a single expansive bedroom with gold and yellow vertical-lined wallpaper; and the study, with its black lacquered walls and windows overlooking the river. Throughout, the apartment was adorned with an eclectic collection of art: drawings by Klimt, Matisse, Kandinsky and Picasso, along with a Hellenistic portrait of the Roman emperor Marcus Aurelius, oil paintings by Luca Giordano and, next to George's bed, a sketch of his daughter Laura by the artist Molly Bishop.

To one side of the room was the author, David Pryce-Jones, and his lawyer. Facing them was a Mr Ferriman, the solicitor representing Sir Oswald Mosley, former head of the British Union of Fascists. In between sat George Weidenfeld, publisher and mediator. They were surrounded by towering bookshelves. Above the fireplace was hung Francis Bacon's *Screaming Pope*. Through the window they could see the choppy, brackish waters of the Thames.

At issue was Pryce-Jones's new book about Oswald Mosley's sister-in-law, Unity Mitford. According to Ferriman, the Mitford family was distraught about the author's approach, particularly his revelations about Unity's close connections with the German Nazi Party. This was the summer of 1976, and George was still smarting from the savage press coverage following the announcement of his peerage. What he really didn't need right now was another fight with the fourth estate.

Finally, Ferriman had had enough. 'If you don't withdraw this book immediately,' he barked, 'we are not responsible for the consequences to Mr Pryce-Jones.' Taken aback, the author's representative asked what that meant. 'Work it out for yourself,' replied Ferriman, threateningly. On hearing this, Pryce-Jones's first instinct was to leave immediately and fetch his children from their school, so worried was he for their safety. Mosley's henchman's words were not an empty threat. Ever since leading mass rallies of Blackshirts back in the 1930s, Mosley had been known not only as a man of grand oratory but also violence.

After Ferriman had left, George turned to the author. 'Whatever they do,' he said, 'we're going to fight. And I'm fighting with you.' Pryce-Jones was deeply grateful for the words of support. He was determined to see this through.

Unity Valkyrie Mitford was born in 1914, the fifth of David and Sydney Mitford's seven children, a clan notorious for their extreme views and colourful lives. Two of Unity's siblings, Tom and Diana, were fascists, the latter marrying Oswald Mosley (at the home of

Joseph Goebbels; Adolf Hitler was guest of honour). Jessica was a self-confessed Communist. Nancy a well-known novelist. Deborah married the Duke of Devonshire. While Pamela had a passion for rural life.

Of all her siblings, however, Unity Mitford held the most extreme views. As a young woman, she had been a supporter of the Nazis. Later she lived in Germany and befriended Hitler (he gave her a flat in Munich). 'I hate all Jews,' Unity had told the press at one point. 'I want everybody to know I am a Jew-hater,' she had written to the pro-Nazi rag *Der Stürmer*. On another occasion, when she had heard reports that some Jews were beaten up, Unity had said 'Jolly good, serves them right we should go and cheer.'

David Pryce-Jones had known the Mitford family since childhood. Like George, he had been born in Vienna. His mother was from the aristocratic Fould-Springer family; his father was a member of parliament with aristocratic English lineage who had attended Eton College, where he had met Unity Mitford's brother Tom and became a frequent visitor to the family home in Swinbrook. This is how, in the early 1970s, David Pryce-Jones came to be staying at the home of Unity Mitford's sister Jessica in Berkeley, California. They had swapped houses for the summer. One day he and his wife were going through the library when they found the book *Jew Süß*, a nineteenth-century anti-Semitic novel about a Jewish banker. Inside the flap, he found Unity had signed her name. 'Through possession of this very copy of *Jew Süß*,' Pryce-Jones later wrote, 'Unity leaped into a living dimension.' This was the start of his quest for her.

By the time Pryce-Jones was thinking about his new book, he and George Weidenfeld had been working together for more than a decade. Indeed, Weidenfeld & Nicolson had published five of his novels (including the bestseller *Sands of Summer*) and four of his non-fiction books (such as *Next Generation: Travels in Israel* and *Evelyn Waugh & His World*). In early 1972, Pryce-Jones formally proposed the book about Unity Mitford to George Weidenfeld, who was immediately supportive. The book was commissioned, and a contract agreed.

Weidenfeld & Nicolson's reputation as a publisher of important works of fiction and non-fiction was, by this point, second to none. Between 1969 and 1972 they had published Tom Wolfe's *The Electric Kool-Aid Acid Test*, Edna O'Brien's *A Pagan's Place*, Norman Mailer's *A Fire on the Moon* and Margaret Drabble's *The Needle's Eye*, along with memoirs by Andy Warhol and Charles de Gaulle, and the genre-breaking *Religion and the Decline of Magic* by Keith Thomas, which had a huge impact on how history is written.

Even more impressively, Weidenfeld & Nicolson had released two Booker Prize-winning books in as many years. First came John Berger's novel *G* in 1972, followed by J. G. Farrell's *The Siege of Krishnapur*. Both books had been championed by Tony Godwin, who was by now the company's managing editorial director. Berger's book – a novel on the theme of Don Juan and written in long, infrequently punctuated sentences – had been rejected by a score of American publishing houses, much to Godwin's frustration After it won the Booker Prize, Godwin wrote to the American editors who had spurned the manuscript. 'You can imagine how delighted I am,' he told Andre Schiffrin, publishing director at Pantheon Books, 'and I am only sorry that, having published his previous books, you didn't take *G*.' To Roger Straus, Godwin crowed, 'It is a marvellous vindication as far as I am concerned, I do occasionally get my hands on a good novel.'

It was within this context of risk-taking, widespread acclaim and team bravado, along with high hopes of commercial and critical success, that George took on Pryce-Jones's project, *Unity*. From the very beginning, both publisher and author had understood that there would likely be significant resistance from the Mitford family and their powerful and well-connected friends. That they would worry about damage to the Mitfords' reputation. That the book would reflect poorly on those at the heart of Britain's aristocracy. That it might challenge the myth that Britain's story around fascism was not just about standing up to the German Nazis, but that in the country of the Magna Carta, the Mother of Parliaments and Shakespeare, fascism had also spread its tentacles. Cooperation with Unity's sisters, they agreed, would be key. Which was why, early on, Pryce-Jones asked George to put him in touch with Nancy Mitford, Unity's eldest sister. George responded that, sadly, he could not, 'for I do not know her well and I don't think there is much mutual fondness'. He would, however, reach out to Antonia Fraser's mother Elizabeth Longford, who had possible connections with the Mitford family. Perhaps she might be able to help.

While David Pryce-Jones continued researching Unity Mitford, George's family was hit by a traumatic event, one that both revealed and amplified his political understanding.

It was dark at 7 p.m. on 30 December 1973 when thirty-two-year-old Ilich Ramirez Sanchez walked along Queen's Grove in St John's Wood, London, his way illuminated by a few street lights. Seeing the house he was looking for, number 48, a large two-storey red-brick Georgian property, he pushed through the wrought-iron gate, stepped across several paving stones, and knocked on the glossy black front door. This was the home of Teddy Sieff, George's sixty-eight-year-old former father-in-law, and grandfather to his daughter Laura. Teddy was president of Marks & Spencer and vice-president of the British Zionist Federation. Ilich Ramirez Sanchez was also known as 'Carlos the Jackal' and worked on behalf of the Palestinian Liberation Organisation.

When the door was opened by a butler, Carlos the Jackal pulled a 9mm Beretta from his pocket, pointed it at the butler's ribs and told him to take him to Teddy Sieff. Seeing the intruder downstairs, Teddy's wife Lois hurried to the bedroom and called the emergency services. Meanwhile, the butler took the Jackal upstairs to the master bathroom where Teddy was dressing for dinner. Seeing his target, the terrorist shot Teddy in the mouth at point-blank range. The victim fell to the floor, unconscious. The intruder fired again, but the gun jammed. Thinking he had done his job, and fearing that he would be caught, the Jackal fled the house. Lois turned Teddy over, into the recovery position, thus saving his life. Two minutes later, the police arrived, then an ambulance, which rushed the injured man to hospital. Remarkably, the bullet had narrowly missed his jugular. The next morning, following an operation to remove the bullet, Teddy was giving interviews from his hospital bed.

In the following day's press coverage, the assassination attempt was widely seen to have been connected with the victim being Jewish. The *Daily Mirror* reported that Teddy Sieff was 'known for his work with Jewish causes', and the *Birmingham Post* declared him to be 'one of the most prominent members of the Jewish community'. Meanwhile, beneath a large front-page headline: TOP JEWS ON DEATH LIST, the *Liverpool Echo* reported that a number of Jewish people in Great Britain had received telephone calls informing them that they were potential targets, including an unnamed woman who was second on the list and the Tesco chief, Sir John Cohen, who was third. Scotland Yard, they continued, had issued a 'be vigilant' warning to Jewish leaders in Britain.

George was distraught when he heard what happened to Teddy Sieff, who he thought of not only as his ex-wife's father but also as a friend. He called his daughter, Laura, who was now twenty years old and studying in Austria, and gave her the news. They agreed that she did not have to return to London as her grandfather was not in mortal danger. George also sent a letter of support to Lois, Teddy's wife. For the publisher, the failed assassination of Teddy Sieff demonstrated that supporting the state of Israel had potentially dangerous personal consequences. It also was a reminder, if he needed one, that anti-Semitism had not ended with the downfall of Nazi Germany.

*

On 6 January 1974, David Pryce-Jones provided a progress report to George. He had been in touch with Unity's younger sister Jessica (with whom he had swapped houses years before). Jessica was not only happy to introduce the author to other members of the Mitford family but, remarkably, she was willing to share letters between herself and Unity. He had also visited Diana Mitford in Paris. Diana agreed that if Pryce-Jones returned to Paris, both she and her husband Oswald Mosley would speak 'at length' about the book and, when it was ready, she would read a draft of his manuscript. 'I therefore feel confident,' he told George, 'that I have a working relationship with her.' In addition, he had tracked down one of Unity's confidantes in Paris and another in Munich. In summary, despite the 'fear of the Mitfords', his leads were 'quite unexpectedly stronger' than he had anticipated. George was pleased. He shared a number of contacts with the author and encouraged him to keep him updated on the research.

Over the next several months, Pryce-Jones met with scores of people who remembered Unity's time in Germany before the war. He learned that she had often visited the Osteria Bavaria restaurant in Munich, waiting around for Adolf Hitler. From her bright face and gleaming eyes, he was told, it was clear she was in love with the Führer. Given that she was an Englishwoman, some were surprised at how much access Unity was allowed. Hitler and Unity would argue, but the Führer appeared to appreciate her honesty. They never slept together. Later, when Unity shot herself in the temple with a pistol, after feeling she had to choose between Germany and England, it was Hitler who paid for her medical care. Hitler was shocked when Unity shot herself, Pryce-Jones was informed, and felt responsible for her attempted suicide. She survived, and the Führer organised her passage by train back to England.

Adolf Hitler and Unity Mitford, circa 1937

When he had started his research, Pryce-Jones had been thinking of writing a portrait of a fanatic, a woman swept up in a movement, not a true believer. But after spending many weeks in Germany, meeting with those who remembered Unity's time there in the 1930s, he more fully understood that she was an extreme ideologue, a Nazi. He felt that it all had to be exposed. On 6 February 1975, therefore, and now more than two years into the research, the author wrote again to his publisher back in England. 'One of the things wrong with my life is that I never see you,' he started, warmly. 'The fault's mine as I'm always in Germany *auf die Spur der Unity* [on the trail of Unity]', adding that 'The Unity research has been fascinating. I have now got it together except for a few loose ends, and very remarkable it all is. I never thought I would be able to get so far. I move in circles where *Onkel Adolf* [Uncle Adolf] is very much alive.' He concluded, 'As you see, I am terribly pleased so far, and have still hopes of further last-minutes success.'

Upon his return to England, whenever Pryce-Jones mentioned his new project to friends and family members, he was warned that there would be trouble. He was told that by revealing the true story of Unity Mitford he was betraying his class and that it was a disgraceful thing to point out that somebody of that background was a Nazi. Such things, he was told repeatedly, had to be forgotten. If he proceeded, he would be completely 'breaking the rules'. And if he did proceed, it was certain that Oswald Mosley would sue.

Which he did. On 22 June 1976, after Oswald Mosley was sent a copy of the typeset proof, Weidenfeld & Nicolson received a letter from his solicitors informing them that certain statements and passages contained within Pryce-Jones's book were untrue. In particular, Mosley's lawyers asserted that it was false that a party insignia and a rubber truncheon were delivered to Unity Mitford on his behalf, as stated on page 59. Nor was it correct to say on page 249 that Mosley and the fascists were regarded as a 'dangerous fifth column' or that he and his followers were 'Quislings and Vichyites'. As to the line, 'Mosley appeared in his pyjamas' on page 57, their client 'informs us he never slept a night in the house in question'.

On receiving these corrections, David Pryce-Jones quickly assured George that he was happy to take in all the changes. Indeed, he was delighted that this was all that Mosley and his wife Diana Mitford were calling for. There would be a cost to adjust the layout of the book and print new pages, the author was told, in total £2,909 74s. Pryce-Jones agreed to split this 50/50 with the publisher. To make the modifications, the book's release would have to be delayed till the autumn. It was now that letters of protest started arriving at Weidenfeld & Nicolson's offices. Many of those writing had titles associated with their names: Lady this, Lord that, Duke and Duchess of the other, Countess of somewhere else. Some demanded corrections. Others retracted support for the project. The complaints broke down into four categories: the letter-writers had been misquoted by the author; he hadn't taken notes during interviews; he claimed to have the support of the Mitford sisters who were clearly hostile; and, lastly, he had failed to send proofs for checking as promised. Pryce-Jones reassured George that he had never claimed to have the support of all the sisters; he did send out proof copies; he corrected any errors that he was made aware of; and he did take notes. Why, then, all the hostility? A letter from Lady Harrod, a friend of the Mitfords, provided possible explanation. 'We loved Bobo [Unity's nickname] of course,' she said. 'We would never think of saying anything nasty about her, we loved her. She had a sort of innocence, but I suppose this is difficult to put across now.'

It was around this time that George received a particularly noxious letter from Anthony Claud Frederick Lambton, the 6th Earl of Durham, also known as Viscount Lambton, or more simply, Tony. This was the same man who had recently been forced to resign from the cabinet after the *Daily Mail* took photos of him having sex with two prostitutes while still married. He had also had an affair with the Duchess of Devonshire (Unity's younger sister Deborah), who had apparently urged him to make an intervention on the family's behalf. From Biddick Hall, Lambton Park in County Durham, Lambton wrote his letter to the publisher in looping blue ink. The book, wrote the viscount, was 'pornographic', 'full of innuendo', and 'very badly told'. He urged George to halt publication, for his own sake, before accusing him of putting money and ambition before all else. 'I have always admired you as a man,' he added, but if publication was pursued, he, Lambton, would be forced to write negative reviews in the press.

On 26 August 1976, David Pryce-Jones wrote once again to George. 'The letters of intimidation you are receiving are unprecedented in my experience,' he said, 'it is a concerted war of nerves.' As to Tony Lambton's letter to George, the author continued, 'if he accuses you of vulgar money-making tastes, he will be quite exposed for really the public cannot have forgotten the reasons for his downfall'. Pryce-Jones added in a further letter, 'I think the implications of the upper-class behaviour are contemptable. These people are making themselves post-facto accomplices of Nazis. Anti-Semitism lurks in Lambton's letter. It seems to me.'

Another of those to write to George was Hugh Fraser MP,

husband of Antonia Fraser. 'I have just seen a copy of David's book on Unity,' he wrote on House of Commons letterhead. 'I find it thoroughly distasteful and remarkable only for achieving, for those who knew her, a quite unrecognisable degree of prurience.' He then added, 'Its publication will not only cause many people real and lasting pain [...] but ethically and historically I believe this book will cause damage to your reputation as a publisher.' He finished by recommending that 'as it stands it is one which I feel should be withdrawn'. This perhaps, after all the years of friendship, was one of the hardest of the letters for George to read. On 31 August the publisher wrote back, saying how sorry he was to receive Hugh Fraser's letter. He then added, 'I have faith in the integrity and sense of responsibility of the author, whom I have known and whose books I have published for many years.'

In September three of Unity's sisters (Diana, Deborah and Pamela) made further requests of a relatively minor nature to the publisher, and the book was delayed again. Even though their corrections were taken in, they then made public their opposition to the book's release in a letter to *The Times*.

At last, and in the face of considerable and growing pressure, *Unity Mitford: A Quest* was published in the first week of November 1976. The *Evening Standard* was typical of the overwhelmingly positive reviews. Under the headline THE DEB WHO FELL FOR HITLER, the reviewer stated that the story 'is told with all the clinical detail of a police report and turns out to be not so much a biography as a psychological thriller of commanding intelligence'. The *New York Times* was also positive, quipping that the book was 'less a testament to the "frivolity of evil" than to the evil consequences of frivolity'. Further reviews appeared in the *Sunday Telegraph, Sunday Times, Birmingham Post, Daily Express, Daily Mail* and *Glasgow Sunday Mail*. The book was, according to the vast majority of critics, a triumph.

A week later, David Pryce-Jones was invited to face Oswald

Mosley on BBC1's *Tonight Show* with Melvyn Bragg. The three men – each wearing a suit, white shirt, stiff collar and tie – gathered around a small table, on a simple, well-lit set. At thirty-seven and forty years old respectively, the presenter and author looked positively youthful compared to the octogenarian fascist. During the conversation that followed, Mosley denied that he or his British Union of Fascists had ever been anti-Semitic, provoking astonishment on the author's face. Mosley then spoke live on British national television of 'the use of Jewish money power to promote a world war'. When pressed by Bragg, he countered that he had meant 'not all Jews, but some Jews'. Pryce-Jones attempted to point out that the Jews had nothing to do with the start of the Second World War – in fact, of course, they were the Nazis' greatest victims – but Mosley pushed on, stating that if things had been so bad in Germany for the Jews, why didn't they all leave?

'Devoid of any capacity for self-criticism, Sir Oswald is never nonplussed when caught out: he simply rattles on with undiminished brio,' noted the cultural critic Clive James later that week. 'To know that the shameless old spell-binder has been peddling these whoppers is one thing. To have him produce them right there in front of you is another.' James then commended the author for being 'brave' for standing up to Oswald Mosley who had now been reduced to no more than a 'terrifically silly man'.

Mosley was not the only person to criticise Pryce-Jones or George Weidenfeld following the release of *Unity Mitford*. When the columnist Alastair Forbes submitted his review to the *Times Literary Supplement* it was spiked by the editor, John Gross, for its anti-Semitic content. Central to Forbes's critique was that because he had a Jewish mother, Pryce-Jones was not sufficiently objective to write a book about Unity Mitford, a fascist. Unhappy with his rejection by Gross, Forbes made a hundred copies of his review and circulated these around his literary friends in London along with the remark that 'this was the piece the Jews rejected'.

One of those to receive Forbes's article was Tony Lambton. Outraged by what he saw as media censorship, the viscount threw himself into the anti-*Unity* campaign with even greater fervour. From his Tuscan palace in Italy, Lambton submitted a review of the book to the *Spectator* that was published on 13 November 1976. The viscount repeated many of his earlier criticisms before calling *Unity Milford: A Quest* 'a shoddy, inaccurate, dull little book'. He then turned on George Weidenfeld. The publisher, he wrote, was a member of the 'Jewish establishment' and 'recently ennobled for politeness to Sir Harold Wilson and Lady Falkender'. It was 'unforgivable,' he continued, that George Weidenfeld had published a book 'attempting to pin political responsibility upon a reckless young girl'. Lambton then questioned whether George had even read the book. 'It is said in defence of Lord Weidenfeld that he does not enjoy reading,' the viscount wrote. 'This is unfair, but his full-time occupation of genuflecting and sycophanting to every notable, and visiting notable in England, swirling daily through the drawing rooms of London in a series of *palais glides*, whispering obsequiously, leaves him breathless for such a mundane task.'

Many within the publishing industry and beyond were outraged by Lambton's review. One of those was Thomas Wallace, editor-in-chief of the American publishing house Holt, Rinehart and Winston. On 3 December he wrote to David Pryce-Jones saying that he was 'appalled' by the 'vicious attack on you and George Weidenfeld'. He would try and get *Publishers Weekly* to write a story about the 'disgraceful situation'. Another of those to act was Tom Rosenthal, the publisher at Secker and Warburg, who was also a child of Jewish refugees. In early December he sent a letter to the *Spectator*. Lambton's review, he said, was 'as vulgar a piece of writing as I have seen in your distinguished journal'. It was, he added, 'a mingling of anti-Semitic innuendo and personal invective'. He then went on to make a broader point. 'I believe that one of England's greatest virtues was, and is, its ability to accept and absorb strange and foreign people of all sorts and conditions and to give them equality of opportunity and freedom of speech. I think that Lord Lambton's vituperation has abused these privileges and, in the manner of his doing so, denied them.'

George was deeply moved by Tom Rosenthal's defence. On Christmas Eve he wrote back, thanking him for his 'gallant intervention' and saying how 'touched' he was for his friendship. 'Although I am almost wholly inured to this genre of innuendo as a result of the press campaign throughout the Harold Wilson resignation and honours crisis,' George wrote, 'I felt very badly about the Unity Mitford campaign and the Lambton article and your intervention was most gratifying.'

Of all those who provided support, perhaps none was more meaningful to George than that of his former fiction editor, Barley Alison. 'The attacks on the Mitford book and you personally are MONSTROUS from every possible point of view,' she wrote. 'The spectacle of the upper classes' relapsing into early Victorian snobbery and anti-Semitism is quite repulsive.' In her opinion, Lambton's review had had the opposite effect to that which he had wanted. 'Those members of the publishing "establishment" who do not love you because they are envious of your enthusiasm and success will not be anything but loyal colleagues now lest they be thought to be Mosleyite.' In his reply to Barley, George said he was 'touched' by her 'kind letter', and though he had been 'appalled' by the *Spectator* 'stooping to so low a level of abuse and irrelevant invective', he assured her that he was not 'unduly upset' by the whole business.

Viscount Tony Lambton, though, would not drop it. He now wrote a novel loosely based on David Price-Jones and George Weidenfeld. According to those who have seen it, the manuscript was full of anti-Semitic tropes. Yet, despite sending his manuscript to numerous publishers in London, nobody would take it, including the publisher of Quartet Books, Naim Attallah, who said it was unprintable. 'Not only could it be interpreted as libellous,' Attallah later wrote, 'but the fact that it was mainly fired by Tony's splenetic loathing of his subject came over more strongly than the storyline.' In the end, George Weidenfeld and David Pryce-Jones had won the battle of ideas. It would be their version of Unity, their version of history, that would be remembered.

'I suppose more than anything else,' remembers David Pryce-Jones, 'George wanted success.' The publisher was always on the lookout for the next project. 'Once I went to a memorial service with George. Afterwards, when we came out he said, "Look at all these people, do you see, there's a book in that?" How many people leave a memorial service thinking about how to make a book out of the congregation? It was the way George was. He had an incredibly fertile mind. He was full of ideas.'

'I was with him one day in his flat overlooking the Thames,' Pryce-Jones continues in a more sombre voice, 'and he said, "I want to show you something." There was a family tree, going back to a rabbi in the sixteenth century in Prague. George said, "You see, I came from a very famous stock, these are great men and I'm just a publisher" and he started to cry.' Pryce-Jones pauses for a moment, thinking about this story, what it meant. 'I think he needed reassuring,' he concludes, 'and he needed love and he was looking for it all the time.'

George in the late 1970s

CHAPTER 13

Yoni: Hero of Entebbe

1979

'Sometimes I smell a book and the book smells right.' – GW

'Most journalists value what passes for integrity in our trade, but almost all of us have sometime tarnished it in one fashion or another [...] but if this story is to be an honest one, I must describe one of the sorriest episodes of my own career.' This was how the much-lauded journalist and historian Max Hastings began the twelfth chapter of his autobiography published in 2000.

Twenty-four years earlier, on 4 July 1976, Hastings was in New York to report on the bicentennial anniversary of the founding of the United States. He turned on the radio and heard some extraordinary news: a week earlier, on 27 June, pro-Palestinian terrorists had hijacked an Air France plane flying out of Tel Aviv with 248 passengers on board and forced it to land at Entebbe airport in Uganda. Over the next few days around 140 passengers were released. The terrorists then threatened to kill the rest if their demands were not met. Overnight, a small, highly trained unit from the Israeli army had landed at Entebbe airport in Uganda and, miraculously, rescued 102 out of the 106 hostages, most of whom were Israelis. The paratroopers had suffered few casualties, with the exception of one of the commandos who had been killed during the raid. The raid at Entebbe became a massive international story, dominating the television headlines for weeks to come. It also played a key role in the transformation of Israel's image:

professional, well-organised, technologically advanced and made up of courageous and well-disciplined warriors. This was in stark contrast to the portrayal of Jewish people as passive victims of Nazi aggression which had become so dominant since the Second World War.

Four months after the Entebbe rescue, the thirty-one-year-old Hastings received a message from George Weidenfeld. Could Max come to see him at his flat on Chelsea Embankment? The journalist had met him a few times and, like so many others, had been invited to write a book. In his case, the suggestion had been to tell the story of Rufus Isaacs, the first Jewish Lord Chief Justice and the first British Jew to be made a marquis. Back then, Hastings had declined but the door was left open. Hence the call. They met soon after and George suggested that Hastings write a book about the Israeli commando who had been killed at Entebbe. This man, Hastings now learned, was named Yonathan ('Yoni') and was the son of one of Israel's leading families, the Netanyahus. Hastings was immediately excited by the prospect, but he worried that he would not be allowed to reveal the inner workings of Israel's secretive army. The Israeli government was behind the project, George reassured him. Shimon Peres, the Minister of Defence, had given him a personal assurance that access would not be a problem.

With this promise, Hastings agreed to write the book. The advance was £20,000: a third payable on signing of the contract, a third on publisher's acceptance of the manuscript and a third on publication.

George Weidenfeld's claim to have Tel Aviv's support was no empty boast. By this point, Israel's survival and success had become one of his prime concerns. In 1935, as a schoolboy, he had visited Palestine, returning home full of dreams and personal commitments. Later, as a university student in Vienna, he had been a member of a Zionist organisation, studying the writings of Theodor Herzl and other proponents of a Jewish homeland. On 15 May 1948, George had stood outside the Israeli delegation in Manchester Square, London, with hundreds of others to celebrate the arrival of the Jewish state. Then, just months after the founding of Israel, and after being introduced by a member of the London Jewish establishment, the twenty-eight-year-old novice publisher had been invited to work as chief of staff to Chaim Weizmann, Israel's first president. It had been a difficult choice for George as he had only just launched Weidenfeld & Nicolson, but, with the blessing of Nigel Nicolson's father Harold, he had taken the position in Israel, promising to return after a year. During his time with Weizmann, he had two assignments. First, to write speeches and keep the president informed on world events. And second, to help run the media campaign against the internationalisation of the city of Jerusalem. Through these efforts, George met many of those who would play a central role in Israel's future.

Once the year was over, George's commitment to Israel was even deeper than before. He was strongly tempted to remain in Jerusalem but felt under an obligation to Nigel Nicolson. After his return to England, George put his new contacts to good use, over the next decades publishing books by numerous Israeli grandees, including memoirs by David Ben-Gurion, Yitzhak Rabin, Golda Meir, Abba Eban, Moshe Dayan, Yigal Allon, Teddy Kollek, not to mention Shimon Peres.

George and Chaim Weizmann, 1948   *George with Moshe Dayan, 1970s*

Before a contract could be agreed, Hastings had to be approved by Yoni's family, in particular his father, Benzion Netanyahu, a sixty-six-year-old professor of history at Cornell University in New York with strong ties to Israel. George had suggested other candidates to Yoni's family, but as yet none had been selected. So it was that in the afternoon of 13 January 1977, Benzion Netanyahu and Max Hastings met at the coffee shop of the Royal Garden Hotel in Kensington, London. The following day, Hastings wrote to George on *Evening Standard* letterhead with a report of the meeting. His first line did not inspire much confidence. He said that he had met with Yoni's father, though he wasn't sure how to spell his last name. At first he typed 'Nethanayahoo', then in pen corrected it to 'Netanayahu', neither of which was correct. The conversation about Yoni was 'obviously not easy', he reported, Benzion having lost his son only a few months before. The father – who at times he called 'the old gentleman' and at others 'a nice old man' – clearly 'worshipped' his son, and Hastings was 'a little embarrassed' that he didn't know more about Yoni. From what he had so far gathered, however, the subject of the book was looking like a 'classical romantic hero'. He added that he was concerned that Benzion might try to interfere with the project and, to ward this off, Hastings had told him that this would not be an 'official biography' or in any way a 'propaganda exercise'. He, Hastings, must be free to write the book the way he liked.

Almost exactly a month later, George heard from Benzion Netanyahu, who provided his account of the meeting with Max Hastings in London. It was good news. He was pleased that the young journalist had said he was a 'romanticist' and that he 'liked heroes'. This fitted well with his own view of his son. 'Judging by Mr Hastings' literary and research capacities,' he continued, 'I would be only too happy if he undertook the life of Yoni.' While he had concerns about the young journalist's limited knowledge of Jewish history and Zionism, he had been reassured that this was a matter of research. By return of post, the publisher wrote to Benzion in Ithaca, New York. The terms would be as follows: Benzion would have the 'right to see the manuscript with a view to vetting facts and dates, the author will have the freedom to produce his own account and interpretation, in other words the freedom to exercise the discretion of a serious writer and journalist'. Several days later, George told Hastings he had passed the test. Over the next few months, a contract was negotiated and finally signed in April 1977. The project was on.

As it happened, Hastings had also been commissioned by the publisher Michael Joseph to write another book, *Bomber Command*. With two not insignificant advances in his pocket, he stepped away from full-time journalism (at the time he worked as a freelance foreign correspondent for the BBC and the *Evening Standard*), bought a home in Ireland – Jerpoint House in Thomastown, County Kilkenny – and moved across the Irish Sea with his pregnant wife and their child. The first book he would work on would be *Yoni*.

In the spring of 1977, Hastings flew to America and for two weeks interviewed Benzion Netanyahu and his son Benjamin (also known as 'Bibi', Yoni's younger brother and future Israeli prime minister) at the family home in Ithaca, New York. On 9 May, Yoni's father reported to George that the trip had been successful. 'I am quite confident that, as time goes on, he will develop original and important insights into Yoni's life,' Benzion wrote, adding that, 'Mr Hastings has the skills and talents to write a great book: all he needs is to become fully acquainted with Yoni – that is, to fix his gaze on him until he really sees him.' Next, Hastings travelled to Israel. He went on exercises with army patrols near the border. He spent time in a Centurion tank, bouncing along the rocky ground. He visited sites of historic, military and cultural importance. He interviewed soldiers who had taken part in the Entebbe raid as well as their senior officers. 'It was,' Hastings later wrote, 'one of the most fascinating experiences of my life.' Most extraordinarily, perhaps, he was given access to the inner workings of the Israeli army's most secretive unit, the *Sayaret Matkal*, the special forces of the Israel Defence Forces – like the British SAS or the US Navy Seals – also known as 'The Unit'.

Not all of those Hastings encountered in Israel were supportive of his efforts. One of the most critical was Ehud Barak, a *Sayaret* senior officer and an architect of the Entebbe rescue mission. Barak had been in the Israel Defence Forces for almost twenty years, himself leading several high-profile operations, including 'Operation Isotope', the attempt to free hostages who had been hijacked at Lod Airport in Tel Aviv in 1972, and the raid on Lebanon in 1973, in which three high-level PLO leaders were assassinated. Later, Barak became chief of the IDF and, after that, prime minister (1999–2001). 'This book should not be written for another 10 years,' said Barak, adding, 'the family has suffered a great deal and they would not want to be hit below the belt.'

In 1977, as spring turned to summer, the mood in England rose. It was Queen Elizabeth II's silver jubilee and celebrations were rolled out across the nation. In London alone there were more than 4,000 street parties. The next few weeks were marked by hot weather and then on 1 July the British tennis player Virginia Wade won the women's championship at Wimbledon, adding to the ebullient national mood. The following day, however, George heard some bad news. His long-time author and friend Vladimir Nabokov had died, aged seventy-eight, in Montreux, Switzerland.

Ever since the publication of *Lolita* in 1959, George had published all of the author's work. They had exchanged birthday and New Year's greetings. He had visited Nabokov and his wife Véra on an almost annual basis at their home in Switzerland. He had answered numerous letters about royalty payments, book-cover quotes and media interviews. On 4 July, George sent Véra a cable:

Deeply grieved tragic news of death of not only
greatest writer English language and naturally
our most treasured and esteemed author. But also
of man most profoundly admired whose working
relationship and friendship meant more to me than
I can express. With all love and sympathy from my
colleagues and myself.

To this he added a eulogy which was published in *The Bookseller*. He spoke of twenty years of a 'truly wonderful professional and personal relationship' and his periodic visits to the family home in Switzerland, which 'will stand out in my mind forever. A meal, a talk, a walk with Vladimir Nabokov was an event: warming, puzzling and happy-making.'

It is unsurprising that George would have more intense feelings for Vladimir Nabokov than for his newly acquired authors, such as Max Hastings. That did not mean, of course, that there was not the potential for friendship. Nor opportunity for literary excellence and cultural significance. It did, however, put George in a solemn, contemplative mood as he waited to hear how Hastings's research was proceeding in Israel.

By the summer's end, Hastings was back at his home in Ireland, where he began to write. As the sentences and paragraphs mounted, he realised the Netanyahu family might not approve of the way he was telling the story. Contrary to what they had told him, he had learned that the hero of Entebbe was disliked by some of his men, was at times lonely and depressed, and wasn't a great intellectual. In early October 1977, Hastings finished the manuscript and had it delivered to John Curtis, who had been assigned as his editor at Weidenfeld & Nicolson. A few days later, the author sent the editor a postcard from Pakistan. 'I hope you got the MS [manuscript] ok and aren't too disappointed,' he wrote. 'First chapter is the weakest. There is probably too much Zionism in the book as a whole.'

On 13 October, Curtis wrote to Hastings saying that he had read the manuscript. 'Let me say at once that I think the book is a success,' the editor wrote, 'it is a very moving and saleable story.' With this favourable reading, Curtis now sent the manuscript to Benzion Netanyahu in New York.

Two weeks later, on 1 November 1977, Hastings spoke by phone with the professor's son, Bibi Netanyahu. Bibi had also read the manuscript and was not happy. The family fundamentally did not agree with Hastings's portrayal of Yoni. Where was the hero they had been promised? Bibi said that without his and the family's support, the Israeli censors were unlikely to approve the draft. In particular, the description of Yoni's unit would have to be made more vague and non-identifiable. Bibi suggested that the author fly out to see him in Boston and he would go over his notes. Worried that the problems were about principle, not detail, Hastings declined. They were at an impasse. Hastings reported on this telephone call to John Curtis that same day. 'At the bottom of my heart, even though it was apparent early on that the Netanyahus are rotten through and through,' he concluded, 'I cherished a sneaking dream that Bibi would ring up and congratulate me on doing a sensitive job with the story.'

Max Hastings reported that he had also heard from Ehud Barak, the *Sayaret Matkal* commander. Barak said that it would be impossible to publish the book in its present form. Hastings' protestations that this was unfair, given their previous agreements, made no difference.

A week later, the situation was summed up for George in an internal memo sent by John Curtis. The Netanyahu family believed the biography was 'malicious' and 'not serious'. They were 'adamant' that all references to the military unit should be deleted from the book. In addition, Yoni's letters – currently the heart of the book – could not be quoted at length. There could be no mention of Bibi or the youngest brother Iddo. Furthermore, Yoni was to be treated as a serious academic scholar and more attention was to be paid to his senior officers, who were likely to present a more sympathetic picture, rather than the men under his command. For the family, these demands were non-negotiable. They suggested that there would be 'a lot of trouble' if the manuscript was submitted to Israel.

The following day, Hastings wrote again to his editor at Weidenfeld & Nicolson. He admitted that while in Israel and in the presence of Bibi Netanyahu, he had signed a document agreeing to share his manuscript with the censors, but he dismissed this as a 'formality' which all journalists working in Israel had to face. He had amended the document he had signed, he said, limiting it to the 'vital security interests of Israel'. Any factual errors would of course be corrected, but the book should be published as it was.

A letter now arrived at Weidenfeld & Nicolson from Max Hastings's agent, Graham Watson of Curtis Brown. Where was the next installment of the advance, he wanted to know? His author had delivered his manuscript as promised. Payment was now due. The author and his agent were not the only ones whose patience was wearing thin. From New York, George now received a message from James Wade, publisher at Dial Press, who would be releasing the book in America. 'Dear George,' he began, 'I would deeply appreciate if you would give us a report on where matters stand with Max Hasting's [sic] *Yoni*. I gather you are taking steps to resolve the difficulties and I am anxious to know more.'

Sometime towards the end of 1977, George had the manuscript sent to the Israeli censors. On 5 January 1978 word came back from Tel Aviv that it was under official review and had been given a reference number: 1634. Once this process was complete, it would then be separately reviewed by the army spokesman and the Department of Field Security. John Curtis then received a letter from Ina Friedman, who worked in the Weidenfeld & Nicolson office in Jerusalem (which had been set up in the late 1960s to sell Hebrew editions of the company's books). Under the heading 'Eyes Only', Friedman wrote that she had been in touch with Major General Yona Gazit, director of publication relations in Tel Aviv. 'Gazit,' she wrote, 'seems to be up to his neck in the plot, at least he's informed about the details, including the approach to AGW [Arthur George Weidenfeld] to suppress publication.' She added that though he was the 'villain' of the story, Gazit was actually 'sweet as sugar over the phone'. Crucially, she added, Gazit had made it clear that given Hastings was not an Israeli citizen, the army had no legal control of the manuscript, and the 'final decision on what to do with this book <u>rests with the publishers</u>'. In other words, George.

Over the next several weeks, George received numerous messages from his high-level contacts in Tel Aviv that the Israeli government did not want the book published in its current form. Of most concern were the author's revelations about the highly secretive *Sayaret Matkal*. Weeks turned to months and no decision was made on publication. Hastings pressed again for his payment. Much to his consternation, Weidenfeld rejected the request. According to the fine print, payment was only due if the manuscript was accepted by the publisher, which it hadn't been. 'It was the beginning of a nightmare period,' Hastings would later write.

The Netanyahu family now wrote letters demanding that George withdraw the book. This was followed by missives from various Israeli figures, many of whom Hastings had interviewed, saying that he had got the story wrong. One generously wrote that 'the writing of any biography is difficult', before adding 'your book reads simply like an adventure story about an imaginative figure, but in no way does it constitute a true biography of Yoni'. Others said that he had misunderstood the story because he was not Jewish. The journalist was now experiencing financial stress. It had been many months since he had been employed and, though he had received partial advances for two books, he was living on his overdraft. He called George Weidenfeld and, according to his later account, 'pleaded' for the next part of his advance to be paid. Payment was still held back. 'George's relationship with Israel had been a dominant force in his life,' Hastings later wrote. 'He had no intention of quarrelling with the Jewish state about me.'

The journalist now felt he had two choices: He could walk away from the project, giving up all his hard work and, importantly, the much-needed money. Or the book could be published in a bowdlerised version. In the end, after much internal debate, he chose the latter. It was, he later recalled, 'one of the least principled and most humiliating moments of my life'. According to one source, the manuscript was cut by a third and became a sort of 'deification exercise'.

So it was that in April 1979, almost exactly two years after the contract had been signed, *Yoni: Hero of Entebbe – Life of Yonathan Netanyahu* was published by Weidenfeld & Nicolson in Great Britain and Dial Press in America. Hastings was paid what he was owed but he did no publicity to support its release.

In the following years, Max Hastings wrote a string of bestselling books, won renown as a foreign correspondent, perhaps most notably during the Falklands War, and became editor of both the *Daily Telegraph* and the *Evening Standard*. His disdain for George Weidenfeld, however, never diminished. Even as late as 2021, when asked what he thought of the publisher, Hastings wrote, 'I thought George in every way a loathsome human being.'

Why was it that George Weidenfeld who had championed authors such as Vladimir Nabokov, Mary McCarthy and Henry Miller failed to defend Max Hastings's right to publish? It was, apparently, a question of priority. 'As a Zionist my purpose is to secure the survival of Israel,' George later told William Shawcross. 'All considerations, which run counter to this survival whether they are logical or not, have to be suppressed.' Apparently, this included the suppression of British authors like Max Hastings.

George viewed his loyalty to Israel as paramount. On 21 June 1967, for instance, eleven days after the conclusion of the Six Day War, George was part of a group (including the financier Edmund de Rothschild in Paris and the businessman Marcus Sieff in London) who wrote to Israeli Prime Minister Levi Eshkol offering to create informal pro-Israel public relations offices in England, the United States, France, Germany and Australia. This 'close-knit group of active people, well connected in the political and informational fields' would help challenge the 'frontal attack from every conceivable source, ranging from outright condemnation to wavering and growing doubts among our friends'.

More evidence can be seen in George's correspondence with the Israeli Embassy two decades later. In early June 1984, before he gave a speech on Lebanon in the House of Lords, George first ran a draft by the Israeli Embassy in London. On 18 June the reply came back. The Embassy requested a number of edits, including adding the following three points: Europe should 'urge the cessation of communal bloodshed and the withdrawal of all foreign troops from Lebanon'; Europe should 'help Lebanon to achieve true sovereignty'; and Europe should 'oppose Syrian tendency to dominate Lebanon'. Four days later, on 22 June, George rose in the House of Lords and gave his speech. The text echoed the suggestions made by the Embassy, including the three proposed changes to Europe's policy, repeated almost verbatim.

According to Ron Prosor, a career diplomat who is currently the Israeli ambassador to Germany, George's relationship with Israel had evolved over the decades. Originally in his youth, and even more so after the Holocaust, the relationship had been about securing a safe haven for Jews. After the creation of the state of Israel in 1948, it became about military strength and survival, about not being told what to do by others. Finally, in the late 1960s, it became about wanting to make Israel a better society. 'George understood that the fight had to move from the battlefield to the international arena,' says Prosor. 'It was no longer a military issue anymore. Zionism had to be reframed.'

By the time that *Yoni* was published, George was widely respected in Israel. 'Weidenfeld is a jewel in the crown of Israel and the Jewish people,' proclaimed the journalist Douglas Davis in *Jewish World*, 'one that is surrounded by all the romantic, fable and mystery of say Koh-I-Noor. A most rare and priceless jewel.' Ruth Cheshin, who ran the Jerusalem Foundation for decades and who first met George in the 1960s, put it another way: 'I used to say to mutual friends, Israel was the only woman he was loyal to all his life.' Hella Pick, journalist and George's friend, agrees: 'His first loyalty was to Israel'. Such comments would likely have been warmly received by the publisher. An appreciation of his ability to bedazzle and then woo those he encountered through charm, a recognition of his intellect and the glitz of his remarkably wide-ranging contacts. A sprinkling of humour. On a deeper level, he also would have enjoyed the declaration of belonging. That he was not only part of, but central to, Israel and its people. Which is why, when these same people came after him, it stung so much.

There is a possible second motive that might have been at play in George's treatment of Max Hastings. Around the time of *Yoni's* publication, the publisher agreed a series of contracts with various Israeli politicians. One of these was for Yitzhak Rabin's memoirs, signed in September 1977, and written in 1978, the very time that Hastings was struggling to have his book published. Teddy Kollek's book *On Jerusalem* would also be released in 1978, as would Abba Eban's autobiography. All three of these books were serialised in the national newspapers and rights were sold around the world, bringing in considerable revenue to Weidenfeld & Nicolson. Meanwhile, Martin Gilbert was about to release his book *Exile and Return: The Emergence of Jewish Statehood*, there was a biography of Shimon

Peres by Matti Golan in the works, and Michael Bar-Zohar had just completed his manuscript on David Ben-Gurion. In other words, George Weidenfeld's motivation to bowdlerise Hastings's book may have been more about commerce than politics.

Another of Weidenfeld's inner circle says that George always had his eye on improving the fortunes of his business, even if people were bruised along the way. The ends, they summarised, justified the means. According to this line of thinking, Max Hastings's work had been trimmed not because of George's fierce Zionism, though this still played a part, but because the publisher held the needs of his company above those of his author.

CHAPTER 14

In the Eye of the Storm

1982

*'As a group we publishers are or must be congenital optimists
and so we must look for more than survival. Indeed, we must
look for salvation by treating the present challenges as blessings
in disguise and as signposts to a new El Dorado.' – GW*

'Good evening, we begin this evening with revelations about one
of the world's most influential international civil servants,' declared
Peter Jennings, host of ABC television's World News Tonight. 'The
New York Times reported today that Kurt Waldheim, the former
secretary general of the United Nations, was attached to a German
army command during WW2 that engaged in mass deportation
of Greek Jews. The *Times* also reports that Mr Waldheim, who is
Austrian and is presently a candidate for the presidency of Austria,
was enrolled in youth in two Nazi Party organisations.'

Earlier that day, 4 March 1986, the *New York Times* had run a
story on its front page based on research carried out by the World
Jewish Congress. In an interview with the paper, Kurt Waldheim
acknowledged that he had served on General Alexander Lohr's staff
in 1942 and 1943, at a time of military operations against Yugoslav
partisans and mass deportations of Greek Jews. General Lohr, also
an Austrian, was executed as a war criminal in 1947. And yet, the
New York Times continued, the former secretary general and now
presidential candidate had not previously disclosed this information. In particular, the paper added, 'In his recent autobiography,
In the Eye of the Storm, he suggests that his military career ended

in December 1941, when he was wounded in the leg on the eastern front near the Russian town of Orel, and that after his recovery in 1942, he was permitted to resume his law studies.'

Eight years before Peter Jennings spoke about 'one of the world's most influential international civil servants', it had been George Weidenfeld who had suggested that Kurt Waldheim write his memoirs. It had been George who sold the book to the American publisher, Adler & Adler. And it had been one of George's editors who had suggested the book's title *In the Eye of the Storm* and had worked with Waldheim to prepare and then edit the text. As soon as the story broke in the American media, therefore, journalists from around the world tried desperately to reach George for comment.

Kurt Waldheim (2nd from left) in Podgorica; today Montenegro, 1943

From the very start of his career, George Weidenfeld had published books authored by Europe's leading fascists. When George had launched the first list in 1949, one of the titles had been by

Benito Mussolini, another was by Hjalmar Schacht (Hitler's finance minister). This was followed by books by Hitler himself (based on his private conversations) in 1953, Martin Bormann (Hitler's private secretary) in 1954, Joachim von Ribbentrop (Hitler's foreign minister) in 1954, Rudolf Hoess (the commandant of Auschwitz) in 1959, Carl Dönitz (the admiral who briefly replaced Adolf Hitler at the war's end) also in 1959, and Albert Speer (Hitler's architect) in 1970.

Publishing titles by the Nazi senior leadership was highly unusual at this time. When books were released about the Second World War, it was far more common for them to be about the Allies, celebrating the triumphs and derring-do of American generals, members of the British Special Operations Executive (SOE) or French resistance fighters. The one exception was the publisher Tom Maschler – who was also Jewish and had fled from Nazi-controlled Europe – who released a handful of Nazi-related books through his company Jonathan Cape, but nowhere near the number published by Weidenfeld & Nicolson.

For their part, the former Nazis saw George as providing an opportunity to get their ideas, histories and points of view heard by a large readership. They also hoped that their work would likely be taken more seriously given that George was a victim of Nazi persecution. If a Jewish refugee was prepared to publish their book, went the argument, then surely their writing was legitimate.

For publishing these books, George was repeatedly attacked by Jewish individuals and organisations. He was criticised for providing a platform for Nazis and for amplifying their propaganda. To this, George would invariably provide the same explanations: first, it was important that the world understood how the Nazi regime functioned, and what better way than to hear from those on the inside? Second, he made sure that each of these books contained an introduction by an expert on the subject. These introductions put the writing into context, often challenging the author's conclusions and correcting factual errors, dissembling and omissions. Third, and perhaps most importantly, George believed that a publisher did not have to agree with everything that an author put down on paper. Quite the contrary, it was the duty of a publisher to make public writing that was worthy of attention, irrespective of personal beliefs. Nevertheless, the criticism cut deep, particularly when it came from his Jewish friends, such as Isaiah Berlin, Marcus Sieff or Teddy Kollek, which it often did.

Of all the Nazi authors George published, he made the most effort with Albert Speer. While Speer was incarcerated in Spandau prison after the war, George had written to him suggesting that he write his memoirs. Speer was released in 1966 after completing his twenty-year sentence and, soon after, George hosted a dinner party for him in Düsseldorf with a group of influential people, including British and German diplomats and journalists. 'Professor Speer,' George asked at one point during the meal, 'what made Himmler so important? Because from all we know he was a mediocre man.' Speer answered quickly. 'No,' he said, 'this man had a genius for finding the best people.' As soon as Speer said this, he realised his error, adding, 'But [Himmler was] a man of satanic disposition.' Then he told another story that was oft repeated by George. 'I must tell you, Hitler had a magnetic personality,' recalled Speer, 'I went to say goodbye in the bunker and he could have had me killed. I left crying.' To the Austrian refugee turned publisher, this was proof that Speer was honest. Why else would he have admitted visiting the Führer at the very end, of having shed tears? George was reassured that Speer was exactly as he portrayed himself, the 'good Nazi'.

Upon its release in 1970, Speer's book *Inside the Third Reich* had received widespread media coverage. The BBC sent a crew from its flagship current affairs programme *Panorama* to Heidelberg to interview the author. When the programme was aired the following week, the former Nazi was introduced to the audience as remorseful and reformed. Under the headline How Spandau changed Albert Speer, *The Times* described Speer as a 'tall, engaging, well-spoken man with a frank, open look'. While the *New York Times* reported that his book was 'not only the most significant personal German account to come out of the war but the most revealing document on the Hitler phenomenon yet written'.

The reception for *Inside the Third Reich* had not all been good. Among the most critical was the *Jewish Chronicle*, the most widely read Jewish newspaper in Britain. In one article, the paper said that Speer had attempted to 'explain away' the horrors of the Nazi regime and 'made a fortune' in the process. In another piece, the newspaper reported that George Weidenfeld had paid Albert Speer £25,000 for the British rights to his autobiography, and then added snidely: 'By one of those touching ironies of history, the ex-Nazi is working for the ex-refugee. Had Sir George tarried in Austria a little longer he might have been working for Speer – though presumably for a lower fee.' Such coverage, though troubling for George, did not appear to impact sales adversely. In the run-up to the book's release, bookseller subscriptions in Britain exceeded 10,000 copies – five times higher than any of the other books Weidenfeld & Nicolson published that week.

Three years after the publication of *Inside the Third Reich*, George heard word that Speer was unhappy with him. Apparently, the former Nazi was aggrieved that the publisher had not responded to his letter congratulating him on receiving his knighthood. George had written a three-page letter to Speer, apologising for his 'gross discourtesy' and said that he had been busy at work. 'I would like to make one cardinal point very clear to you,' he added, 'regardless of the future of our relationship, both as far as human and professional contact is concerned, I am very proud to have published your first book and have a very high regard for you not only as an author but as a person.' George then continued:

Those of my friends who know me well are well aware that I have the fullest understanding for what actuated many Germans in the thirties and forties and for me the final result is whether they genuinely and honestly have struggled through, in their consciences, and in their minds, to a position that is honourable and acceptable to people of my beliefs and attitudes. Of course, I have had a lot of personal attacks for being your publisher but I have invariably counter-attacked and held you up as someone who – to use the title of Hermann Rauschning's famous book – has had his MAKE AND BREAK WITH HITLER.

This, then, was the pattern: George would secure the rights from a Nazi or his relatives. He published their books and then he defended the publication deploying his Austrian-Jewish background, charm and intelligence. Next, he retained the author's loyalty through strong sales, personal correspondence and one-on-one meetings. It was an effective, albeit controversial commercial strategy.

Such was the context when, in March 1982, George began negotiating the memoirs of Kurt Waldheim, the former Secretary-General of the United Nations. Weidenfeld & Nicolson had already published two of Waldheim's books, *The Austrian Example* in 1973 and *The Challenge of Peace* in 1980. A contract was quickly agreed. The book would be 100,000 words; it would arrive no later than 31 March 1984; Weidenfeld & Nicolson would not only have the rights to sell the book in Great Britain and the Commonwealth, but they would also act as the author's agent, selling the book to a North American publisher. A German edition would be published in parallel, but the release dates would be coordinated. The advance paid by Weidenfeld & Nicolson would be $25,000.

Just before Christmas 1983, the first chapters of Kurt Waldheim's manuscript arrived at the Weidenfeld & Nicolson offices in London. On the front page was written the book's title: *Ten Years at Turtle Bay*. This confused George and his editorial team. When they read the partial manuscript, they were confused still further. They had been expecting a full-life memoir, including his time in Vienna before and during the Second World War. Instead, they had received a book limited to Waldheim's ten years as head of the United Nations.

On 9 February 1984, George wrote to Waldheim. 'I am presuming on a long friendship, and on your faith in my frankness and loyalty, as well as deep respect: hence, this frank letter,' he began. 'My candid opinion is that [the manuscript] needs a complete restructuring and rewriting.' The initial deadline of March 1984 was clearly not going to be met. To rectify the situation, George hired Brian Connell, one of his authors, to help Waldheim. Connell would be paid out of Waldheim's advance.

In April 1984, Connell wrote to Waldheim with a new structure for the book. In particular, he stressed the need to include a 'more vivid account of your war service'. Eight months later, and after spending three weeks interviewing Waldheim, particularly about his early years, a revised draft was ready under the new title *Man in the Middle*. At 110,000 words, the book was a little long, but Connell felt it read well. A publication date was now set for 15 November 1985. All appeared to be going well until the start of February when Alexandra MacCormick, the thirty-nine-year-old senior editor at Weidenfeld & Nicolson who had been put in charge of the project, received a letter from Waldheim. There were, he said, 'serious shortcomings' with the revised manuscript and he was 'working day and night to correct the errors and supplement the text'. On hearing about this from MacCormick, Connell wrote 'I hope to goodness his nibs is about to cough up.' Which he did. Soon after, Waldheim's corrections arrived at the publisher's office in London along with an additional 28,000 words plus the promise of a further two new chapters. This would bring the total book length to 150,000, well beyond the originally agreed 100,000.

In the spring of 1985, MacCormick flew out to see Waldheim at his home in Vienna. They had dinner together, prepared by Waldheim's wife Elisabeth. Once more, MacCormick pressed him to reduce the length of the book and again Waldheim resisted. She also raised another issue of concern. 'While I do want to reduce the text length,' she said, 'you have written no more than a couple of vague sentences about your wartime years. Surely, you would like to add some information about such an important period?' The readers would want to know how he spent this period, she added, and reviewers would ask questions if they noticed a gap. To her surprise, he said 'no', he didn't want to talk about his wartime years. Back in London, she worked to reduce the length of the manuscript and prepared it for publication. Throughout this time, Waldheim's assistant, Rosemary Zaleski, sent page after page of corrections. To make matters more complicated, the German publishers were working on their own version of the book based on a separate text supplied by the author. It was becoming increasingly difficult to keep track of which changes had been taken in.

In the summer of 1985, Weidenfeld & Nicolson told its book-sellers that it would be publishing Waldheim's title early the fol-lowing year. Then, to George's great surprise, Waldheim announced that he was running for president of Austria. This meant that to take advantage of the likely public interest the manuscript had to be ready three months earlier than previously planned. Weidenfeld & Nicolson scrambled to accelerate the editorial process. In the end, the book was published in October in Germany and three months later in the UK and America. The first reviews were lukewarm. The *Sunday Telegraph* commiserated that 'it is hard to produce a book about the UN which is either readable or inspiring'. The *New Statesman* called it a 'catalogue of well-intentioned failures'. While the *TLS* identified the problem: as a diplomat, 'you can no longer be revealing even when you decide to write your memoirs'. In other words, the book was boring.

That was, until the *New York Times* article was published on 4 March 1986, disclosing Waldheim's wartime omissions. This was followed by newspapers around the world, including *The Times* in London, which went with a headline that must have turned George's stomach: WALDHEIM DENIES HOLOCAUST ROLE. Over the next few days, investigative journalists discovered that the German publishers had included material on Waldheim's wartime experience that had not been in the English edition, including a significant passage that placed him in the German army for at least two more years than he had previously disclosed. The newspapers doubled down on the story.

To coordinate a response, George Weidenfeld spoke to George Walsh, the editor at Adler & Adler in New York, saying they needed to protect the author, even if it had negative consequences for the publishing companies. Walsh agreed and recommended they reach out to Thomas Carrocio, head of a law firm in Washington DC specialising in public relations. Carrocio quickly jumped into action. He told the two publishers that they needed to establish an alternative narrative to rebut the 'Waldheim denies Holocaust role' story. Key to this effort would be an affidavit from the editor at the centre of the saga, Alexandra MacCormick. By fax, the lawyer now sent a guide to what MacCormick needed to say. First, she had to confirm that there was a 'variance' between the text prepared by the author and the publisher. Second, that the German and English editions were different. Third, that the author had made numerous efforts to correct the text but had been stymied by Weidenfeld & Nicolson. Fourth, it had been the publisher, and not the author, who had insisted that the book did not 'warrant an extensive emphasis on detailed background in the non-UN-chapters'. Fifth, and perhaps most importantly, when the author had included earlier material, the publisher had cut it to limit the length of the book.

On 26 March, MacCormick wrote a four-page statement and sent it by fax to Thomas Carrocio. Having first explained that she was in charge of preparing the manuscript for publication in both America and Britain, she explained the ups and downs of the editorial process. How Waldheim's first effort had been rejected as too academic and that they wanted something 'more lively and anecdotal to increase sales in bookshops.' A second version had been produced by Brian Connell which was then amended by Waldheim, creating a third version that was 40,000 words too long. It was now that she had cut various passages, including the following key paragraph:

> At the end of my study leave and after my leg had healed, I was recalled to military service. Shortly before the end of the war I was stationed in the Trieste area. When the German troops in Italy surrendered, I made every effort to avoid capture and reach home.

At the time, MacCormick wrote, this 'seemed insignificant', it was one of many cuts that were made. When Waldheim said he wanted to add more material that was to be included in the German edition, such as the above paragraph, the editor had replied that it was not possible, there was just not enough room. The alternative narrative was in place: if a mistake had been made, it was a cock-up, not a cover-up. And, most importantly, it was the publisher's fault, not the author's. The statement did not tackle the central question head-on – why had Waldheim failed to disclose his Nazi past? – but it did confuse the issue. 'When you think back on it,' MacCormick recalls about the entire episode, 'it was mortifying.'

With the editor's affidavit in place, George Weidenfeld went on a media tour, telling any journalist who would listen that Kurt Waldheim was not a Nazi sympathiser. He knew this because when he, George, had been a student in Vienna in the late 1930s, Waldheim had been one of the few to treat him with decency. When George had been forbidden from attending classes at the Diplomatic Academy, it had been Kurt Waldheim who had brought his books and homework to his house, allowing him to continue with his studies. This took some courage, George said, particularly given that his father Max was being held in prison at the time. To further evidence his argument that Waldheim had not been a Nazi sympathiser, George also shared a copy of a confidential report written by a top Nazi official declaring that Waldheim and his family were 'untrustworthy'.

If George thought this would be the end of the matter, he was entirely wrong. Waldheim's wartime record and its omission from *In the Eye of the Storm* became a key issue in the Austrian presidential elections. During the campaign, further documents were made public by the World Jewish Congress in New York, including Waldheim being on the list of war criminals compiled by the United States and United Kingdom in 1945. Those who opposed Waldheim's presidential bid, including Chancellor Fred Sinowatz from the Social Democratic Party, now questioned whether he had been involved in war crimes. Meanwhile, those in Waldheim's party, the Christian Democrat Austrian People's Party (ÖVP), responded aggressively, arguing that Waldheim was under attack from an international Jewish conspiracy and that it should only be Austrians who chose their next president. The election was held on 4 and 8 May 1986. When the tally for the second round was counted, Waldheim had won 53.9 per cent of the vote. He would be the next president of Austria.

The election of Kurt Waldheim triggered outrage around the world. Politicians, academics, journalists and survivors began openly discussing what had long been whispered: Austria denied its role in the Holocaust. A campaign was mounted to add Waldheim to the US Watch List, prohibiting him from travelling to the United States, including his beloved United Nations. Austria now found itself increasingly isolated from the world community.

*

Why did George Weidenfeld stick his neck out for Kurt Waldheim? This was the question that many Jews around the world were asking, including Teddy Kollek, the mayor of Jerusalem and the publisher's long-time friend. In a letter to Kollek, dated 4 September 1986, George tried to explain himself. During their time together at the Diplomatic Academy in Vienna in the late 1930s, Waldheim was one of the small number of students who had been humane and friendly. 'This was not wholly without inconvenience or indeed danger to him,' George wrote, 'since my father was a publicised prisoner of the new regime and our home was thus "out of bounds".' As to Waldheim being a war criminal, the publisher continued, the 'accusations and insinuations against him do not stand up against scrutiny'.

So far, George had said all this before in public. But, in his letter to Kollek, he now went further. 'My main interest,' he said, 'is to mend fences.' He saw his support of Waldheim as part of an effort to reverse the 'long-term deterioration' in the relationship between Austria and world Jewry. 'There is no doubt that if the present campaign persists – either to force Dr Waldheim to resign, or to humiliate his country by denying him landing rights in the United States – it will gravely disturb the relationship between Austrians and Israel, and will also spill over into the Federal Republic [of Germany].' He then continued, 'So you see I am approaching this not at all as an appeaser, or "Assimilant" but, frankly, as a "political Zionist" whose primary concern is the well-being of the State of Israel and the position of Jews wherever they live.'

Absent for a while from Jerusalem, Teddy Kollek took some time to respond. On 14 October he wrote back to George. 'I very much respect your efforts in this connection, particularly as you are truly swimming against the tide, and I agree with these efforts,' the mayor began. 'But with all this there is no question that over the years, the Austrians have behaved abominably, much worse than the Germans.' Whereas the Germans had honestly faced up to their history, he continued, 'NO Austrian ever accepted responsibility.' He therefore declined to join with George in his public support of Waldheim. 'This has nothing to do with Waldheim personally,' he concluded, 'but it is part of an entire picture.' George must have been disappointed by Kollek's response, but he did not let it affect their friendship. For the mayor's next re-election campaign, he contributed $1,000.

In public, George continued to support Kurt Waldheim. In private, however, as more revelations about Waldheim's wartime years surfaced in the media, the publisher expressed his increasing disquiet. 'George was shocked and very disappointed' by the disclosures, Alexandra MacCormick recalls. 'He felt he had been made to look a fool.' Though she added that she found the fact that George had stood up for Kurt Waldheim, despite it all, both 'admirable and amazing'.

In 1996, a decade after the publication of *In the Eye of the Storm*, Waldheim completed another book: *Die Antwort* (*The Answer*). In this account of his wartime military experience, Waldheim admitted to vague knowledge of the deportations and concentration camps, but still claimed that he had no knowledge of the killings of civilians. *Die Antwort* was released by Amalthea Signum in Austria. George chose not to publish this book.

In the end, for his Nazi past and publishing deception, Waldheim was barred from entering the United States and many other countries. In effect, he became an international *persona non grata*, casting an uncomfortable shadow over Austria and its population. The intense negativity of the global response to what became known as the 'Waldheim Affair' caused many in Austria to re-examine their country's wartime history and led to Chancellor Franz Vranitzky's decision to focus on the country's complicity in the Holocaust and to initiate reparations for the victims. Over the next two decades, increasing numbers of Austrians began to question the story that their country had been the victim of Nazi aggression and had played no role in the persecution of the European Jews. This profound shift culminated, in November 2021, with the opening of the Shoah Wall of Names Memorial in a prominent square close to Vienna's city centre. Etched into a series of granite slabs were the names of more than 64,000 Jewish children, women and men of Austria who were murdered during the years 1938–45. Among those listed were George's two grandmothers, Deborah Laura Eisenstein and Jetty Adele Weidenfeld. At the memorial's entrance was a statement that would have been inconceivable before the Waldheim Affair: 'Countless Austrians participated in their mass murder.'

While the vast majority of Jewish and world opinion had turned against Waldheim, triggering an Austrian cultural reckoning, the publisher had played a different but perhaps no less important role. In defending the Austrian president, and by extension the Austrian people, George had built a bridge where, once it had come out the other side of its period of self-reflection, Austria could rejoin the international community chastened, more self-aware, but with its pride intact. The net result was exactly what he wanted: Austria has acknowledged its role in the mass murder during the Holocaust and provides ongoing and significant support for the state of Israel.

Nevertheless, the experience with Kurt Waldheim was bruising for George Weidenfeld. For a number of years it tarnished his reputation with many key figures in the Jewish community in the United States, Britain and around the world. It did not, however, distract him from his other publishing projects. There was one celebrity memoir in particular that he was chasing after, right at the time when he was being swept up in the Waldheim storm. A book that was so big it might well eclipse all of George's previous efforts. And it involved an extremely famous rock star.

CHAPTER 15

Mick Jagger

1985

*'Hardly ever since the days of Gutenberg has it
been more difficult for the serious writer or the
talented beginner to make ends meet.'* – GW

Towards the end of 1981, George Weidenfeld made an offer. It wasn't just any offer. The publisher was inviting the world's most famous rock star to write his memoir. If agreed, it would attract global headlines and was guaranteed to sell millions of copies. The price on the table was $2 million. This was an extraordinary figure and would be the highest advance paid for many years on either side of the Atlantic. Weidenfeld & Nicolson would retain world rights for the book. This was also unusual. Typically, the publisher shared the risk of a project with other companies. But not in this case. George was so confident that he would more than cover his costs that he was willing to take the book on for himself. Excitingly, for him, the offer was accepted. The name of the artist who had agreed to the deal was Michael Philip Jagger, better known as Mick Jagger.

On first appearance, the two men had little in common. Now in his late thirties, Jagger, with his succulent lips and thrusting hips, was considered one of the world's sexiest men, the Great Seducer, with a reputation for enjoying booze and class-A drugs, and consistently performing to ecstatic sell-out crowds. Over the previous three years, the Rolling Stones had enjoyed a string of hits, doing particularly well in America: 'Miss You' which had reached no. 1 in the US charts; 'Beast of Burden' which climbed to no. 8; 'Emotional

Rescue' which peaked at no. 3; and, just that year, the rock anthem 'Start Me Up' had reached no. 2 in America. For his part, George was a teetotalling book publisher in his mid-sixties who wore suits from Savile Row or his personal tailor in Vienna and occasionally gave ill-attended speeches in the House of Lords.

Yet, George Weidenfeld and Mick Jagger had certain things in common. They both shared a friendship with the banker Prince Rupert Loewenstein, managing director of the merchant bank Leopold Joseph & Sons Ltd. Loewenstein had been the Stones' financial advisor since 1968. George had been working with the prince for about the same amount of time. In the mid-1960s, it had been Loewenstein who had advised George during the negotiations with Frederick Praeger and Encyclopedia Britannica. It was Loewenstein who provided a £150,000 loan to George's company when he had been short of cash. The prince had also sat as a director on the board of George's publishing company and frequented the publisher's private parties at his home on Chelsea Embankment. At the very least, therefore, the publisher and the rock star were connected by a man known for his commercial savvy.

George's idea was that Jagger should write an autobiography with an emphasis on his early life and career. At its core, the book would be based on a series of conversations conducted by a ghostwriter and then Jagger would review the transcripts, provide notes, and the text would be revised. The first challenge, then, was to find the right ghostwriter. Over the summer of 1982, Jagger met with the prospective candidates at his room at the Savoy Hotel in London. On the shortlist were John Ryle, the thirty-one-year-old deputy literary editor at the *Sunday Times*; Philip Norman, who wrote the celebrated book *Shout!* about the Beatles; the novelist and film critic Adam Mars-Jones; and the journalist and royal biographer Anthony Holden. At one point, the music journalist Maureen Cleave had also been considered, but Jagger made it clear that he preferred to work with a man. Inside the room – dressed in a cat-stippled

T-shirt, tight white trousers and bare-footed – Jagger asked the candidates various questions. He appeared polite, genial, intelligent. Champagne and smoked salmon sandwiches were offered and consumed. At one point, he asked to see if they could roll a large joint made from three sheets of cigarette paper. In the end, he chose John Ryle.

On the morning of 13 December 1982, John Ryle travelled to meet the editorial team of Weidenfeld & Nicolson. The company had recently moved to South London, they needed more space and the rent was cheaper. Located next to a second-hand tailor's shop and above some old council offices, the new headquarters at 91 Clapham High Street made a poor first impression. To reach Weidenfeld & Nicolson, Ryle had to first walk up five flights of stairs – there was no lift – then along a dank corridor and through a set of doors with mesh wire set in a small inset window – the kind that might be found in the wing of an old hospital. After checking in at reception, the writer was escorted to the interior, down another drab corridor with worn brown carpeting, past the library, which held every title released by Weidenfeld & Nicolson, and into a room which, unlike the rest of the place, was rather grand. This was the publisher's office. Its walls were draped in tobacco-coloured felt, tastefully adorned with expensively framed works of art. A few carefully selected books stood on the shelves. On one side of the room was a long suede sofa, upon which perched the editorial director, John Curtis, and the writer's literary agent, Gillon Aitken. On the other side, behind a large wooden desk, sat the publisher, George Weidenfeld.

During this meeting, the men discussed the scope of the project. The book would be an autobiography between 80,000 and 100,000 words long. Its provisional title was *Mick Jagger by Mick Jagger*. The focus of the book would be on the life of the musician up to 1971 and would cover all the major milestones including tours. Ryle would need to deliver a book outline with forty or fifty sample pages by 28 February 1983. Once the outline had been approved by Jagger, the ghostwriter would have to complete the manuscript by that November. The book would then likely be released the following year. The contract would be between Ryle and Jagger's company, Promopub BV, based in Amsterdam. Ryle would be paid a substantial five-figure advance. He would be provided with a word processor and training how to use it. In addition, Promopub would take out insurance on the writer's life, in case of accidental death. It would be up to the ghostwriter to check the facts and to make sure none of the material was libellous or obscene. Also, and this was stressed a few times, Ryle could not disclose any information about Mick Jagger or his family or friends, without the rock star's explicit consent. Finally, and perhaps this should have been a warning, Jagger could decide if and when the book was published.

George was untroubled by any of these stipulations. He had plenty of experience of working with famous people and publishing their memoirs. He could handle Mick Jagger.

Mick Jagger

By the early 1980s, George was well-known for publishing books by and about the rich and famous. It had become a cornerstone of his business. A reliable source of income. In 1979, for instance, he bid for and won the rights to publish a book by his long-time friend,

Henry Kissinger. The book was called *The White House Years*, becoming a bestseller. At the time, Kissinger was the most recognisable diplomat in the world. To many he was a hero, brokering peace in Vietnam and forging a new relationship with China. To others he was a villain, responsible for the bombing of Cambodia (which resulted in the deaths of over 100,000 civilians), and signing off on Indonesia's genocidal assault of East Timor. In 1981, Weidenfeld & Nicolson published a collection of Kissinger's interviews and statements titled *For the Record*, followed by *The Years of Upheaval* in 1982 recounting his time as Secretary of State under Nixon. Also in 1979, George published the memoirs of Antony Armstrong-Jones (Lord Snowdon), *Snowdon: A Personal View*; the singer Max Boyce's *I Was There*; along with Thomas Bob's biography of the film and television actress Joan Crawford, released just a year after her death. Most successful of all, George had just published *Charles, Prince of Wales* by the journalist Anthony Holden, the first full biography of Britain's heir to the throne, which had remained on the bestseller list for weeks.

This is not to say that celebrity titles were all that Weidenfeld & Nicolson published at this time. Included in the roughly 130 titles that came out annually during this period were also *The White Album* by Joan Didion (1979), *Civilizations of the Holy Land* by Paul Johnson (1979), Vladimir Nabokov's *Lectures on Literature* (1980), and A. J. Ayer's *Philosophy in the Twentieth Century* (1982). Nevertheless, celebrity memoirs – of film stars, football players, comedians, television hosts and musicians – were considered a dependable route for delivering a bestseller and were aggressively pursued by Weidenfeld & Nicolson and most of the other leading publishers in London, New York and around the world. Many of these titles were published under the stewardship of Christopher Falkus, a former historian and academic, who was by some accounts a brilliant and mercurial managing director. George had recruited Falkus to the firm in 1970 to run the Art and Illustrated list. Since then, he had created the 'Kings and Queens' series, edited by Antonia Fraser, released in conjunction with Book Club Associates, which became a major source of revenue for Weidenfeld & Nicolson.

Celebrity books were not, however, without their problems. Princess Margaret's biography was a case in point. The book had been commissioned by Alexandra MacCormick for Weidenfeld & Nicolson in 1981 and was written by Chris Warwick. At first it appeared to be progressing well. 'Of the Princess herself I have nothing but praise and she and I continue to get on swimmingly,' Warwick wrote to his editor on 5 January 1982, 'She has been <u>most</u> helpful in arranging appointments for me – with people who wouldn't normally say a word.' Adding, 'in her own words, "I am enjoying all this enormously".' The project, however, was besieged by a number of issues. Much of the subject matter was, according to Warwick, 'tedious', particularly the middle years during the 1940s and 1950s. This is not an unusual problem for books about celebrities or royal figures where their backstories are frequently less interesting than details of their colourful present lives. Next came the finances. Paying out large sums to celebrities or their biographers placed an inevitable strain on the company's fiscal resources which, in turn, could result in late payment of invoices. 'I am furious I have not yet received my latest cheque,' Warwick wrote on 17 January. 'It really is not good enough, nor indeed is W&N's perennial and tiresome excuse about a cash-flow problem.'

Then there was the question of publicity. The celebrity or royal figure was glad to accept the generous advance or attention, but typically didn't want to do the work of promoting the book. On 24 November 1982, Alexandra MacCormick wrote a memo to George in preparation for the launch party of the book now titled *Princess Margaret*. The princess apparently 'prefers parties where she meets people other than the ones she would normally be invited to lunch with, ie not Debretts, not stuffy,' MacCormick warned. 'If we invite her to a private party and she arrives and the Press is waiting at the door, she may turn round and go home.' Also, Weidenfeld & Nicolson frequently received intense pressure from a celebrity's famous associates. In this instance, it was Princess Margaret's former husband, Lord Snowdon, another of George's authors. On 21 September 1982, Snowdon wrote to the publisher requesting that a line be added to the acknowledgements stating that 'The Earl of Snowdon, although invited to do so, declined to make any contribution for personal reasons, but sent his best wishes for the success of the book.' And yet, when the manuscript was complete, Snowdon demanded not only to be sent a copy, but then issued a series of letters which included long lists of corrections that he insisted be made. Such interventions distracted the publishing team and added to an already heavy workload.

For his part, George was unfazed by tantrums of the rich and famous. At the end of March 1983 he hosted the launch for Princess Margaret's book at his flat on Chelsea Embankment. The event was attended by the author, along with scores of journalists, actors and book critics. A few days later, the princess wrote to the publisher from her home in Kensington Palace. 'Dear George,' she began, 'Thank you so much for that delightful evening you gave for Christopher Warwick's book about me. Some of my friends who have read it like it and I do hope you are pleased with it.' She then sent her appreciation to 'all your charming employees whom I had the pleasure of meeting over the book', before signing off 'yours very sincerely, Margaret'.

Despite the painful editorial process and tepid reviews, the book became a bestseller. Like every book, key to its success was that it had first been written, then printed, and then copies were made available to be purchased in shops. Such steps, though basic, would also be necessary if the Jagger autobiography was to fulfil its stratospheric potential.

*

John Ryle's first task was to interview Mick Jagger. Not easy given the rock star's hectic globe-trotting schedule. They finally met in New York on 4 October 1982. Then in Paris on 29 November. A week later, Ryle, sent three pages of interview transcripts entitled 'Mick Jagger Talking' to his editor at Weidenfeld & Nicolson.

Page one started with Jagger's earliest memory: his mother removing the blackout curtains on 8 May 1945, Victory in Europe (VE) Day. He would have been twenty-two months old. 'We won't be needing these anymore,' he recalled his mother saying. He then spoke about his childhood. His family was 'respectable'. They lived in Dartford in Kent, on the outskirts of London. His mother came from Australia. His father worked as a teacher in Manchester before coming to London. The cultural difference was as big as moving from England to America. He never met his grandfather on his mother's side, but his grandmother played a big role in his childhood. So did her garden. He could still recall the smell of the apple tree in her garden. He was baptised, but religion was not important to his parents. Jagger said that he initially met his future band mate Keith Richards as a young child, before they went to school. Richards was really into cowboys, Jagger remembered; he wanted to be Roy Rogers. Before Jagger's first day at school he cried, worried how terrible it would be. It met his expectations. The children were mean to each other and the food was awful. They learned to write with chalk on boards of slate. Discipline was strict. Following one infraction, the school principal made his whole class stand in the yard and then she hit each child in turn with a ruler across the knuckles. Jagger recalled they were 'like prisoners in a concentration camp'.

By the second page, Jagger moved on to his early teenage years. 'In those days, the two most important things in your life were sex education and career guidance, you got told nothing about that at all.' At school, they listened to a bishop who warned them about the dangers of venereal disease and made them watch a film about rabbits. The children laughed uncontrollably. There was one story that stood out in the transcript. The rock star recalled a 'gypsy' woman with a headscarf and gold earrings coming to their door selling lucky heather and clothes pegs. He said his mother thought his dad fancied this woman. As with the other early memories, Jagger didn't provide further details, nor did he provide insight into what this story meant to him.

Starting on page three, Jagger was fifteen years old. He hung out with his friends at a neighbourhood coffee house playing snooker. They listened to music they couldn't hear on the BBC: Elvis Presley, Buddy Holly, Cliff Richard, The Shadows. He said that some of the boys had jobs and rode around on motorbikes, but he stayed at school and only had a bicycle. Some days, they went into central London to look at clothes in Carnaby Street. He tried out many different styles. 'It was a way of getting out of the way of the life of your elders,' he said, 'who want you to wear brown suits.' He added that at this time in his life he had a 'lean time with girls'.

There was one more memory, tucked into the final paragraph of the third page. Jagger talked about taking trips from south of the River Thames through a long pedestrian tunnel to the East End, which was filled with 'streetwise villains' and was more 'romantic'. He said it was the Blackwall Tunnel, which back in those days was open to foot traffic. 'I used to love going there, going through that dark tunnel as a child was like going into a new world.' That's where the transcript ended. There was some interesting material but to write a book, the ghostwriter would need much more.

Ryle and Jagger met for a third time on 15 December, again in Paris. Two days later, the ghostwriter wrote to the rock star saying that he thought their last session had gone well. But this was only the start. To produce the forty or fifty sample pages, he continued, they would need to meet for at least twenty-five more hours. Given that Jagger was planning to spend February recording the Stones' next album (*Undercover*), Ryle suggested they meet again in New York, perhaps between 17 and 23 January 1983. It would be best to meet every day for a few hours. They could then talk further about the 'tone you want to adopt in the book and exactly what you want to include in it'. Before then, Ryle asked if it would be appropriate for him to meet Jagger's parents; this would help him prepare for 'another session on your childhood'. He also hoped to transfer various Rolling Stones concerts onto video so that they could later go through them together, as this might trigger some memories. Finally, he planned to reach out to Bill Wyman, the Stones' bass player, to look at tour schedules and other documents. From this Ryle would construct a reliable chronology of events. The most useful 'memory-prompting device', he said, would be if he and Jagger could walk through the streets of Soho and Dartford, where the musician had spent so much of his childhood. In the end, Ryle would take the walking tour of London with the singer's younger brother Chris.

On Wednesday 9 February 1983, George approved a press release announcing that they would be publishing Mick Jagger's auto-biography. It was sent out to media contacts in Britain, America and around the world. Word had already leaked out about the forthcoming autobiography, with stories in both the *New York Post* and the *Evening Standard*. The coverage had been followed by various discreet letters of interest from top American publishing executives. With the press release, though, the floodgates opened. By the end of the month, George received formal inquiries from Bantam Books, St Martin's Press, Doubleday and Simon & Schuster.

By the middle of March, however, it became clear that the project was running into serious trouble. Ryles spoke with the rock star by phone, who was then in Kenya, and then reported the conversation back to Weidenfeld & Nicolson. Jagger apparently said that he didn't want to work on the outline while he was in Africa. When Ryle 'pressed him' for a date upon his return, he was 'vague' in his response 'whilst expressing keenness to get on with the book'. The ghostwriter didn't think Jagger's enthusiasm was 'flagging', more that he just 'wanted a break'. This news caused George tremendous anxiety. His company was on the hook for $2 million, not to mention the enormous amount of time his editorial team had invested in the project. They needed to come up with a solution, urgently.

On 29 March, having checked the contents with Prince Loewenstein, George sent a telex to his celebrity author. 'Dearest Mick', he began:

Undue delay in initial outline material upsets overall schedule and affects my negotiating position and splendid opportunities with America and the rest of the world. Urge you, in the interest of producing book of real quality and meeting our contracts, to find the essential one continuous week necessary to complete first stage. Since end of March impossible, could you please assure me without shadow of doubt that you can give access and co-operation to Ryle for this phase to be completed by 23 April, or very latest, end April. Five to seven days should be enough and I can co-ordinate dates with Ryle for you. Beyond that, delay would jeopardize all future dates and affect not only quality but practical possibilities of meeting schedules for next year. Rest assured that we have tremendous faith in the book and only want the best for all concerned, but are under pressure from prospective publishing partners and through long experience aware of dangers. Deeply aware of your many commitments and need to relax after past heavy recording work, but need assurance from you that you are really in earnest and anxious to receive confirmation of above specific dates.

Much love

George Weidenfeld

On 7 April, Prince Loewenstein left a telephone message at the publishing house. John Ryle was welcome to visit the rock star at his home near Tours the following week and could remain for a week to ten days. Loewenstein added that 'If Mick Jagger is not there please leave a message with either Jerry Hall or his Indian manservant.' Ryle duly went to Tours, the musician did in fact appear, and while playing backgammon or driving in the car, Ryle taped a number of further conversations. When he returned to his house in Essex the following week, the ghostwriter started writing up his notes.

In the third week of May, John Ryle submitted the outline to his editor at Weidenfeld & Nicolson, John Curtis. There would be ten chapters in all. Epigraphs would be included from the Jagger–Richards songbook and other sources. The material would be bolstered by additional interviews with family and friends. Curtis was disappointed. 'While [the outline] undoubtedly contains some very good things,' the editor wrote to his colleagues at Weidenfeld & Nicolson, 'I think we must all agree that taken as a whole the material is rather thin.' For his part, George had two notes. First, Jagger should recount his early life chronologically. And second, 'Among the topics which he proposes to give his views should also be "sex".'

A week later, George met Jagger in New York. In a memo back to his colleagues in London, the publisher reported that the rock star was 'delighted' with Ryle's outline. However, it was time to bring someone else in, to add 'spontaneity and freshness'. Additional interviews should be completed by Brooke Hayward, the forty-six-year-old American actress who had recently published her bestselling childhood memoir, *Haywire*. Brooke Hayward would undertake five or six one- or two-hour interviews over the next three months. The publisher suggested these might include Keith Richards, Chris Jagger, Andy Warhol, Jack Nicholson, Diana Vreeland, Michelle Philips, Bo Diddley, David Hockney, Roman

Polanski, Bianca Jagger, Marianne Faithful and others. John Ryle would incorporate the new material generated by Brooke. George left the meeting feeling a little more optimistic.

On 7 September, John Ryle delivered his revised book outline. According to an internal Weidenfeld & Nicolson memo, this was accepted by both Jagger and George. Three weeks later, Bud MacLennan, the publishing house's much admired and hard-nosed head of rights and sales, flew to New York. Ahead of her arrival, George sent telexes to the five publishing houses who had expressed the most interest. Each was now invited to visit MacLennan at the Carlyle Hotel where she was staying and make their best offer. After multiple bids were submitted, Bantam – America's largest mass-market paperback publisher – won the deal by offering $1,650,000. 'It would be impossible for me to exaggerate their enthusiasm for the book,' Jagger was told by a senior executive at Weidenfeld & Nicolson. The executive added that the deal with Bantam was 'probably the biggest publishing deal for many years'.

Publishers in six other countries now agreed to purchase the rights, including Canada, France and Germany. Seven more countries were expected to sign up in the next two months. Meanwhile, the *Sunday Times* had acquired the serial rights for a six-figure sum. Weidenfeld & Nicolson's share of all this income would be close to $300,000, more once he received his share of the American income. While he was confident that they would more than make up the difference in book sales, the stakes were high. George's anxiety levels climbed, his health declined, most notably seen in his gain of weight.

In the first week of October 1983, George sent Brooke Hayward a telex – by this point she had not yet completed her list of interviews – telling her that he had airmailed her a draft of the Jagger book outline and that Bantam Books had signed up to publish in America. A few days later, he sent her a follow-up letter. 'As we are under some pressure to complete the work by 31 March, your collaboration is not only desirable and appreciated but has a ring of urgency!' The problem was that Jagger was now travelling extensively, promoting the Stones' new album. He would be in Europe in November for a fortnight, then two weeks in Barbados, and then the next three months in Los Angeles.

While Ryle and Hayward were working on the text, the editorial team back in London were energetically discussing the other aspects of the publication. Colour posters were made for the London Underground and the sides of buses. There would also be a media tour, including travel by Concorde to and from the United States. Meanwhile, Jagger had been sent mock-ups of the book jacket using a David Bailey photograph, along with the current title suggestion: *Mick Jagger: My Life and Opinions.* If all went well, the text would be sent for copy-editing in May, with a view to publish on 15 October. All the time, tensions were running high. Everyone working on the project knew that George's company faced an existential financial loss, let alone a reputational disaster, if the publication was not a huge success.

At the start of April, Weidenfeld approached another writer to work on the project. This time it was Barry Coleman, who had previously written a biography of the motorcycle racer Kenny Roberts in just ten weeks. 'We've got a problem,' Coleman was told on the telephone, 'Can you come in... tomorrow?' When Coleman arrived at the Weidenfeld & Nicolson office on Clapham High Street, he was briefed about the Jagger autobiography and the difficulties they were having. 'The story I was told, was that the previous ghostwriter had gone to a lot of celebrity parties and met people like Michael Jackson, and then lost the plot,' Coleman later reported to a *Guardian* journalist. 'I don't know if that was the pressure of the book.' Coleman was asked if he could draft two new chapters within the next two weeks. He said he would try, and jumped on a TWA plane to John F. Kennedy airport in New York.

All the while, the editorial team at Weidenfeld & Nicolson were becoming increasingly frustrated with John Ryle. In one memo, an editor described him as having a 'relaxed attitude'. George sent an urgent message to Ryle in New York:

I MUST STRESS ABSOLUTE NECESSITY TO HAVE REMAINING CHAPTERS – REPEAT, TEXT FOR EVERY SINGLE CHAPTER, EVEN IF ONE CHAPTER WILL REQUIRE FAR MORE EXTENSIVE REVISION THAN THE OTHERS, MUST STRESS AGAIN THE POINT THAT NON-DELIVERANCE OF A COMPLETE M/S [MANUSCRIPT] BETWEEN 80,000–100,000 ON 13TH APRIL COULD BE CONSTRUED BY BANTAM AS BREACH OF CONTRACT AND CANCEL OR RE-NEGOTIATE TO OUR INCALCULABLE LOSS.

On 13 April a parcel was delivered to Tobi Sanders, senior editor at Bantam. It was the full manuscript of Jagger's autobiography. She read the text and was not pleased with the quality of the writing. Having consulted her colleagues, Tobi now proposed that they write jointly – Bantam and Weidenfeld & Nicolson – to Jagger and his representatives and say, clearly, that the 'first draft of the manuscript shown to publishers on April 13, 1984 has been found to be unacceptable by both publishers'. The project could only continue if the author, Mick Jagger, had 'greater involvement'.

Over the next few days, George updated the international publishers and newspapers who had contracts for the book. This prompted numerous distressed messages. Many wanted their money immediately repaid. By return, he sent letters of reassurance. To Andrew Neil, for instance, the editor of the *Sunday Times*, George wrote that 'In Mick's and our view this is a very good beginning', but that it needed two or three months' more work. The book would therefore have to be held over until later that year. Through the summer and into the autumn, the editorial team at Weidenfeld & Nicolson valiantly kept going, trying to wrangle the project over the finish line. The publication date was delayed once again. And then again. Finally, shortly before Christmas 1985, George met with John Ryle and told him that the manuscript had been formally rejected. Publication was now unlikely to take place. George sent back the money he had received from the various international publishers. Mick Jagger, who had by this point been paid $450,000, returned his advance to Weidenfeld & Nicolson. George's financial losses totalled £42,500, but the damage to his reputation was unquantifiable.

Over the past few decades, two narratives have emerged to explain what went wrong with the Mick Jagger autobiography. The first, very public account, comes from the musician himself. 'When I actually started to get into it, I just didn't enjoy reliving my life,' Jagger told the journalist Dave Simpson in the *Guardian*. 'If you wanna write an autobiography, you can't do it in a week. It takes a lot out of you. It takes a lot of reliving emotions, reliving friendships, reliving ups and downs... I just didn't enjoy the process.' He then added, 'So I just said: "I can't be bothered with this", and gave the money back.' When asked in an interview with the BBC why he had started with this project given his busy schedule and his reluctance to talk about his childhood, Mick Jagger, one of the world's most charismatic figures, thought about it a moment. He then said that he, the Great Seducer, had fallen prey to the charms of the publisher. He had been 'seduced', he said, by George Weidenfeld. But later, and this was the other end of the narrative arc, Jagger had managed to re-assert himself, putting his personal enjoyment above the sordid needs of commercial publishing. In other words, he had walked away with his bohemian credentials intact.

The second, much more private explanation, comes from the publisher George Weidenfeld and his editorial team. Mick Jagger's book simply wasn't good enough. George's view was that Jagger may have had many talents, including being a world-class performer, but, according to this theory, telling the story of his life wasn't one of them. This was why the manuscript had been rejected by both Weidenfeld & Nicolson and Bantam Books. For Jagger to say that he 'wasn't bothered' showed, at least to George, a lack of respect for the efforts of the publishing team. It was also a personal affront. After all, George had given the rock star a gold-plated opportunity. According to this narrative, Mick Jagger just hadn't invested sufficient time or energy in the preparation and writing of the book. Therefore, no amount of effort by the ghostwriters, researchers, editors or publishing executives could render his manuscript of sufficient quality. Barry Coleman suggested in his interview with the *Guardian* that 'there was always this sense in the transcripts that Mick was holding back, or trying not to hurt anybody's feelings.' Working with Mick Jagger 'was a huge mistake,' George later told a journalist. 'It was a terrible odyssey; the man was never there when you needed him.'

Whichever of these explanations was correct – and perhaps they all were, at least in part – George's tryst with Jagger gave him, the publisher, an even greater taste for New York. He felt comfortable here. He enjoyed attending dinner parties with the great and the good. This was also where the United Nations was based, the centre of global politics, nectar to the Austrian who as a young man had attended the Diplomatic Academy. A plan began to emerge. Instead of constantly selling rights to American publishers and receiving only a small commission in return, why not set up his own firm here, at the centre of world publishing? And so, in the mid-1980s, while he was in the midst of grappling with Mick Jagger's writing career, George's attention turned to New York, New York.

CHAPTER 16

Catcher in the Rye II

1987

'The cult of the best-seller has become truly idolatrous.' – GW

George sat at the corner of the long, oak boardroom table. Next to him at the head was Ann Getty, company president and chief investor in his American venture: Weidenfeld & Nicolson New York. In her early forties, Ann was a tall, extremely attractive woman with long red hair. Also in the room were various senior staff members including Dan Green the CEO, John Herman the editor-in-chief, and Juliet Nicolson (Nigel Nicolson's daughter), who was head of publicity and subsidiary rights. This was a meeting to discuss which books they would next take on, a so-called acquisitions meeting.

The meeting was taking place in the offices of Weidenfeld & Nicolson New York at the Harper and Row building on East 53rd Street, around the corner from St Thomas Church on Fifth Avenue. The carpet was a lush green and custom-ordered. Just outside the boardroom was a small kitchen with a walk-in fridge fully stocked with champagne. In the air hung the sweet smell of cigar tobacco. This meant that George had been in the office for at least an hour.

After discussing various possibilities, Ann Getty said she had a project she wanted to go after. Her favourite book was J. D. Salinger's *Catcher in the Rye*. She had heard, though she did not say from whom, that Salinger was thinking about writing a sequel, and their firm, Weidenfeld & Nicolson New York, should acquire it. 'But we don't know anything about the book,' stammered Dan Green. Mrs Getty, as she was known to her employees, said she didn't care. 'And you don't mind that not a single word has been written?' the chief executive pressed. She didn't mind. The money would be coming out of her pocket, not the company's. What was the maximum amount she was willing to pay? Ann Getty thought about this a moment and then replied: '$1 million.'

The group was stunned. There was nothing solid about the book. They had not been approached formally by the author or his agent. Worst of all, the advance was excessive. Ridiculous even. George Weidenfeld's business partner was unflinching. They were to dedicate themselves to this project, even if it was a phantom.

George with Ann Getty (left) and Arianna Huffington (right)

George had long thought about setting up an American branch of his publishing company; it suited his self-image as a global powerbroker. It must of course be located in New York, home to the country's leading houses: Simon & Schuster; Random House; Knopf; Farrar, Straus & Giroux; Holt; and Viking. Like Weidenfeld & Nicolson, many of these American firms had benefited from the influx of European intellectuals who arrived in the years before the war. They had shaken things up, challenging the bluebloods and stuffy shirts from Yale, Vassar, Princeton and Harvard, broadened the tastes of both the commissioning editors and the public at large. But the New York publishing scene of the 1980s was very different to that of London in the 1950s. The budgets were much more tightly controlled, the publishing houses more corporate, less boutique. For George to break in, it would take not only a keen eye for talent, but also considerable money. For this, he needed an investor.

George had first met Ann and Gordon Getty in 1977 at a mutual friend's dinner party. Gordon was the son of Paul Getty, the oil tycoon and one of the world's richest men. Ann was a philanthropist who sat on various charitable boards. George and the Gettys established a friendship based on a shared appreciation for opera. The Gettys stayed as George's guest in Salzburg during the summer opera festival and, in subsequent years, he stayed with them. They also went twice on vacation together. 'I can't find words to thank you for the most wonderful holiday,' he wrote to Ann after one of these trips, 'which combined intellectual and artistic enjoyment with perfect happiness. I have become an addict of the Getty family – a dangerous thing to be, for it is habit-forming and eminently spoiling.'

It was during these social encounters in the late 1970s and early 1980s that Ann and George began talking about jointly setting up a publishing business in America. Ann asked how much money it would take to acquire and develop a publishing operation in the United States. He estimated that they would need around $10 million. The years went by, the conversation continued, but no action was taken.

Then in 1984, Weidenfeld & Nicolson had a particularly bad year. Following the debacle of the Jagger autobiography and other dubious projects, George's London company was losing significant amounts of money. That year alone they would lose over £140,000 on sales of just over £5 million. George decided the way out of his trouble was to persuade Ann Getty to invest in him and his business. This was not a new strategy. After all, in the 1940s, he had set up Weidenfeld & Nicolson using money from the Nicolson family. In the 1950s the father of his first wife, the chairman of Marks and Spencer, had given George an important book contract which had provided much-needed cash flow in the early years. In the 1960s, Frederick Praeger had subsidised George's books and then invested in the company. Later, in the 1970s, the publisher's third wife, Sandra Payson, had helped him purchase the enormous house in Hyde Park Gate that played host to endless book parties and other publishing-related events. Now in the 1980s, George needed his next financial backer.

So it was that early in the New Year of 1985, George and Ann Getty agreed to launch their joint publishing venture. They set up a new company called the Wheatland Corporation, named after Getty's home town in California. Ann Getty was appointed president and George chairman and chief executive. Marc Leland, a former assistant secretary at the US Treasury, was engaged as the legal advisor. As part of the deal, George received a salary plus share options which he could cash in at some future point, a so-called 'put option'. With the organisational structure in place, George pursued a three-part plan. First, George had proposed purchasing a well-established publishing house in America, a fast-track into the book industry. Getty thought this a good idea, and suggested the firm whose books she had avidly consumed in her twenties: the legendary Grove Press.

A small, independent publishing house of great literary repute, Grove had been set up by Barney Rosset just after the end of the Second World War. Rosset had championed some of the most iconic books of the mid-twentieth century, such as Henry Miller's *Tropic of Cancer*, William Burroughs's *Naked Lunch* and D. H. Lawrence's *Lady Chatterley's Lover*. Many of these titles were initially banned because of their perceived obscenity and Rosset had fought vigorously and tenaciously in the courts for the right to publish. He had also been the first to publish many of the key Beat poets, including Allen Ginsberg and Jack Kerouac, as well as the bestselling *The Autobiography of Malcolm X*. He also published Samuel Beckett's works in America, including his masterpiece *Waiting for Godot*. If George Weidenfeld was a man who aspired to be part of the Establishment, Rosset was the exact opposite, relishing being anti-authority. Yet, and here was both the opportunity and the challenge, Grove Press was leaking enormous amounts of money. Their remarkable backlist was not able to provide sufficient funds to acquire and publish new titles. Rosset may have been a genius at spotting new talent and defending freedom of speech, but he was not, according to many observers, a great businessman.

George went to meet Barney Rosset at his offices in a four-storey building on West Houston Street in Greenwich Village. The two men knew each other well, having worked in the same business for four decades. The owner of Grove Press was a slight man, compared to George, but he could hold his own. He would sell the company, he said, but he wanted to stay on as editor-in-chief. He had a relationship with the authors, and he was best placed to move the company forward. George agreed that Rosset could stay on, though this would be at the discretion of the board, in other words himself and Ann Getty. The deal was done.

On 1 March 1985 it was announced that Wheatland had purchased Grove for $2 million, with an additional $1.5 million made available for operating costs. As news broke of the purchase, George received a flood of cables and phone calls. One from Teddy Kollek, the mayor of Jerusalem, 'Warmest congratulations on your and Ann's new acquisition, Grove Press. Wishing you both much success on this venture.' Another came from the journalist and TV presenter, Barbara Walters:

Read of grove press acquisition. Congratulations
terribly happy and excited for you. Means we will
see more of you in New York and that's wonderful

Ann Getty was delighted; she now owned her favourite publishing
house. George was also thrilled. He would be working with some
of the most important authors in American literature. It was, he
thought, a strong start for his ambitions in the United States.

With the purchase of Grove Press now complete, George had
moved into the second part of his plan: enabling Getty to gain a
foothold in the British publishing market. In return for investing $1
million in Weidenfeld & Nicolson Holdings, the parent company of
his London-based publishing company, she received a 36 per cent
stake in the firm. With additional infusions of cash, this later grew
to 47 per cent. A further £1 million was also made available as a
loan, this money being used to stabilise the company's cash flow
and help it grow over the next few years. It also enabled George
to increase his annual salary to £250,000, a significant sum at that
time. 'Ann Getty certainly came at a point when she could be a
tremendous boost to us,' George later told a reporter from *Vanity
Fair*, 'but it's absurd to think that she saved the company from
disaster.'

Now came the third part of George's great plan: expansion of
the American publishing operation. 'The strength of Grove is also
its weakness,' George wrote in an internal memo on 11 March 1985.
'Grove has a very clearly defined image and profile, i.e. it is known
for its avant-garde list of American and European novelists and
playwrights, for the radical tendency of many of its books and a
special appeal to the young reading public.' George now proposed
that they establish a second publishing house called Weidenfeld &
Nicolson Inc. in New York, 'to fulfil the purpose of complementing
Grove and rounding off a programme for a comprehensive general

trade publishing operation'. The aim would be to publish twenty-five books in the first year, rising to forty by year three. Ann approved the plan, and the new company was set up under the Wheatland Corporation, separate from Grove Press.

Early in the summer of 1985, George flew to New York and asked his contacts in the publishing industry for a list of people with literary talent. Over the course of the next few weeks, and headquartered in the lobby of the Carlyle Hotel – cigar in hand, cup of Earl Grey on the table before him – he embarked on a long round of interviews. His first big catch was Dan Green, who was hired as CEO of the new publishing house. Green had been a senior executive at Simon & Schuster and was known for a number of bestsellers including *Pumping Iron* and *Jane Fonda's Workout Book*. He also reeled in John Herman from Simon & Schuster, who would become editor-in-chief for the new imprint. With no more than a Rolodex of contacts and a telephone, Herman started calling literary agents and others he knew in the business and invited them to pitch him ideas. 'I was given the opportunity to build a list from scratch,' he remembers, 'it was a dream come true.'

By the end of 1985, W&N NY – as it was soon abbreviated to – released its first book catalogue which was received with polite but not overwhelming praise. Over the next few months, Herman worked tirelessly to grow his stable of authors. As is often the case in publishing, particularly for start-ups, they had mixed success. For instance, they acquired the novelist Robert Stone's *Outerbridge Reach* for $400,000, which went on to be a finalist for the National Book Award and proved commercially successful. But they also paid $500,000 for *The Pizza Connection*, a non-fiction account of the longest-running trial against the American Mafia, printing more than 100,000 copies but selling only 26,000.

George was now spending at least a week a month in New York. Ann Getty had rented an apartment for him, just below her own, at 820 Fifth Avenue overlooking Central Park. There were stories circulating around the office that they were having an affair. Those promoting these rumours pointed to a picture in George's apartment of Ann Getty sitting on his knee with an arm around his shoulder. The romance was not inconceivable. George was single at this time and had a penchant for affluent, attractive, younger American women. Others believed that Ann Getty and George Weidenfeld's relationship was purely platonic. Later, it was revealed that Ann Getty's husband, Gordon, had a second, secret, family at this time.

In the evenings, George circulated among the cultural elite of New York. He was warmly greeted at dinner parties, gallery openings and other high-society gatherings that marked the city's social calendar. *Vanity Fair* ran a nine-page spread on the publisher under the headline 'Lord Big' in which they called him a 'paradox: an outsider who has become Mr Inside', adding 'Lord Weidenfeld was always London's power publisher. Now the party-giving plenipotentiary has joined forces with Mrs. Gordon Getty – and he's conquering America.'

Yet, behind his back, people spoke about the fragility of his list. They mocked his naivety. They told each other wisely that you can't buy yourself into publishing success. It took decades of hard work, luck and perhaps most importantly, taste. Apocryphal stories were shared and retold. Like the time George took the hand of a young woman and said, 'My dear, have you thought of harnessing your talents to write a book?' To which she responded, 'You son of a bitch! You've already published two of them!' Or the dinner party that he hosted at his own apartment and then left, halfway through, because he wanted to join another more interesting gathering. There were echoes of the same old mutterings that had dogged him for years, though now with an American accent. George Weidenfeld was a 'social climber', a 'cosmopolitan', a 'Gatsby'. In the meantime, Grove Press, the totem of Wheatland's publishing venture, was running into staff trouble.

*

Dan Green, the CEO of W&N New York, was finding it increasingly hard to work with Barney Rosset at Grove Press. The idea had been to let the former owner stay on, both for his remarkable publishing abilities as well as for the sake of continuity. By the spring of 1986, the arrangement was threatening to fall off the tracks. Frustrated and fed up, Dan Green wrote to George detailing his concerns. Rosset had flown to Paris without his permission. Even worse, he complained, when the former owner submitted an inflated budget and it was rejected, he resubmitted it without change, and when that was turned down, he sent it in once again. Rosset was publishing books 'which have minimal commercial or literary value,' Green continued, and 'goes blithely ahead spending money as he sees fit'.

In the last week of March 1986, George drafted a letter to Rosset. 'I beg and urge you, as a friend of forty years standing and I speak as one who not only respects but loves you,' he wrote, 'to make the mental change and realise that there is a new ownership who has spent a great deal of money and wishes to spend a great deal more, and wishes to exercise its right, not only to make decisions but possibly even to make mistakes.' After encouraging Rosset to cooperate, George said that 'neither you nor we want a kind of inter-company guerrilla war' and pleaded that the former owner give him the 'benefit of the doubt'. In the end, George didn't send this letter. He decided it was best first to discuss the matter with the board.

On 3 April 1986, Barney Rosset met with George, Ann Getty, Marc Leland and Dan Green at the headquarters of Grove Press. Midway through the meeting Rosset asked, 'Who is the CEO of Grove?' 'Why, Dan is,' replied George. 'How can this be?' stammered Rosset, shocked, 'you told me you wanted to keep me.' To this, Green called Rosset an 'onerous burden' and 'iconoclastic', prompting Rosset to respond that Dan was a 'hatchet man' who would be the next to be fired.

At this point, the opera singer Placido Domingo walked into the room to discuss a book deal. George stood up and welcomed the famous tenor. All the while, Rosset sat in his chair glaring. Picking up on the tension, Domingo apologised for interrupting, 'Perhaps this is not such a good time', and departed. A few moments later, the group returned to the matter at hand: the future of Barney Rosset. Little could be agreed. At the meeting's conclusion, the board made a decision: Rosset would be demoted from chief executive officer and president of Grove Press to senior editor.

After the meeting, Rosset told *Manhattan, inc.* magazine that he was 'traumatised' and 'stunned'. To another journalist at *Publishers Weekly*, he acknowledged that as the sole owner of the company, Ann Getty 'had a perfect right' to change his position, but he described it as an 'unresolved idea'. As far as he was concerned, Grove Press was his. He had built it from scratch. Two weeks later, on 17 April, Rosset wrote to Dan Green, saying that he felt demeaned and degraded. 'Frankly all of this is pushing me to the limits of my emotional endurance.'

Rosset now launched a campaign against George Weidenfeld and Ann Getty. First, he had his lawyer send them a letter saying that he had been deliberately humiliated and had been charged with 'deception', 'dishonesty' and 'abuse', all of which was libellous. Next he reached out to his many literary friends – including Samuel Beckett, William Burroughs and Allen Ginsberg – and asked them to sign on to a press release calling for his reinstatement as chief executive. 'Together, Grove Press and Rosset are major forces in American publishing', the press release boomed. 'In the second half of this century, there has been no one and no company as daring, as contrary, as imaginative in publishing and we are all the better for it.'

Finally, Rosset urged other publishing executives to put pressure on George directly. In the first week of July, for instance, George received a letter from Dick Seaver, the head of Henry Holt in New York, reporting that he had recently returned from the annual American Library Association conference where he had been approached by more than a dozen people who said how 'terrible this Grove Press business is'. Seaver added that the media coverage of the matter had been 'one-sidedly bad' for George, and that he was worried that 'this whole episode could tarnish your brilliant debut in American publishing'. Seaver then concluded that 'in the best of all possible worlds' Rosset could buy Grove back and George could invest the funds into his other New York publishing house, Weidenfeld & Nicolson.

In the end, they came to a solution. Rosset agreed to walk away from Grove Press but, as part of the deal, he took the 'adult' Victorian Library Books and was compensated for the lease of the building where the publishing house was located. He could continue to publish books, but he would not recruit authors published by Grove. Perhaps most importantly, he promised to stop issuing negative statements to the press about Ann Getty and George Weidenfeld. Overall, the settlement cost Wheatland Inc. an additional $1.2 million.

The takeover of Grove Press had proved more difficult and more expensive than George had anticipated. But now that it was over, he was relieved the matter was resolved and, ever optimistic, he looked forward to a more positive future for his American publishing operation.

The lead title for W&N New York's first list in the autumn of 1986 was Princess Michael of Kent's book *Crowned in a Far Country: Portraits of Eight Royal Brides*. That she wanted to write a book, unusual for members of the royal family at the time, is another testament to George's powers of persuasion. The plan was to use the princess's star power to build a strong media campaign and, from this, launch the book and promote New York's newest publishing house.

The book had not, however, been without its problems. In June 1985 the academic James Bentley provided a reader's report saying that the quality of research gave him 'considerable alarm', adding that 'almost every page of typescript contains research errors, sometimes several, some of them appalling mistakes'. To address these problems, George encouraged the princess to hire Bentley as an outside editor. The project appeared to be back on track, but then the publisher received a five-page letter from the author written on blue Kensington Palace letterhead. The princess wrote of her 'dissatisfaction' with her researcher and 'unhappiness' with the editor that George had made her employ at vast expense. Worse, W&N New York had included the wrong cover photo, the wrong title and wrong chapter headings in the most recent catalogue. On 22 July, George replied. 'I would so much like to avoid anything that could lead to an acrimonious and unhappy correspondence,' he wrote, and then proceeded to address her complaints. He ended with 'You would be truly pleased if you saw how much work, how much effort and how much loyalty towards you are displayed both in London and Manhattan and I sincerely hope that the net result will please you.'

Then on 22 September, just weeks before the book was due to be launched, Princess Michael was accused of plagiarism. The *Observer* reported that parts of her chapter on the Empress Eugenie were taken from another book that Weidenfeld & Nicolson had published by Harold Kurtz. That same day, the princess wrote to George saying that she was 'appalled' to read the story in the newspaper. She said that the mistake was 'inadvertent' and demonstrated that she was a 'beginner'. She then explained that her writing method was to make a note of the author's name when copying a direct quotation, but in this case she must have 'omitted' Kurtz's name from her notes. Again, she apologised.

Notwithstanding the legal furore, the book launch went ahead, and in mid-October the princess arrived in the United States for a promotional tour. Starting in New York, she travelled on to Los

Angeles, Chicago, Houston and then Boston. She appeared on three national television programmes. It all seemed to be going well. And then, a second accusation of literary theft hit the headlines. PRINCESS PAYS THE PRICE FOR HER PLAGIARISM, proclaimed the *Aberdeen Press and Journal* on 24 November, before explaining that Princess Michael of Kent had paid compensation to Daphne Bennett, who accused the princess of copying 'page after page' of her book without permission. 'I have won and I want other people to know I have won,' Mrs Bennett told the paper, continuing, 'I want other writers to take heart and take action when their work is plagiarised.' Four months later, in February 1987, the *Evening Standard* ran a story that three more authors now claimed their work had been taken by the princess without permission. One of these was the journalist Alastair Forsyth, who said a passage in the book 'relied heavily' on one of his articles. When the reporter asked for a comment from Weidenfeld & Nicolson, they were told 'We are not embarrassed by this. We cannot take responsibility. You cannot check everything. No one else has complained.' The paper quipped, 'Well that's a relief.'

Despite the legal distractions, the book sold 20,000 copies in the United States. According to George this was something to be celebrated. On 9 June 1987, having praised Juliet Nicolson and Dan Green for their hard work promoting the book in America, the publisher wrote to the princess that 'I believe, with my forty years' experience in publishing, that you have every reason to be extremely pleased with the result.' The author was not convinced. Two weeks later, her private secretary, a Colonel Farmer, responded that the book sold well in Britain not because of Weidenfeld & Nicolson's marketing or advertising efforts, but because of the 'ridiculous publicity surrounding the book's publication'. In a separate letter, Colonel Farmer wrote that 'your company was still too new with its first list of publications last October'. It was a stinging blow for George. He wrote to the princess and called Colonel Farmer's remark 'not only unflattering but wholly untrue', and repeated the assertion that the 'overwhelming consensus of the American book trade was that we did remarkably well with this book'.

Despite George's assurance, the release of the princess's book, with all its ancillary noise, following so hard on the very public bust-up with Barney Rosset, was hardly the auspicious start to the W&N New York venture he had hoped for. Yet, George's relationship with Ann Getty was more solid than ever. On 13 September 1987 she hosted a sixty-eighth birthday party for him at the Foreign Press Association in London. Getty had hired the elegant Council Room, with its baby-blue painted walls, floor-to-ceiling windows looking onto the garden, and impressive pictures of generals and kings overseeing the proceedings from the walls. It was meant to be a small, select group of guests, but word of the festivity had leaked, and more than fifty people arrived for dinner.

At the meal's end, George stood up to say a few words. 'I am particularly touched because this is a very common-or-garden birthday,' he began. 'It is not my eightieth, seventieth, fiftieth nor any round figure. In fact, the only round figure in this room is the birthday boy.' His self-depreciation drew immediate laughs and applause. George continued that he wished to toast Ann Getty: 'I would like to drink to our friendship and partnership and the success of many exciting ventures and adventures on which we are embarked on both sides of the ocean.' He raised his glass, and the group repeated his words, 'To Ann'.

After the glasses were returned to the table, George declared that he wanted to propose another toast. Born under the sign Virgo, he said, he was a planner and an optimist, who thought more about the future than the past. Each year on his birthday he made a resolution. The previous year, he had resolved to pursue a double life. His time had been split between New York and London. 'Sometimes I think I have succeeded and sometimes I think I have failed, by being in both or neither.' For the next year, he continued, it would be a year of friendship. Harold Nicolson, Nigel's father, had once said that a year in which one failed to make at least one new friend was a lost year. George said that his figure was three to five. 'The need for friendship is visceral and vital,' he told the group of intimates gathered before him, 'and my idea of a real friend is one who plays the dual role of Don Quixote and Sancho Panza rolled into one. They must pull you up and bring you down to earth, condone your dreams and correct your follies. Many of you have done this in the past, please continue.' With that he raised his glass. 'To my friends,' he said. The crowd echoed back to him, 'To friends'.

Over the next four years, vast amounts of money continued to pour out of Wheatland Inc. and its sister non-profit the Wheatland Foundation. Stratospheric advances were dished out, set high enough to attract the literary world's royalty, including Arthur Miller, Milan Kundera, Walter Laqueur and Peter Ackroyd. There were sales conferences at the luxury Pierre Hotel in New York and glitzy parties at the American Booksellers Association conference in San Francisco. International literary gatherings were hosted in Washington DC, Lisbon and Budapest, with guest speakers featuring Susan Sontag, Martin Amis, Ian McEwan, Salman Rushdie, John Updike, José Saramago and Mario Vargas Llosa. All of which was funded by Ann Getty. George was repeatedly flown from New York to California and back on Ann Getty's private plane. Amid this cascade of money, W&N authors appeared on the *Today* show and *60 Minutes*, their books were reviewed by the *New York Times* and other literary magazines. Sales, however, remained disappointing. At one point, when Ann Getty was asked by a journalist if she had lost $15 million, she responded, 'I don't feel I've lost at least $15 million, I honestly feel I have merely *invested* the money. I am still enthusiastic.'

According to his later telling of the story, George tried to convene board meetings to address the deteriorating financial situation on numerous occasions, but Ann Getty was seldom available. Her attendance, he told a friend, was 'erratic'. The publisher turned to the company's lawyer, Marc Leland, and urgently discussed ways of saving money. To this end, in 1988, the firm moved out of its expensive offices at the Harper and Row building on 53rd Street and into a smaller loft space in Greenwich Village. Even this was not sufficient to stem the outflow of cash. So George suggested a further cost-cutting measure: the merging of W&N NY and Grove Press. But when he raised the idea, he was told that Ann Getty wouldn't countenance the loss of Grove's independence.

At a board meeting on 2 February 1989 it was revealed that the true size of Ann Getty's investment in the Wheatland publishing company amounted to $30 million. It was projected that in the upcoming year the company would need an additional $8 million. In late March the decision was made to make radical changes. Dan Green was fired. The operating budget was severely cut. Then, on 4 May, the *New York Times* revealed that Grove Press and Weidenfeld & Nicolson were after all to be merged. The new company would be called Grove Weidenfeld. Several days later, John Herman was encouraged to find other pastures. Over the next few weeks, George had a number of difficult conversations with Ann Getty's attorney, Marc Leland. 'It was at this point,' the publisher later told his English lawyer, 'that relations between Ann and Marc and myself deteriorated rapidly.' By the end of April, it was agreed that George would have to 'modify' his position. He would no longer be responsible for day-to-day operations in New York, he was told, though he would remain chairman of Wheatland Corporation.

In the second week of September 1989, and now back in London, George celebrated his seventieth birthday. 'It's comforting to know,' wrote Henry Kissinger in one of many letters of support that were gathered to honour the anniversary, 'that unlike fine wine, you haven't mellowed with age. All the best from a younger vintage.' Other messages arrived from the violinist Yehudi Menuhin, the proprietor of the *Washington Post* Katharine Graham, and the TV host Barbara Walters.

Another missive came from Simon Michael Bessie, the American publisher who had published *The Double Helix* with George. 'To recount George's progress from little Arthur to today's Lord Weidenfeld might require the talents of Boswell <u>and</u> Pepys,' wrote Bessie. 'A friendly witness of the past forty-five years can only assume that surprises will continue.' A party was hosted in George's honour at the National Portrait Gallery attended by 400 guests, including the media mogul Rupert Murdoch and the former prime minister, Ted Heath. Also present was Nigel Nicolson who gave a warm speech, at one point calling George the 'Spencer' to his 'Marks'.

George's seventieth birthday provided an opportunity for journalists to look back at the publisher's many decades in the public eye. Among these was Peregrine Worsthorne, editor of the *Sunday Telegraph*, who wrote a profile piece on George. 'He is famous, but then not everything is known about him,' said the editor. 'Above all, it is not generally known about him how supremely cultivated he is. Nor how funny.' Worsthorne then noted that George Weidenfeld had recently taken part in a meeting with Pope John Paul II at Castel Gandolfo, twenty miles south of Rome. 'There are not many publishers on either side of the Atlantic,' he concluded, 'who would be included in such company.'

Not all the press coverage was so flattering. It was around this time that the fortnightly satirical magazine *Private Eye* began printing a cartoon strip about a fictional publishing house called 'Snipcock and Tweed'. The name was apparently spoofing Weidenfeld & Nicolson. Snipcock presumably referring to the practice of circumcising Jewish boys. Tweed relating to the world of the tweed-wearing aristocrat. 'It was brought to my attention not that long ago that it was an epithet,' says Nick Newman (in 2022), who

George with Pope John Paul II

drew the cartoon for more than twenty years. 'It never occurred
to me, I was rather horrified when I realised it. I've stopped doing
the strip now.'

Two weeks after celebrating his seventieth birthday, George
returned to New York for an emergency meeting held at Ann
Getty's apartment at 820 Fifth Avenue. Just after high noon,
according to the minutes of the meeting, 'Mrs Getty said that she
had already invested far more money in the business than she had
been led to believe would be necessary and that she had no further
funds to invest in Grove Weidenfeld.' It was then agreed that two
executives from Weidenfeld & Nicolson in London would take over
as joint managing directors of the company with the purpose of
implementing 'whatever steps were deemed necessary to make it
a viable business'. The meeting finished after just eighty minutes.

A month later, on 22 October, the *New York Times* published an
article by Adam Begley entitled ANN GETTY: PERISH OR PUB-
LISH. The first paragraph reported that the 'partnership of Ann
Getty and George Weidenfeld – fabulous wealth wed to expansive

ambition – should have been the perfect match', before adding, 'It didn't turn out that way.' For George, the next 4,000 words made for difficult reading, particularly the ninth paragraph:

> George Weidenfeld feels at home in the House of Lords. At lunch
> in the dining room where peers may bring their guests, he breaks
> off his discussion of international publishing to explain with the
> delight of a linguist the arcane rhetoric of parliamentary speeches.
> The indirection of the discourse evidently pleases him; it's also
> evident that he has mastered the subtleties of the genre. But in the
> faded, clublike atmosphere of the dining room, a hint of the foreign,
> of the exotic, still clings to him.

Then, after listing the various people who helped him financially over the years, including Ann Getty, the article quoted Roger W. Straus, co-founder of one of New York's most established publishing houses, Farrar, Straus & Giroux, 'George has always been able to find help when he needed it.' Finally, in a third punch to George's pride, the journalist quoted a British publishing analyst who said that Weidenfeld & Nicolson in London 'is only marginally profitable. It's a company that's been going nowhere fast.'

A few days after reading Begley's piece in the *New York Times*, the publisher wrote a letter to a Texas friend saying that the article was 'manifestly unfair and tendentious'. Later, he would describe these few months in New York as 'harrowing'.

Nevertheless, his torment was not yet over for though he was no longer supervising the American publishing company, it was still named after him and could damage his reputation. In late March 1990, the story that Grove Weidenfeld was up for sale was reported by the press in America and England. 'This attracted much unfavourable publicity,' George later said, 'and also had a very unfortunate fall-out on the London company as it raised questions about its financial prospects and the relationship between myself and Ann Getty. To counter the rumours, George made sure that he was photographed with Ann Getty at as many social functions as possible and he made it clear to any journalist who would listen that there were no issues between them. As for Mrs Getty, when asked if she and George had fallen out, she replied, 'Far from it', adding that 'he is still my CEO and we get along just fine. In fact, George and I have never had a cross word.'

Meanwhile, Random House, Simon & Schuster and Penguin were expressing interest in purchasing Grove Weidenfeld, attracted by the remarkable backlist (Allen Ginsberg, Samuel Beckett, Henry Miller, Malcolm X etc.) that brought in $3 million every year. It was at this point, in May 1990, that Ann Getty announced the company was no longer up for sale. 'After hearing the strong feeling among authors, agents and booksellers that we should not be swallowed by a publishing conglomerate,' she said in a statement, 'I have become convinced that the best course is for Grove Weidenfeld to remain an independent publishing house dedicated to publishing quality works.'

Eventually, in February 1993, Atlantic Monthly Press – a literary publisher established by the Boston magazine *The Atlantic Monthly* – would purchase Grove Weidenfeld. Ann Getty would keep a share of the new company and remain on the board. And, to his great delight, Barney Rosset would be brought back in to manage part of Grove's operations.

Whatever happened to Ann Getty's desire to purchase J. D. Salinger's sequel to *Catcher in the Rye*? According to the filmmaker Shane Salerno, Salinger spent more than four decades working on 'continuations' of the Caulfield family story. But, no evidence has yet been made public confirming that the author ever intended to embark on this project, let alone that he had begun work on it. There is, however, a short twelve-page unpublished story, 'The Last and the Best of the Peter Pans', that some have labelled the sequel to

Catcher in the Rye, a copy of which is to be found at the University of Princeton Firestone Library. Perhaps this is what Ann Getty was referring to when she said she wished to acquire the sequel.

More probably, according to those who knew her at the time, Ann Getty had simply heard a rumour at a party and wished for it to be true. Or perhaps there was a third explanation. She may have been trying to entice the famous author to write the book by dangling a large amount of money in front of him. Along the lines of: '"I've got a million bucks sitting on the table . . . Whataya say?"' suggested John Herman, who had attended the meeting that day at the Harper and Row building. 'Something like this may have been going on with Salinger and Ann Getty.'

With Grove Weidenfeld now sold to Atlantic, where was George Weidenfeld? He was not in New York giving quotes to the press about the rise and fall of his part-eponymous publishing company. Nor was he attending the founding board meeting of the renamed firm, Grove/Atlantic. In fact, unlike Mrs Getty, he had not been invited to join this board. Nor was he on a Concorde, shuttling back and forth across the Atlantic to save his American adventure. For now, at least, that chapter of his life was over. Instead, George was in London, trying to stave off what was, at least for him, a more existential threat. He was there to save Weidenfeld & Nicolson from financial collapse. He was attempting to save his legacy.

CHAPTER 17

Remembering My Good Friends

1994

'Throughout my life and starting at an early age, I have been attracted, fascinated, at times dominated, by political ideas and ideals, and looking back, the root of this deep concern lies in the Vienna and central Europe of the 1930s. In those formative years, I became aware, very tangibly and dramatically aware, of the problem of freedom versus oppression.' – GW

With the fall of the Berlin Wall in November 1989, George was increasingly preoccupied with European politics. For him, the way forward was obvious. Germany, for so long divided between East and West, Communism and Capitalism, must unify. In speeches to the House of Lords, in articles published in newspapers in Britain, Germany and elsewhere, and in private conversations with politicians, academics and journalists, George was campaigning for reunification.

In a letter to Helmut Kohl, the chancellor of Germany, dated 23 February 1990, George made clear his reasons for supporting reunification. 'A united Germany can and must play a vitally important part, not only politically and economically, but also in the sphere of human rights, and especially in the struggle against racism, chauvinism and anti-Semitism, as it helps the emergent democracies of Central and Eastern Europe to enter the civil society.'

On 13 July 1990 the publisher met Kohl for two hours at his home in Bonn. The following day, George summarised his thinking:

'Germany's auspicious progress on the road to unity is not only a vindication of the Federal Republic's achievement in building a functioning democracy, vibrant economy and civil society but also renews a link with all that was most promising in the early part of the Weimar Republic and in the past century. This provides a pedagogic opportunity and challenge for young Germans and others to rethink the course and meaning of German history.' He then suggested that the chancellor write a short book 'containing your quintessential ideas and thoughts on Germany's role'. He also offered to bring a small, informal group of distinguished European Jews to Bonn for an open and friendly discussion to continue their conversation about a united Germany, European Jewry and Israel. After one of these meetings, George reviewed what had taken place in a memo and sent this to the Israeli prime minister, Yitzhak Shamir. A few days later, Shamir replied, thanking George for the 'detailed account', and adding 'The Chancellor's initiative in convening such a group for a lengthy session was interesting in itself.'

Over the course of the summer of 1990, and following the economic collapse of East Germany, it was agreed by the East and West German governments that they should reunify. Reunification finally took place on 3 October. Eight months later, in May 1991, George received the Knight Commander's Cross (Badge and Star) of the Order of Merit from the German government. 'Whatever modest service I might have rendered to the cause of German unification,' George wrote to the German president, Richard von Weizsäcker, upon receiving the award, 'stemmed from a deep feeling that all of us who cherish human rights and the ideals of civil society owe a great debt of gratitude to the new Germany.'

In later years, George tried to explain his desire to engage with German politics. 'The effort to build bridges between the Jewish people and the Germans,' he told the German ambassador in London, is 'not only a duty but a visceral purpose.' He then continued, 'it also corresponds to a much deeper empathy, with respect and – if I may say so – love for the Germans. For someone who was brought up in the German language, which in my formative years was not contaminated by the bitterness and anguish of the Hitler period, my faith in that "real Germany", which is now represented by [President] Weizsäcker and [Chancellor] Kohl and the younger generation, is unshaken.'

The engagement with senior German leaders and the cause of reunification was an example of a wider trend in the publisher's life: the increasing blurring of the lines between politics and literature. One connection created another. It wasn't long, for instance, before George shared his German network with an up-and-coming British politician. 'Thank you so much for helping to arrange my meeting with Chancellor Kohl last week,' wrote Tony Blair, leader of the Labour opposition. 'As I expect you heard, we got off to a good start together.'

As his power grew, as his contacts list expanded, as his appetite for influence deepened, George was more and more using his platform as publisher to shape the world around him.

George (left) with Chancellor Kohl

Around the time that George received his accolade from the German government, he travelled to Israel to celebrate the eightieth birthday of Teddy Kollek, the mayor of Jerusalem. This was shortly after the conclusion of the Gulf War and the Israeli population was getting used to taking part once again in public events; for the past few months every time they went outdoors they'd had to carry a gas mask, fearing a chemical attack from Iraq.

During one event, the publisher was standing by a buffet loading delicacies onto his plate, when a tall, blond woman approached him. She introduced herself as Annabelle Whitestone. They had first met in the late 1970s, she reminded him, and, like George, she was a friend of Kollek. She lived in Lausanne, Switzerland, she added, and managed classical musicians. At forty-five years old, she was twenty-seven years George's junior.

They started a conversation. Annabelle said she had just read a book by an excellent writer which had been a bestseller in France – perhaps he would like to publish it? Later that evening, George invited her to join him at his table for dinner. She found him smart, curious, funny. They were both staying at the King David Hotel. At the end of the week, when George had to get up early to take a flight back to London, Annabelle woke up early too. She wanted to see him off, which George found charming.

They saw each other the following weekend when George visited Annabelle in Lausanne, staying at the Beau Rivage hotel in Ouchy. The weekend after that he took her to Vienna, where she had never been. He showed her where he had lived as a child and the schools he attended. Then on to a concert at the Musikverein (home to the Vienna Philharmonic orchestra). It was shortly afterwards, two or three weeks later, that she came to London at his request. 'Without warning he whisked me off to stay with the Keswicks in the country for the weekend.' Annabelle recalls. Henry Keswick (chairman of the Fortune 500 company Jardines) and his wife Tessa (special advisor to politician Kenneth Clarke) were old friends of George.

Their home, Oare House, was a large, eighteenth-century, red-brick mansion outside Marlborough in Wiltshire. 'They entertained in great style with wonderful lunches and dinners and delicious food.'

The next time that Annabelle was in London, she came to visit George at his flat on Chelsea Embankment. And the next. She soon became part of his social scene, though not without nerves. She was terrified of boring him. Of not being smart enough. That she didn't have enough general knowledge, history, literature, all the things that George might know. She felt totally ignorant. She was also intimidated by his highly accomplished friends. At one dinner party, she sat next to the eminent philosopher, Isaiah Berlin. 'My God,' she thought, 'what are we going to talk about?' Luckily, Isaiah Berlin started speaking about her area of expertise, music. The conversation turned to Chopin and then the philosopher said, 'You know, who was the greatest interpreter of Chopin? It was Arthur Rubinstein. And what a wonderful man he was. He left his wife and then ran off with his mistress. And he died a happy man.' Annabelle laughed, but didn't tell Isaiah Berlin that she was the one who had been Rubinstein's mistress. At the time, she had been twenty-three years old, Rubenstein eighty-three.

As the weeks went by, Annabelle realised that she was becoming fonder and fonder of George. She called her younger brother and told him about George, that he was a wonderful man. She said, however, that he was going through a terrible time financially. That his company, Weidenfeld & Nicolson, might not survive.

George was indeed having a terrible time financially. Although he was enjoying getting to know Annabelle during the evenings and weekends, by day he was fully focused on rescuing his company.

With Ann Getty refusing to offer further investment, he needed a new source of money. Publishing in general was going through a difficult period. Both America and Britain were in the middle of a recession. This was made worse by the political upheavals gripping the Soviet Union after the fall of the Berlin Wall, the financial drain of German reunification, as well as the global economic impact of the Gulf War. Paper prices had rapidly increased. Book sales were generally down. Agents and their authors were demanding ever-higher fees. There was another problem. Weidenfeld & Nicolson was going through one of those cycles that sometimes beset a publisher. They hadn't had a huge success for quite some time.

George was becoming increasingly worried. He reached out to a few of his close contacts in the media sector. One of these was Reed International, an information and technology company which showed signs of interest. Before one meeting, Annabelle spoke to George on the phone and wished him luck. He sounded anxious that he might not be able to secure the deal. Could he pull the rabbit out of the hat one more time? What would happen if he couldn't, to all the employees at Weidenfeld & Nicolson? 'He was very concerned,' Annabelle recalls, 'because he thought he was going to face redundancies. And he didn't want to do that.' The meeting with Reed went as well as could be expected. George delivered his pitch and showed them the numbers, but, and this was truly disappointing, over the next few days, their interest petered out. The publisher was back to square one.

Weidenfeld & Nicolson was now facing a real cash-flow crisis. Invoices went unpaid. Salary cheques were delayed. A freeze was put on new staff hirings. Book acquisitions were more carefully reviewed than ever. George grew increasingly stressed. Unlike other people, this did not show itself by him talking louder or losing his temper. Instead, he grew ever more pensive. He spent hours in his study alone staring into the distance. Occasionally making notes on paper in his illegible scribble. Most unusually of all, he became quiet. Not speaking on the phone. Not entertaining guests. Withdrawing into himself.

Finally, he made a decision. George swallowed his pride and reached out to Ann Getty. Their relationship had not fully recovered since his executive position had been 'modified' a couple of years earlier. The humiliation of those emergency board meetings still stung, as did the press coverage that followed. This, however, was about business. Getty owned 47 per cent of the London company; surely she wouldn't want to lose her investment. By phone from his apartment on Chelsea Embankment, George called her and explained that the company was running out of cash. His plan was to raise money for the firm, and while he knew that she was not going to invest any more, would she provide a bridge loan? This would be used to cover expenses for the near future until the new money arrived. To sweeten the deal, he suggested that in return for waiving his significant share options with the Wheatland Corporation, valued at around $3 million, Ann Getty would relinquish a little over half of her shares in Weidenfeld & Nicolson. In effect, George was walking away from certain substantial financial gain in America to protect the legacy of the British company that bore his name. Over the next few weeks a deal was struck. Ann agreed to swap the American share options for reduced equity in the UK company and transferred £250,000 to George's personal account. In turn, he lent the money to Weidenfeld & Nicolson so that it could pay the bills. George was now personally underwriting Weidenfeld & Nicolson. It was a colossal risk, but he had given the company a few more months to survive. The clock was ticking.

Over the summer of 1991, George tried to raise money from scores of potential investors. He spent hours in his study on the phone, a list of names and telephone numbers before him, a cup of Earl Grey tea by his side. It was exhausting, tedious work. For each call, he had to sound fresh, hopeful, clear-minded, enthusiastic, rigorous. Most importantly, he could not sound imploring or beseeching. He knew from long experience that investors would run a mile if they smelled desperation. He called wealthy friends who had previously expressed interest in publishing. He spoke with well-connected politicians, hoping they might know someone who could be interested. He reached out to senior executives in the pub-lishing industry. Was their company trying to grow? Perhaps they were looking to take on a literary imprint? In return, he received a lot of respect, and not a little sympathy, but nobody was willing to take the next step. No one was interested in making an offer.

On Thursday 10 October, and with time fast running out to raise much-needed capital, George flew to Frankfurt for the international book fair. This had become something of an annual pilgrimage for the publisher. It would be his forty-third visit. The fair had changed enormously during his career, from a small, intimate affair in the late 1940s, to an enormous week-long extravaganza. This year there would be 8,417 exhibitors from ninety-one countries. The American exhibits alone numbered 673. It was also expensive. Once flights, hotels, exhibition fees and meals were tallied up, the costs to a publishing house could total hundreds of thousands of dollars.

Just six years earlier, in 1985, George had given the opening speech at the Frankfurt Book Fair. Standing on the main stage in front of a warmly receptive crowd, he had declared that 'No other city has provided so vast, so effective, so compact a meeting ground, not only for intellectual product, but also for the exchange of ideas. It has not only been a barometer of material trends and a thermo-meter of the health or infirmity of the whole metabolism or indi-vidual parts of the world publishing body, but also a seismograph of future turbulence or calm.' He had then given one of his favourite quotes from the English historian G. M. Trevelyan, who said that so often the people most involved in the turning points of history are the last to know when history really turns. He then added, 'This applies also, of course, to the history of the publishing profession.'

Now, in October 1991, George was plying his usual trade. He spent little time in the crowded halls, cafés and corridors of the fair. They were too busy, too noisy, too public. Instead, he sat in the lobby of the Hotel Hessischer Hof and held court. A large Davidoff cigar in hand, glass of apple juice or cup of camomile tea on the table, entertaining publishers, authors, agents and journalists in German, French, Italian and English as they walked in and out of the hotel. Sharing anecdotes about the latest famous person he had met – the Pope, Henry Kissinger, Helmut Kohl, Princess Margaret, Mick Jagger. Discussing book ideas. Swapping gossip. Exchanging ideas on politics, art and culture. Yet, by the week's end, and despite all the bonhomie and conviviality, when he flew back to London, George's mood was seriously down. He remained without an investor.

In the week after he returned from Frankfurt, George met with the publisher André Deutsch, the agent Ed Victor and the financier Evelyn de Rothschild. On 18 October he chaired a board meeting at the office. Two days later he celebrated Annabelle's birthday and on the 22nd he had dinner with the Israeli ambassador. The following day, he met with his lawyer Harold Paisner at his office and two days after that, the American ambassador came to see him at Chelsea Embankment. All the time George was considering how he might change his company's fortunes.

Then George had an idea. He asked his rights director Bud MacLennan to reach out to Anthony Cheetham. They had known each other since 1972 when Cheetham had written *The Life and Times of Richard III* for Weidenfeld & Nicolson. In the intervening years, Cheetham had built an impressive career in publishing. He had run Futura for the tycoon Robert Maxwell. He had then set up Century Publishing with Gail Rebuck, Peter Roche and Rosie de Courcy. Century had been sold to Random House in 1989 but then, two years later, Cheetham had been fired, much to his chagrin. Despite this setback, Cheetham had a reputation for being a savvy publishing entrepreneur and this is what George wanted to talk about.

During the course of the 1980s, the international book industry had been swept by a series of mergers and consolidations. In 1985, E. P. Dutton (one of the longest-running publishers in America) was acquired by the paperback publisher New American Library, which was then purchased the following year by Penguin Books (itself owned by Pearson). In 1986 two of America's most famous imprints – Doubleday and Dell – were sold to the West German publisher Bertelsmann. A year later, in 1987, the New York-based Random House purchased four members of the British publishing establishment: Chatto & Windus, Virago, Bodley Head and Jonathan Cape. That same year, Paul Hamlyn's Octopus Books and Heinemann were both sold to Reed International. Then, in 1989, Rupert Murdoch's News Corporation became sole owner of Collins, before merging it with another of its acquisitions, Harper and Row, to form HarperCollins. Soon after, HarperCollins acquired another British publishing legend, Allen & Unwin.

This trend towards greater amalgamation would accelerate over the next three decades with the arrival of computerisation and online book sales, along with the increased reliance on financial reporting and accountability. Farrar, Straus & Giroux would be purchased by the German-based Holtzbrinck Publishing Group in the 1990s, as would Macmillan (including Pan Books and Henry Holt). In 2002, John Murray would be taken over by Hodder Headline, which was purchased in 2004 by Hachette Livre, itself owned by the French multinational Lagardère Group. Two years later, Hachette acquired Time Warner's book publishing division, and later purchased Hyperion Books from Disney. Finally, the year 2012 saw the greatest merger of all, the joining of Penguin and Random House, forming the global mega publishing empire of Penguin Random House, which is now exclusively owned by Bertelsmann.

Back in 1991, therefore, as George Weidenfeld considered the sale of his precious publishing house, the industry was moving at speed towards consolidation. Which is why his desire to retain Weidenfeld & Nicolson's independence appeared to many as both unlikely and foolhardy.

*

At 9 a.m. on Tuesday 29 October 1991, George met Anthony Cheetham for breakfast at Claridge's. George said he was looking for a new investor. Weidenfeld & Nicolson was losing money. The culture and vision were strong, but the financial model was no longer viable. Might Cheetham be interested? He was.

Over the next few weeks, they met on a several occasions. They discussed various structures and legal instruments. Most importantly, to George at least, Cheetham showed him immense respect. For his backlist, for his legacy, for his genius as a publisher. Cheetham asked George what was important to him. George said he wanted the company to keep its name, to remain a distinct imprint. As for himself, he would like to continue in an emeritus position. If he brought in books that were released, he would appreciate a commission. He would also like an office, an expense account, a modest annual salary, and to keep his secretary, Pat Kinsman.

'George wanted me to take over the company. He was in quite a big hurry,' recalls Anthony Cheetham. 'The company was financially in dire straits.' He adds, 'George saw me as part of the intellectual set. He didn't see it as a business proposition. He said he would be my "impresario", he would introduce me to everyone. I would be his successor.'

A few weeks after the meeting at Claridge's, George and Annabelle spent the weekend in the country with Anthony Cheetham and his wife Rosie de Courcy. When they arrived at their bedroom, they found a sheet of paper providing the outline of the deal. Weidenfeld & Nicolson would be purchased by Cheetham's new company Orion Books Limited and George would stay on as chairman. 'Anthony got it all drawn up between October and the end of the year,' Annabelle recalls, 'it was like a miracle.'

In early December 1991 the terms of the acquisition were agreed. Orion would purchase Weidenfeld & Nicolson for £1.75 million. In addition, George would be repaid the £500,000 loan he had made to the company, half of which he immediately transferred to Ann Getty for the loan she had made him. After paying all his legal costs, interest accrued and taxes owed, and taking account of the loan payments, George walked away with £1,455,575.90. In one blow, therefore, he had not only put the company on a sustainable footing, he had also freed himself from the day-to-day stresses of running the organisation and secured his personal long-term finances. It was a cause for both satisfaction and celebration.

News of the deal broke on 13 December, when the *Bookseller* announced that CHEETHAM BUYS WEIDENFELD. They concluded that the development was 'satisfying' as it ensured the 'continuity of the publishing house which Lord Weidenfeld founded forty-four years ago, saving it from the maws of conglomerates and solving what the seventy-two-year-old Lord Weidenfeld calls the "vexed problem" of the succession of leadership'. *Publishing News* also carried the story, including the following quote from George: 'I never wanted Weidenfeld to be cannibalised and become two rooms in a corridor,' adding that, 'It is not only a great relief but a real pleasure to have an association with Anthony whom I have always very much admired.'

Soon, letters of congratulations arrived from around the world, ranging from the politician David Steel to the press magnate Rupert Murdoch. In his note, John Curtis – who was associated with some of Weidenfeld & Nicolson's greatest books and now ran his own imprint John Curtis Books within the firm Hodder & Stoughton – wrote it was a 'relief' to hear that George had secured the deal with Orion. He was also pleased that the company had not been 'swallowed up by one of the big conglomerates'. He then added, 'I hope it gives you all the satisfaction you require, both to continue your own publishing activities and for the assured future of the most prestigious publishing company to have been created in this country since the war, to which I am proud to think I made a contribution.'

*

One evening in early January 1992, Annabelle was in George's flat on Chelsea Embankment getting ready to go out. She was standing in front of a mirror applying make-up when she heard him speaking on the phone in the next-door room. She wasn't eavesdropping, but she couldn't help but overhear. She could only hear George's side of the call, but by what he said, she guessed it was Barbara Walters on the other end. Barbara had just visited them in London, it had been a good time. Annabelle liked the American TV journalist and clearly Barbara was fond of George. They had known each other for years. On the phone, it appeared to Annabelle that George was being encouraged to do something and George was agreeing. 'Yes, you're right,' he said, 'Yes, I think I'll do it. Yes, I will.' The next afternoon, George and Annabelle were sitting on a sofa in his study with the black painted walls. He turned to her and said, 'Don't you think we should get regularised?'

By this point, George had told Annabelle about his three other marriages. During the first marriage to Jane Sieff he had been hyperactive, always busy, working and socialising, which had proved difficult for her, his much younger wife. His second marriage to Barbara Skelton had been 'completely crazy'. Like a compulsion. And the third, to Sandra Payson, who was a bit out of her depth. Who missed her children in America. Who was a quiet drinker. For Annabelle it was not a difficult decision to make. Yes, she would love to marry George.

That spring was filled with wedding preparations. Venues had to be booked, invitations drafted, designed, printed and mailed out. Fortunately, George was able to lean on his secretaries Pat Kinsman and Sally King, the latter taking on most of the administrative effort. There would be two events, one in London and the other in Jerusalem. This was a chance to celebrate the love between George and Annabelle; it was also a chance to mark a significant turning point in George's life, as he moved from publisher to chairman. Although he was now seventy-two years old, few believed that he would likely slow down, at least not any time soon, but the change in his outlook had been remarkable in these short few months. Optimism was in the air.

George and Annabelle's wedding took place on an extremely hot and humid 14 July – Bastille Day. First off, they were married at a small, private ceremony held at the Chelsea registry office. This was followed by a lunch for more than 150 people hosted by Drue Heinz, the American actress and philanthropist. After this, a reception was held at the National Portrait Gallery for 400 people. By this time Annabelle was exhausted, but still they had to go on. They next attended a dinner at the home of Donatella and Gerd Rudolf Flick (she the daughter of an Ossetian prince, he the son of a wealthy German industrialist), for all those who had come in from abroad. At the night's end, jacket- and tie-less, George sang Austrian student songs.

Four months later, on 15 November 1992, the party moved to Jerusalem. Just as the sun was setting, Annabelle and George were married under a *chuppah* overlooking the old city. George wore a dark blue suit with a pink zigzag tie and a scarlet handkerchief in his breast pocket. Atop his head was a white kippah. Annabelle was dressed in a two-piece guipure cotton lace outfit by Ungaro. Her head was draped in a veil of the same colour. On her left wrist shone a gold band. Annabelle's father had recently died, so she was given away by Teddy Kollek, the mayor of Jerusalem. After the service, she and George signed an ornate *ketubah*, a Jewish wedding contract. Later, a private dinner was attended by some of the most powerful figures in Israel, including President Herzog, Shimon Peres and Teddy Kollek. From London, the group was joined by Isaiah Berlin, Ed Victor and Lord Sieff.

The Israeli wedding was 'the one that counted,' Annabelle later recalls, 'it was the real wedding'. She then adds, 'It was all very moving. Very romantic.' For George, holding the ceremony in Jerusalem was equally important. 'I've always been very conscious of my Jewish heritage,' he once told an audience, 'and while not necessarily very religious, I certainly don't regard myself as an agnostic. For me being Jewish is really more an attachment, a sense of belonging to a worldwide family and respect for their values, for one's ancestors, traditions and institutions. A warming glow of kinship is, to me, one of the most striking and enjoyable sensations of being Jewish.' Marrying Annabelle under a *chuppah* overlooking the old city, while surrounded by the leaders of the nation he so deeply cared for, was a culmination of George's Jewish identity. A fulfilment of his obligation to his rabbinical ancestors. The delivery of his youthful Zionist dreams.

George and Annabelle's wedding, Jerusalem, with Teddy Kollek (left)

In addition to the sale of his company and his wedding to Annabelle, George was preoccupied with a third project throughout the early 1990s: the writing of his autobiography.

There had been a previous attempt to help the publisher produce his memoirs. In the mid-1980s, the effort was undertaken with the help of Victoria Glendinning, author of a string of successful biographies including *Elizabeth Bowen, Vita: The Life of Vita Sackville*

West and *Rebecca West: A Life*. 'I was a Weidenfeld author,' she says, 'I went to his parties. I was a Weidenfeld pet.' Over the course of a few weeks, she sat down with him and recorded their conversations. The plan was that she would edit these into some kind of shape and submit them to him for approval. Then, Glendinning was approached by another publisher offering her a large advance to write a biography of Anthony Trollope. She wrote to George saying that she was moving publishers. By return, he asked her to come to see him, which she did. 'Darling,' he said, 'I would have given you £100,000.' At which point, Glendinning said the other publisher was offering more. The following day, according to Glendinning, a staff member from Weidenfeld & Nicolson had turned up at her door and demanded she hand over the recordings and any transcripts she had made of her conversations with George. She was never asked to another of the publisher's parties.

Ever since Glendinning's aborted attempt, George had been encouraged by friends to revisit the idea of producing his autobiography. Finally, he relented. He decided not to publish with his own firm, however, to avoid accusations of nepotism and hagiography. Instead, he signed up with HarperCollins, explaining his reasons in a letter to its publisher, Simon King: 'I had a great admiration for the late Sir William [Collins],' George wrote, 'who was a generous colleague and who, unlike others, was well-disposed to a new entrant into the publishing world when I first started. I am also a great admirer of Rupert Murdoch [the owner of HarperCollins].'

Gina Thomas, London correspondent for *Frankfurter Allgemeine Zeitung*, agreed to help George write the book. For over a year in 1989 and 1990, Gina and George had met almost every week. She recorded their conversations, typed up the manuscript and gave him the text for comment. Getting him to focus proved difficult. Their discussions were often interrupted by a phone call which the publisher always had to take. Nevertheless, she felt they were making progress. George's autobiography began to take shape.

*

There have been several books written by or about English-language publishers. Most have been panned by the critics as self-involved and niche, preferring to dwell on the famous authors with whom the publishers have dined, cajoled and claimed credit for over the years, rather than build a compelling narrative. Few have sold well. This is perhaps surprising, given the skills and experience of those involved. One of the main criticisms of these books is that little effort has been made to place the subject in context. How do they compare to their peers? What choices did they make for which they stand out from the pack?

Given that George was active for more than six decades in the publishing industry, he had scores of peers. In Britain, some of his key contemporaries included Tom Maschler of Jonathan Cape, André Deutsch of the eponymous company and Allen Lane of Penguin. In America, perhaps the nearest equivalents were Peter Mayer of Penguin and Roger Straus of Farrar, Straus & Giroux. Of these, it is maybe most productive to contrast George with Tom Maschler, as their backgrounds were so similar.

Both George and Tom Maschler were Jewish and had lived as young boys under Nazi rule in Vienna. Both lost grandparents in the camps and then fled with their families to England. Both frequently travelled to America to acquire books and both had for decades attended the Frankfurt Book Fair. Finally, both had also published great works of literature. In Maschler's case, examples included Joseph Heller's *Catch-22*, Bruce Chatwin's *The Songlines* and Gabriel García Márquez's *One Hundred Years of Solitude*.

There were, however, notable differences. While Maschler prided himself on the hours spent in the office, George rarely remained at his desk, preferring to do business at his flat, in a restaurant, by telephone or during a taxi ride. Maschler's passion was literary fiction, whereas George's personal taste was non-fiction. And while Maschler had run an existing business, George had founded his.

More importantly, perhaps, whereas Maschler tended to view books as discrete cultural objects, George leaned into the politics of publishing, keenly interested in the cultural impact of the books. Thus, when faced with the difficulties of publishing Salman Rushdie's *The Satanic Verses* – for which the author faced a fatwa – and despite publishing many of Rushdie's previous books including *Midnight's Children* and *Shame*, Maschler professed relief when Peter Mayer (the head of Penguin) took on the burden. In contrast, George fought for the publication of *Lolita* and *The Group* and felt it crucially important to provide a platform for unheard voices from around the world. This is perhaps why Maschler focused on editorial and promotion, while George spent most of his energy coming up with or inviting book ideas and persuading people to write them. On this point, Maschler once told a journalist from the *Telegraph*, 'George is the best in the country at inventing books.'

More than this, Tom Maschler – like the vast majority of publishers – restricted his professional life to the publishing of books, whereas George viewed books as part of a far greater mission to build bridges between people. Thus, while the former proudly proclaimed an aversion to committees and any other non-publishing related activity, George gladly took up the responsibilities as a committee member, trustee, governor, member of the House of Lords, and assorted other roles in the charitable and political world, both in England and overseas.

It was because of all these factors, and more, that George Weidenfeld's name was perhaps best known outside the world of publishing. And which was why so many were keen for him to write his autobiography.

Starting in late 1992, George began sending early drafts to Michael Fishwick, his editor at HarperCollins. In the first chapter, titled 'Sunny Youth', he made no mention of being locked up by his nanny so she could have sex with her boyfriend, but he did write about his 'solitude' and 'isolation' as a child. He also shared his feelings about his family: his father (a 'gifted teacher' but a 'self-deceiver' and 'not a good businessman'); his mother ('saw things as they were' and with 'a good education'); and his maternal grandmother ('a formative influence [who] instilled in me a sense of near infallibility'). In the next chapters, he chronicled his time at school ('I treasured brotherhood and conviviality more than anything else'); the rise of the Nazis ('I believe that the vast majority of Austrians were passive, listless or hostile to the *Anschluss*'); his first trip to Palestine ('gave me a thrilling sense of solidarity and serenity such as I had never experienced before'); and saying farewell to his father just before departing for England ('At that moment in the prison I felt I had formally come of age').

In April 1993, Fishwick wrote to George saying he was 'delighted' with the book's progress. A few weeks later, George sent several more chapters. The editor responded that these were 'very, very good indeed', adding that 'you must congratulate yourself on them; you have developed, excitingly, the knack of conjuring up a personality, a moment or an era through telling detail, nothing over or underdone'. Then, in October 1993, Fishwick reported that the book 'goes from strength to strength', and 'The Wilson chapter is simply stunning'. For his part, George was having doubts. On 23 December the publisher wrote to his editor that 'I am at that stage of gestation when confidence and self-doubt change in feverish sequence', adding that 'I sincerely hope to confront you very soon with a completed manuscript'.

Gina Thomas and George Weidenfeld continued, however, on the drafting and redrafting. Chapters were swapped back and forth. Edits and comments were taken in. Finally, in early June 1994, George approved the final text of the book. It finished with a sentimental flourish. In the last paragraph of the final page, the publisher said how lucky he felt meeting and marrying Annabelle. 'I love my married life and the companionship of one who shares my interests,' he wrote, then added, 'having known contentment, obsession and the distress of divorce, I have at last found happiness.'

*

George's autobiography – now known as *Remembering My Good Friends* – was published by HarperCollins in November 1994. To launch the book, a party was held at the Hyde Park Hotel in London. It was hosted by the newspaper proprietor Conrad Black and his journalist wife, Barbara Amiel. Over a hundred people were invited, it was a glitzy gala event. When the guests sat down, they found their tables covered with cloths printed from pages taken from George's book. Heavily pregnant at the time, Gina Thomas was seated at a table at the room's edge, far away from the publisher and the VIPs near him, but she didn't mind; she was tired and wanted to get home as soon as possible. Both George and Conrad Black gave speeches full of praise and wit, but neither mentioned Gina's name or her contribution to the book.

Over the next few weeks, *Remembering My Good Friends* was widely covered in the press, the overwhelming consensus being that the book was poorly written, full of errors and, more than anything else, an exercise in name-dropping. Many of the reviewers mocked George for including more than 2,000 entries in his index. The *Independent*, for instance, called this an 'almanac of name-dropping'. Alastair Forbes in the *Spectator* lamented the book's 'many glaring bloomers' and 'lazy gaffes'. The *Financial Times* made a similar point, wondering why a 'seasoned publisher would not have had someone check the proofs'. In his review for *Night and Day* magazine, Christopher Hitchens was equally dismissive, saying that 'for a volume written by a publisher, this book has an appalling number of spelling mistakes'. He also called it a 'rather self-satisfied memoir'. The *Jewish Chronicle* labelled the book 'curiously insubstantial'. The *Observer* felt that the book never revealed the publisher's true self. 'We long to discover [George] in a moment of unencumbered solitude,' they wrote, 'though of course we never do.' Meanwhile, the *Washington Post* described the book as an 'encyclopaedic resource' – in other words, not for those looking for a page-turner.

Some of the reviews verged on being bigoted and anti-semitic. 'This book of schmaltzy memoir tells very little of the inner man, *homo danubis*,' stated the *Scotsman* 'and, the lashings of snobbery and jobbery mask an underlying lack of principle and an unappealing opportunism.' While under the headline THE OUTSIDER WHO TOOK ON BRITAIN, AND WON, the *Daily Mail* declared that 'this uppity Jewish publisher' has a 'certain soullessness, a constant fixation on the bottom line', and that his 'cosmopolitan circle' was 'very un-English'.

There were, to George's relief, some positive notices, but these were almost entirely written by his friends. The literary agent Ed Victor (who at one time had worked for him) gushed in the *Bookseller* that the book 'deserves space on the shelf' along with other books about publishing greats. While the Labour politician Gerald Kaufman, a frequent attendee of George's parties, wrote in the *Manchester Evening News* that the book was 'one of the finest volumes of memoirs I have ever read'. Meanwhile, in her review for the *Tablet*, Antonia Fraser described the memoir as 'remarkable'.

For her part, Gina Thomas was disappointed with *Remembering My Good Friends*. 'He didn't have the application or the concentration. He was far too restless to sit down and write a book,' she remembers. 'I don't think he wanted to do the work.' When she tried to flesh out information on the people he mentioned, to make the text less gushing, he became cautious, not wanting to offend anyone either by leaving them out or saying something that they might take amiss. 'It was,' Gina Thomas recalls, 'an absolute nightmare.' Their close friendship endured, however, despite the difficulties.

Years earlier, George had been warned about the perils of writing autobiographies by his friend Sigmund Warburg. 'As you know I have the gravest reservations in this respect because I hate self-advertising of human beings even more than the various unaesthetic variations of toothpaste advertising,' wrote the merchant banker in a private letter to the publisher, adding that 'I feel autobiography is at least partly a sort of self-advertisement unless it appears post mortem.' Perhaps George ought to have listened to this advice.

Then, to add to his distress, George received some worrying news about the book's upcoming serialisation in the *Sunday Times*. Serialisation had always been a mark of a successful book for George. It brought in considerable revenue and he had often been personally involved in the negotiating of deals with the major newspapers. Just two years earlier, he had been in discussion with Brian MacArthur, executive editor of the *Sunday Times*, about the serialisation of a biography of Prime Minister John Major. MacArthur had made it clear that the newspaper had certain expectations for a book like this. 'We shall expect the biography to contain hitherto unrevealed details of the early life of John Major,' wrote MacArthur, 'his period as a council leader in Lambeth, his rise through the Conservative party after becoming an MP. That means that the book must contain anecdotal and revealing accounts of his relationship with Margaret Thatcher and other Cabinet colleagues.'

For George's autobiography, the *Sunday Times* had agreed to print an extract and had already paid him two-thirds of a £70,000 fee, but, they now told George, there was a problem. For some reason, HarperCollins had allowed copies of the book to be shipped to the shops two weeks early. This was disastrous given that newspapers demand to run their serialisation before the books are available to the public. A letter was now sent to George demanding the return of his serialisation fee. To make matters worse, he was told that the editor of the *Sunday Times* thought his book was 'bloody awful' and couldn't imagine why they had ever thought of serialising it. In the end, after protracted negotiations, HarperCollins agreed to share the reimbursement costs with George.

In contrast, Laura was upbeat about her father's book. By this point, she was in her early forties, married to the headmaster of an English independent school, and with four children. 'Dear Daddy, your memoirs made for compulsive reading,' Laura wrote on 24 November 1994.

'I found *Remembering My Good Friends* fascinating and a good and true reflection of its equally fascinating author.' Unlike the critics who only read the index, she added, she found much of 'substance' in the book. She was also pleased that he had kept some of his favourite epithets – like calling women 'Junoesque' – to a minimum. 'I was touched by the way in which you wrote about the failure of your marriages to my mother and Sandra – without either accusation or self-pity,' she continued. 'You may think that I am too close to the author to be able to properly judge the book, and that is true, but, on the other hand, I could have reacted, for that very reason, with acute embarrassment and distaste and found the memoirs awful. Instead I am very proud of you and of what you have written.'

Amid all the dark clouds that gathered around the publication of *Remembering My Good Friends*, there was a silver lining. While he was at the Frankfurt Book Fair, George had a serendipitous meeting with a thirty-two-year-old journalist called Mathias Döpfner. At this time, Döpfner was editor in chief of the *Hamburger Morgenpost*, the second largest newspaper in Hamburg, and he wanted George to write a column for him.

They stood next to each other in a hotel lobby, face to face, and spoke for an hour. The conversation moved beyond discussing column inches, and soon turned on the latest issues facing politics and culture in general. Despite the considerable age gap – the publisher was forty-three years older than the journalist – an emotional connection was formed; a like-mindedness was established. They agreed to stay in touch but, over the following days and despite his efforts, Döpfner heard nothing back from George.

A fortnight later, George called Mathias Döpfner and apologised for his delayed contact. He said that the journalist had saved his life. 'How did I save your life?' asked Döpfner, surprised. George explained that for the entire hour they had been talking in the hotel lobby, he had been standing in front of an air-conditioning unit and, as a result, George had caught pneumonia and was extremely sick for two weeks. Following advice from the hospital doctors, he had since given up smoking his beloved cigars and, by stopping smoking, Döpfner had saved his life. The journalist laughed when he heard this. He was also tremendously moved by the generosity of George's story.

Döpfner asked again if George would write a column for him, but the publisher once more declined. The *Morgenpost* was a regional newspaper, George said, it didn't have the platform he was looking for. He was, however, interested in getting to know the journalist better. Over the next weeks and months, whenever George was in Germany or Döpfner was in London, they made a point of meeting up with each other.

A little later, when he was appointed editor-in-chief of *Die Welt*, one of Germany's main daily newspapers, Döpfner again asked George if he would write a column for him. This time he agreed. The two men now spent increasing amounts of time with each other. 'You could say,' Döpfner remembers, 'that was the beginning of a more and more intense relationship.'

George with Mathias Döpfner

CHAPTER 18

Letters from Oxford

2004

'I must admit that I am an optimist and I predict nothing but growth and expansion of interest in the field of literature.' - GW

For George, the rest of the 1990s was a period of affluence and influence. Soon after selling Weidenfeld & Nicolson, he handed over the proceeds to his godson, Jonathan Lourie, founder of Cheyne Capital, who set about carefully growing the already sizeable nest egg. In addition, George received income from various non-executive directorships, including a pharmaceutical company in Hamburg, Germany, two asset-management companies, as well as Orion Publishing. He was now, by any measure, a wealthy man.

Though now in his seventies, George, however, had no intention of retiring. He worked as a paid consultant for an array of media organisations, including the Telegraph Group in Britain and Axel Springer, Bertelsmann and Burda Medien in Germany. He was also increasingly engaged in the non-media world. In addition to giving the occasional speech in the House of Lords – on the Middle East, on the funding of the BBC, on the future of the European Union – he was governor for three universities (Ben-Gurion, Tel Aviv and the Weizmann Institute), a trustee of the Jerusalem Foundation, and a consultant for Daimler Chrysler in Berlin. All of these projects kept him busier than ever. His daily diary rarely had a blank hour, let alone an empty day.

Beyond all these time-consuming activities, George still considered himself primarily a book publisher. Each day he was driven to

Orion House on Upper St Martin's Lane opposite the Ivy restaurant. There, he worked in a third-floor corner office, sitting behind a large bureau, surrounded by Feliks Topolski portraits hanging from the walls. Through the window, he could see the rooftops of Trafalgar Square and the stone ball floating above the English National Opera building. Working with him were two secretaries: Pat Kinsman, who had been with him since the 1970s, and Brit Felmberg, a German native, who in addition to her other administrative responsibilities, typed up George's bi-weekly column for *Die Welt* newspaper (George himself never learned to use a computer). All the while, amid the politics and the charitable work and the consultancies, and the extraordinary parties with the A-list guests that he continued to host two or three times a week, the publisher continued to come up with book ideas. He dictated pitches and book summaries and had these passed along to the senior editors at Orion. A few were taken up; most were not.

One of the books championed by George was a memoir by Katharine Graham, owner of the *Washington Post*, who had been in charge of the newspaper during the Watergate scandal (1972–4). He had known her for more than two decades. When he visited Washington DC, she threw dinner parties in his honour, attended by top-ranking senators, journalists and diplomats. When she was in London, George reciprocated by hosting VIP dinners for her. Graham had also attended George and Annabelle's wedding, which she had described as 'beautiful'.

When Katharine Graham first spoke to George about writing her autobiography, he had been encouraging. In September 1996 she sent him a copy of the manuscript, which he swiftly read. He immediately contacted Anthony Cheetham and persuaded the new owner of Weidenfeld & Nicolson to acquire the book, despite what appeared to be its niche appeal. 'I have just finished reading your book,' George wrote to Katharine Graham on 25 September, 'and found it most remarkable and moving and we would be very proud to publish it.'

On 14 May 1997, Katharine Graham's *Personal History* was released in England. Later that day, George hosted a party for her at his flat on Chelsea Embankment. Afterwards, she wrote him a letter on Claridge's pale blue letterhead, thanking him for hosting an 'enchanting, beautiful and glamorous' dinner to celebrate the launch of her book. She then added, 'you were courageous to buy it before we both found it did well in the USA.'

In March 1998, *Personal History* was awarded the prestigious Pulitzer Prize for biography. According to an article in *Publishers Weekly* on 5 April, this had an immediate impact on sales in America. The book 'enjoys a second week on *PW*'s trade paper chart,' the trade journal announced, 'and copies in print now total 125,000; prior to winning the prize, the book's in-print total was 90,000.' Ten days later, on 15 April, George sent Katharine Graham a fax. 'We have just learned of your exciting but well-merited Pulitzer Prize award. I am so proud to be your publisher and old friend!' By return of post, she replied: 'Many thanks for your flowers and your note about the Pulitzer Prize. I am so happy you are the British publisher – so this award has come to both of us.' With the good news arriving from across the Atlantic, *Personal History* now climbed to the top of the UK bestseller lists.

For George Weidenfeld, who had given up control of his eponymous company five years earlier, to be still associated with such a publishing success was delightful. Not all his associations with books at this time ended so happily.

George had known Hugh Trevor-Roper, the Oxford academic and author of various popular history books, for decades. When, in 1953, the publisher had released *Hitler's Table Talk*, a compendium of the Führer's wartime monologues, it had been Trevor-Roper who he had asked to pen the introduction. A decade later, in 1962, George had published the historian's book *Jewish and Other Nationalisms*.

Since that time, they had remained close. Trevor-Roper was a regular guest at the publisher's parties.

Starting in the 1970s, George proposed that Trevor-Roper write his memoirs. He continued to nudge him throughout the 1980s. 'My dear Hugh,' George wrote on 15 May 1989, 'You agreed to my jogging you about your Memoirs. If I am doing so more robustly it is because our enthusiasm is so great that we would like to encase it in solid, precious metal. We would like to offer you $150,000 for world rights in the book.' Still, Trevor-Roper held off.

Finally, in May 1997, the historian relented. He agreed to write his autobiography for George. By this point, the octogenarian historian was suffering from reduced vision, which made it challenging to read and write. The solution was that Trevor-Roper would recall his life, his work and his beliefs in conversation with Frank Johnson, the then editor of the *Spectator*. The book would be called *Crimes, Follies and Misfortunes: The Reminiscences of Hugh Trevor-Roper*. With George smoothing the way in the background, Johnson interviewed Trevor-Roper at his home in Didcot almost every week for more than a year. The historian recalled his childhood, his wartime work in intelligence, and the fierce rivalries between Oxford dons. He also spoke about the low point in his career: his role in the authenticating of Adolf Hitler's diaries (after the diaries were published in the *Sunday Times* in 1983 they were revealed to be a hoax and Trevor-Roper was much criticised by the media and his fellow academics).

When Johnson submitted his 200-page manuscript to Ben Buchan (editorial director at Weidenfeld & Nicolson), Buchan was, mostly, delighted with the text. But when Hugh Trevor-Roper read the draft, he was not happy, giving various reasons for his dissatisfaction. He told Frank Johnson that he had been too indiscreet. He told Ben Buchan that Johnson had not posed the right questions. 'If I'm a tube of toothpaste,' the historian said, 'he hasn't squeezed me hard enough.' Whatever the real reason, Trevor-Roper now instructed Weidenfeld & Nicolson to cancel the project. According to his agent, Frank Johnson was 'seriously disappointed' to hear this news, having invested considerable time and energy in the project, but Trevor-Roper remained insistent. Then, on 26 January 2003, the acclaimed historian died of cancer in a hospice in Oxford. The project was over.

While George was sad to learn that Hugh Trevor-Roper had died, he was even more upset to hear that his former partner Nigel Nicolson was experiencing serious health concerns. Six years earlier, Weidenfeld & Nicolson had released Nigel's autobiography *Long Life*, in which he retold the story of the company's founding and extolled his friendship with George. Over the past fifty years he had written twenty-seven books. He was now too frail to embark on another manuscript, spending increasing amounts of time in bed at his family home in Sissinghurst, Kent.

In the third week of March 2004, George sent word that he would like to visit his old partner. In a letter written a few days later, Nigel said he was 'very touched' by the offer, but a visit was not necessary. He then reflected on their many decades of friendship. 'So long a journey we have made together,' he said, 'I expressed in <u>Long Life</u> all my gratitude and affection for you, and need not repeat them now, except to double both. You have been, for so many years, my chief prop in life, and W&N its chief memorial.' He then finished, 'Bless you and thank you dear George.' It would be the last communication between the two men.

Six months later, on 23 September, Nigel died at home in Sissinghurst aged eighty-seven. 'My life would have been very different without his friendship,' George wrote in the *Observer* the following day, 'and if the publishing firm that bears our names continues in the founders' spirit, it will be Nigel who has earned a huge share of the credit.'

Aged eighty-five years old himself, George was getting

increasingly accustomed to those around him becoming frail, withdrawing and then dying. Each year, it appeared that he was attending more and more funerals. When speaking about this with close friends, George said it felt like another form of abandonment.

Ten months after Hugh Trevor-Roper's funeral, Blair Worden, the Oxford professor in charge of the historian's literary estate, wrote an email to Ben Buchan. 'Now that the dust of the Trevor-Roper/Frank Johnson volume has (I hope) settled,' he wrote, 'may I, as Hugh's literary executor, make a suggestion to you? Knowing Weidenfeld's admiration for Hugh and long dealings with him, I would be glad to see a happier posthumous legacy of that relationship.' Worden now proposed that Weidenfeld & Nicolson publish a book of letters from the young Trevor-Roper to the American art historian and octogenarian Bernard Berenson, written in a colourful style to entertain the old man in the 1940s and 1950s. The correspondence would be edited by Richard Davenport-Hines, the much-admired biographer and columnist for the *Spectator*. Buchan was delighted by the proposition and asked to see copies of the letters.

In early December 2004, Davenport-Hines submitted over 300 pages of letters to Ben Buchan. Reading the missives, the editor grew excited. 'They are extraordinary,' he wrote to Blair Worden, 'I wonder if anyone writes letters like this anymore.' Buchan added, however, that they had a problem. In his voluminous correspondence with Berenson, Trevor-Roper had written at some length about George Weidenfeld. Buchan believed that the publisher 'could not object to' some of the passages, but others were 'aggressively malicious'.

Buchan went to see George in his office at Orion House and told him about the Trevor-Roper letters. 'Oh dear,' the publisher said, looking sad. The editor suggested that he, Buchan, should read the letters again carefully and suggest which parts might be cut. Would that be an acceptable plan? George gave his agreement. The next day, on 9 December, Buchan sent George copies of the seven pages that referred to him and, in thick green highlighter pen, marked the sections he thought could be deleted. 'These are the cuts I am requesting,' the editor wrote, 'ie all the really unpleasant stuff.'

The first of these letters was written on 5 February 1955 and concerned George's first wife. In this passage, Trevor-Roper wrote that around the time that Jane Sieff had separated from George she had met a young French student who had developed a desire for 'simple domestic life, *l'amour du cottage*'. The implication was that Jane had been unfaithful. Trevor-Roper went on to say that her parents ('stiff, boring and respectable Jewish millionaires') had then worked to 'keep the French student at bay'.

The second letter had been written seventeen months earlier, on 22 September 1953. This spoke of George having an 'incorrigible penchant for the flashy and the bogus' and being 'indefatigable alas in producing the memoirs of shady war-criminals and the gossip of those dethroned Balkan monarchs who keep their tawdry courts in Estonia'. In his private notes on this passage, Ben Buchan wrote: 'This is bad!'

The third letter was dated 22 May 1954. According to Ben Buchan's notes it was 'probably the worst'. Trevor-Roper had written the following about George:

> He has no literary judgment, none at all. So he rushes to
> America, to France, to Italy, to Berlin, to Vienna, flashing the
> Sieff profits, offering large prices, wooing Rohwolt [German
> publisher] and Flammarion [French publisher], Farrar Straus &
> Giroux [American publisher] and Mondadori [Italian publisher],
> entertaining authors and editors, but it is no good. He is, alas,
> quite illiterate and doesn't know how to begin to distinguish
> good from bad. He is now publishing the most pitiful rubbish
> [...] The Jews, who blessed his orthodox marriage, now boggle
> at the stream of Nazi literature which he produces; the scholars

whom he madly woos now draw their academic gowns primly
about them as he approaches... and poor George, in the void
around him, is left pursuing disreputable Cockney millionaires
or ambitious French collaborationists for their memoirs, while
the unenterprising mandarins of the English publishing world,
Macmillan and co., smile condescendingly at their effortlessly
preserved monopoly. So if George Weidenfeld is pressing you for
your next work, don't leap too eagerly into his arms just yet.

Having read all seven pages, George agreed with Buchan's assess-
ment. There were only three sections that were truly offensive.
The first about his ex-wife needed 'judicious cuts'. The second also
required deletions. As to the third, it all had to go. Ben Buchan
passed the decision on to Davenport-Hines and Blair Worden, who
took in the request. The book *Letters from Oxford* was published in
July 2006. Its preface revealed that 'several libellous passages' had
been removed, but did not make clear in the text where this had
occurred. Nor did it reveal that several of these passages had been
about George Weidenfeld.

What does it say that George asked for these passages to be cut?
This is the same person who, in the cases of *Lolita*, *The Group* and
many other books, had fought for the right to publish. Who had
been much lauded as a champion of free speech. Is it evidence that
George Weidenfeld had a thin skin? Perhaps there is more to it.
After all, Hugh Trevor-Roper was an old friend, an ally in George's
lifelong interest in the Nazis. A fellow traveller on the murky path
of intelligence, history and European culture. George had proven
loyal to Trevor-Roper time and time again, most notably when
the historian had been lambasted for mistakenly authenticating
Hitler's Diaries. Perhaps the real hurt, the true sting, was that the
historian's letters to Berenson, with their toxic mix of sneering
caricature and titillating gossip, played into George's fundamental
insecurities. That even though people spoke well of him in public,

would embrace him with warm greetings and praise, were only too glad to sup at his dinner parties, he feared that in private, behind his back, he was ridiculed, shunned and rejected.

In the years following the publication of *Letters from Oxford*, George continued to be actively involved at Weidenfeld & Nicolson in his capacity as chairman. So when the company moved from St Martin's Lane in Soho to their new open-plan offices at Carmelite House overlooking the Thames, he was given his own private office – the only private office in the company.

As he moved into his nineties, George remained extraordinarily active. Days packed with meetings. International travel. A crowded social calendar. Frequent public speaking engagements. Many who met him at this time were amazed by the elderly publisher's acuity and impressive cognitive function. Even more, they commented on his seemingly never-ending energy and stamina.

George on the dance floor at grandson Rowan's wedding, 2008

On 30 October 2014, George received a letter from the prime minister of Israel, Bibi Netanyahu. After first congratulating the publisher on his ninety-fifth birthday – which had occurred the previous month – Netanyahu said, 'For the better part of a century, you have been a tireless champion of the Jewish people and the State of Israel, working both to change history and to preserve it.' He then went on to say how much he particularly appreciated George's dedication to publishing stories about Israel and the Israeli people. It was clear that, more than three decades after the publication of Max Hasting's book *Yoni*, Netanyahu's feelings towards George remained strong.

By the autumn of 2015, however, George found himself no longer to be so tireless. He was commuting to Carmelite House less frequently. He preferred to work at home. He found the journey draining. His legs often hurt, he had to use a walking stick. That does not mean that he had withdrawn from his publishing duties, far from it. On 7 October, Alan Samson (publishing executive at Weidenfeld & Nicolson) provided a summary of George's efforts to David Shelley, CEO of Hachette (which now owned Orion and, in turn, Weidenfeld & Nicolson). Although ninety-six years old, George still 'takes an active interest' in the publishing house, Samson wrote, and was 'thrilled' when a few months earlier they were recognised at the Bookseller Industry Awards as Imprint of the Year. He then listed George's involvement in the firm.

First, there was a category of book that 'has been acquired through George's direct connections with the author which has enhanced the prestige of the list and has been commercially successful'. George's relationship with these authors, Samson wrote, 'was significant in their decision to come to Orion/W&N'. Recent examples were *Memory and Identity* by Pope John Paul II (2005) and *Everything is Connected* by Daniel Barenboim (2007). Then there was a category of book that George had proposed but with which he had no further involvement. These included *Celsius: 7/7* by Michael Gove MP, and *No Room for Small Dreams* by Shimon Peres, the former Israeli prime minister. The third category were books that George 'is keen to publish' but were rejected. Alan Samson noted, 'I do my best to manage George's expectations in this regard.'

Samson then went on to outline the books that George was currently pushing, including a book by George Osborne (Chancellor of the Exchequer), Damian Lewis (star of the TV show *Homeland*) and Jonathan Powell (former chief of staff to Prime Minister Tony Blair). There was also a proposal to publish a 'quasi-academic' series funded by George's friend Len Blavatnik, who was currently number one on the *Sunday Times* Rich List.

Finally, Samson reported on the book that he had commissioned from the renowned biographer William Shawcross, provisionally titled *Conversations with George Weidenfeld*. This had been in the works since 2012 and was George's third attempt to have a book written about himself. The manuscript had been delivered, continued Samson, but 'George was unhappy with it' and wanted to go in a different direction. George was now hoping for a new book, a fourth effort, along the lines of *A Dinner Party with George Weidenfeld*, with contributions from eight or nine people, including the author Andrew Roberts, the journalist Hella Pick (who had, by now, worked with George for the past fifteen years), the head of Penguin Peter Mayer and George's daughter Laura. Shawcross would be invited to write the introduction.

At the memo's end, Samson asked his boss for fifteen minutes to discuss George's future. 'For the record, George is an infrequent visitor to the building, much though he likes it,' concluded the executive, 'but he is planning to be in the office tomorrow afternoon, 8th October, and that has precipitated me to send you this along.'

CHAPTER 19

Obit

2016

'I am also convinced that the whole complex of future technological achievement [...] offer the book publisher a Wellsian picture of hope rather than an Orwellian vision of doom.' – GW

It was New Year's Eve 2015 and George Weidenfeld was beginning to feel his age. He was ninety-six years old and walked with the assistance of a cane. He had lost a considerable amount of weight. He no longer went into the office. His kidneys were troubling him. He quickly became tired when guests visited. And yet, George was looking forward to the next few months. There was much to do. A conference to attend. A trip to Israel to organise. Philanthropic work to fulfil. Editors to badger about his latest book ideas.

George did have one complaint, though. Annabelle was spending more and more time with the nonagenarian pianist Menahem Pressler. From February to December 2015 she travelled three times to America. 'It was to help [Pressler] struggle through hospital and rehab in Boston at the age of ninety-two following life-threatening aortic aneurysm repair,' Annabelle recalls. 'He had lost his wife a few weeks earlier, his daughter was finding it very hard to cope as she had serious back problems.' She added, 'We had been closest of friends since 1967 when I managed his trio in London and later Spain. This was not some capricious adventure or love affair!'

Each day, Pat Kinsman came to the flat on Chelsea Embankment to write George's letters and organise his schedule. He told her how much he missed Annabelle. He called his friend Gina Thomas, speaking until well after one o'clock in the morning. They spoke exclusively about the past, including the extreme loneliness he had felt earlier in his life, particularly as a child and in his days as a refugee in London. And he spoke to Mathias Döpfner, the German journalist with whom he had grown extremely close. '[George's] life ended with a surprising tragedy that I could not believe at the beginning when I saw it,' Döpfner recalls. 'George started to be a bit jealous. I didn't take it seriously. I thought well, okay, this guy is in his nineties, come on. I mean it's like a friendship among sisters or friends. But sadly, I started to realise no, this is real, really serious and painful.'

Döpfner noticed how much Annabelle liked Menachem Pressler, how wonderful it was for her to spend time with the great pianist. How supportive she was of him. 'George was so disappointed,' he remembers. At one point, the publisher said, 'Well, Mathias, let's go this summer to Italy. I cannot stay with Annabelle here.' According to Döpfner, at one point George even altered his will.

On 16 January 2016, George woke up feeling weaker than normal. He tried to walk but didn't have the strength. His legs ached with considerable pain. When Pat arrived at the flat, she found him still in bed. She wasn't sure what to do. Annabelle was away. After some discussion, Pat took George to the Chelsea and Westminster Hospital on the Fulham Road. There they spent hours waiting for a doctor and then, after an examination, hours more waiting to be X-rayed. Yet, George didn't seem to mind. Something had changed for the publisher. 'He was peaceful,' Pat says. 'He became sweet. Gentle. Generally relaxed.' He said, 'I like it here.' After speaking with Annabelle, Pat called George's driver to pick them up. Then she called her husband. George was unable to climb into the car himself and even though she thought of him as 'skin and bones', it would take two men to lift him into the vehicle. Not long after they were back in the flat, Annabelle returned.

The next day, the pain in George's legs was even worse. To find out what was going on, Annabelle called an ambulance. George was taken to the Lister, a private hospital in Chelsea. After giving him various tests, they discovered an aneurysm was leaking onto a nerve in his leg. The doctors reassured Annabelle that the problem did not appear to be life-threatening. Throughout the day, the publisher's mood remained warm and peaceful. Members of the family now arrived. His daughter Laura, his grandchildren and great-grandchildren. Old friends came to say hello, including Gina Thomas. The conductor Daniel Barenboim called. And there, with George lying in his hospital bed, they sang 'Gaudeamus igitur' in Latin from his Austrian student days:

Gaudeamus igitur,	So let's rejoice,
Iuvenes dum sumus,	while yet we're young;
Post jucundam juventutem	For when youth's fun
Post molestam senectutem	and age's toil are done,
Nos habebit humus.	the earth will have our bones.
Vivant omnes virgines	Long live all girls,
Faciles, formosae	Easy and fine!
Vivant et mulieres:	And women too,
Tenerae, amabiles	Soft, lovely,
Bonae, laboriosae.	Good and diligent!
Vivat Academia,	And long live Academia!
Vivant Professores,	Long live the Dons!
Vivat membrum quodlibet,	The students too!
Vivant membra quaelibet,	Both singly and united:
Semper sint in flore!	May they ever be in bloom!

At one point, George told his grandson, Rowan, that they should call this the 'Lister interlude', that it was one of the highlights of his life, and joked that they should write a book about it. He appeared happy. At another moment, he spoke by phone to Mathias Döpfner, who happened to be in his car on the way somewhere. They said how fond they were of each other.

Over the next two days George was given morphine for his pain.

He drifted in and out of consciousness. Around one o'clock in the morning of 20 January, Annabelle left her husband's bedside and returned to the flat on Chelsea Embankment. Half an hour later, she received a call from the hospital. George had died in his sleep.

In his conversations with Annabelle and other friends, George had long made it clear he wished to be buried in the capital city of the country that he loved most, Israel. According to Jewish tradition, bodies must be interred within three days of death. Given that he had died on Wednesday and Shabbat started at sunset on the Friday, the family had less than two days to transport George's body from London to Jerusalem and complete the burial rites.

Just before ten in the morning on Friday 22 January 2016 a group of around thirty people dressed in black suits and black dresses walked down the narrow stony path of the cemetery in the Mount of Olives. Annabelle was among them, as was Laura, with her four children and their families. Mathias Döpfner was also there, along with a small number of George's closest friends. It was a beautiful cloudless day. When the mourners arrived at the site, they could see why this spot had been selected with its prime view over the old city. It was also close to the Gate of Mercy, reputed to be where the Messiah would first rise. According to George's grandson Rowan, the setting was 'beautiful', 'humble' and 'fitting'.

Next to a six-foot hole was the body, wrapped in a thin shroud. A rabbi recited some prayers, and then the body was lowered into the grave. 'It was quite tough,' Mathias Döpfner recalls, 'I could see his body falling into the grave. That was awful for me. It was shockingly archaic.' Overcome with emotion, Döpfner walked away from the grave. He continued until he was about fifty feet from the rest of the mourners. Then, at the edge of a terrace, with the hill falling away before him, and now facing the Old City, he stopped – and allowed himself to cry.

*

In the days that followed, George's secretary Brit Felmberg monitored the newspapers for their reporting of the publisher's death. When she found an article, she printed it out and added it to the ever-growing stack on her desk. The coverage was widespread, spanning dozens of countries, which was highly unusual for a publisher and spoke to George's truly international life. In America, there were lengthy obituaries published in the *New York Times*, *National Review* and *Washington Post*. In Britain, *The Times*, *Guardian*, *Financial Times*, *Telegraph* and *Daily Mail* allotted significant space, as did many other newspapers. In Germany, *Die Welt*, *Spiegel*, *FAZ* and assorted others ran notices. Similar extensive coverage was seen in Israel, France, Italy and numerous other countries. Once she felt that enough time had elapsed, Brit Felmberg placed these obituaries in a plastic folder and gave one copy to Annabelle and another to Laura. Contained within these pages were more than 75,000 words of biography, commemoration, evaluation and judgement. More than enough words for a book.

From these notices, various themes surfaced. George Weidenfeld the lover of women. George Weidenfeld the global networker. George Weidenfeld the great supporter of Israel. George Weidenfeld the Jewish refugee who reconciled with Austria and Germany. George Weidenfeld the mentor, the bridge-builder, the leader, the dealmaker. Above everything else was George Weidenfeld the publisher. The man who fought for *Lolita* to be read. The man behind classics such as *The Group*, *The Double Helix* and *The Hedgehog and the Fox*.

'George Weidenfeld was the most enterprising publisher of his day,' David Pryce-Jones stated in the *National Review*. 'Weidenfeld was an outstanding, perhaps a great, publisher,' declared the *Telegraph*. He was 'the last great example of the vanished world of liberal, cosmopolitan, cultured Europe,' declared Melanie Phillips in *The Times*. 'He came to be regarded,' wrote the *New York Times*, 'as the doyen of British publishers.' In a column about George that he posted on his website, Jonathan Sachs, the Chief Rabbi of Great Britain wrote: 'He was bold, he was visionary, he was hard working, and he was fun', adding that, 'He was a giant, and without him the world will seem a smaller and less vivid place.'

In the weeks and months following the announcement of George's death, Annabelle received hundreds of letters of condolence from around the world. They came from authors George had championed, politicians he had worked with, celebrities, friends, acquaintances and many others. For Annabelle, two were particularly memorable. The first came from Angela Merkel, who by this point had been chancellor of Germany for more than a decade. After recalling the various 'unforgettable encounters' she had had with George at the flat in Chelsea, in Salzburg and on numerous occasions in Berlin, she wrote that George's 'wisdom, far-sightedness, knowledge of the entirety of the twentieth century and grace in many things had a great impression on me'. The second letter came from the publisher's old friend Henry Kissinger. George Weidenfeld, wrote Kissinger, 'launched me on my career as an author, publishing a manuscript that had been rejected by eight publishers ... [and] at all crucial periods of my life, George was there with support.' He continued, 'George was a kind of conscience for our world – ubiquitous, committed, civilised and, underneath the accommodating exterior, made of steel.' He concluded, echoing the words of Rabbi Sachs, 'The world is emptier without him.'

On 26 June 2016, three days after the Brexit vote, a memorial service was held for George at the Victoria and Albert Museum in London. In the run-up to the event, George's secretary Pat Kinsman had written to Alan Samson confessing that she had 550 people on her 'must be invited first' list with a reserve of another 200 people. The problem was that the room where the memorial was to take place had a capacity for only 450. In the end, it was standing room only.

The range of those accepting the invitation spoke to George's vast network. From the Austrian, German and Israeli ambassadors to the Jordanian princess Firyal Irshaid. From Labour politician Peter

Mandelson to those in the centre ground like David Owen and on the right, such as Ed Vaizey. There were a large number of authors, including David Pryce-Jones, Anne Sebba and Ronald Harwood, along with an array of journalists and presenters such as Melvyn Bragg, Anne Applebaum, Charles Moore and Anne McElvoy. Members of George's family were also there, as were many of his colleagues from Weidenfeld & Nicolson and the world of publishing.

The celebration commenced with a welcome from George's wife Annabelle, followed by music by Rachmaninoff, Brahms and Chopin played by three of the world's greatest pianists: Evgeny Kissin, Murray Perahia and Menahem Pressler. A poem was read out by George's grandchildren. Eulogies were given by Mathias Döpfner, Antonia Fraser and Isaac Herzog, then leader of the opposition, now president of Israel. According to the printed programme handed out to the attendees, Michael Gove MP (Secretary of State for Justice) was also meant to give an address, but he did not turn up. Years later, Gove would say that his non-appearance was still 'quite an emotional thing'. His decision had been based upon two factors. First, he was in the middle of a 'political maelstrom'. It was just a few days after the result of the Brexit referendum (for which he had campaigned), David Cameron had just resigned and he, Gove, was engaged in conversations that were 'all-consuming'. And, second, he believed that his presence might be 'provocative' and 'distracting', given that George and most of his friends were passionately pro-European. Gove adds that he was 'immensely sad not to be there' and that perhaps, in retrospect, not attending may have been an instance of 'moral cowardice'.

Also in the programme, at its start, were a few lines from Shimon Peres. 'It is hard to believe he is no longer with us,' wrote the former prime minister and president of Israel. 'I miss how he grabbed life with gusto – something we can and must continue in his honour. We must retell his story and act as he did with strong moral consideration. May we continue to remember him, may his memory be a blessing to us all.'

*

George's wife Annabelle talks about the times she was away from him in the last months of his life. She says he would get 'very bitter and he would feel very upset. And he would tell a lot of people about it.' Yet, and she was at pains to make this clear, 'I always went with George's blessing, always.'

Over the years, they had travelled extensively together, including an annual expedition to the Bayreuth Festival in Bavaria, founded in 1876 by Richard Wagner for the performance of his operas. How was it possible for George to have been so passionate about Wagner given the composer's well-known anti-Semitic writings? 'We often spoke about it,' she says. 'But he felt that it's a question of being able to separate the two, separate the art from the artist.' She then adds, 'He adored Wagner, adored the music, adored the whole concept. It had nothing to do with Wagner as a character. He was able to separate the two.'

Annabelle believes there may have been two sides to George, the public side and another, hidden, private. 'What there was certainly with George was a kind of insecurity which I think never left him. And which meant that he needed people very badly around him to have that reassurance. And I think yes, that was a problem which existed all his life. Definitely.'

Annabelle shares two further intimacies. The first was their secret sign. At a social event, when one of them was bored or tired or just wanted to go home, they would rub their nose in a downward motion. Then there was a second private moment, which only she and George knew about. When they came home after a dinner party or other gathering, he liked to conduct what she called a 'postmortem'. They would stay up late discussing who said what, what they'd learned. 'That was absolutely essential,' she remembers, with a smile. 'That he would enjoy. And we could go comparing notes till the early hours of the morning.'

EPILOGUE

'Whatever the future may bring in technological and
scientific change or social innovation, books and writers will
be there in the forefront, fulfilling their age-old role as the
consciences and heralds of human civilisation.' – GW

During his lifetime, George was showered with awards. He received
honorary degrees from universities in Great Britain, Germany,
Israel, and perhaps most movingly for him, Austria – from his
alma mater, the Diplomatic College in Vienna. In addition to
being awarded the Knight Grand Cross (GBE) in 2011 by Queen
Elizabeth II, a rare honour, he received tributes from the German,
Italian, French, Austrian and Polish governments. Various projects were named after him, including the Weidenfeld-Hoffmann
Scholarships and Leadership Programme and The Sussex University
Weidenfeld Institute of Jewish Studies. Now, some years after his
death, with the framed certificates, ribbons and accolades stored
away in rarely opened boxes, what do such honours mean? What
is the legacy of George Weidenfeld?

For those who knew him, George was a memorable character.
In my conversations with more than a hundred people, I heard a
variety of responses. A large number expressed their love, appreciation and admiration for the publisher. But there was also a not
insignificant group, most of whom were unwilling to speak on the
record, who shared their profound dislike of George Weidenfeld.
They used words like 'loathsome', 'appalling' and 'monstrous' when

talking about him. While many, perhaps most, were enthralled by his 'charm' and 'business genius', there were those who found his methods 'underhand', 'unsavoury' and 'unethical'. Equally, while there was a large group of women who revered and cherished the publisher for his humour, intelligence and erudition, there were others who found him 'creepy' and 'inappropriate'. Part of the difference in opinion can be traced back to a single question: is it possible, is it even right, to judge someone's behaviour from thirty or forty years ago by today's standards?

Crucially, for many working at the higher echelons of power around the world – politicians, journalists, authors, religious leaders, business people – George was an exceptional convener. Gifted at high-level diplomacy and working behind the scenes, organising a serendipitous encounter at a conference or in the corridor outside a board room, and arranging the 'placement' (who sat next to whom at a dinner party) that often led to unexpected meetings of minds. All to say, George was a world-class bridge-builder.

There is another group of people who, while never meeting him personally, were affected by George. These included thousands of people who have engaged with organisations that he founded. For instance, the Institute for Strategic Dialogue in London, The Club Of Three, The Europaeum (a network of eighteen universities in Europe), as well as The Blavatnik School of Government in Oxford, whose creation stems from George's close friendship with the benefactor Sir Leonard Blavatnik, whom George advised on its funding and structure. Not to mention the hundreds of Christian refugees for whom George raised funds so they could be rescued from Syria during its civil war; in gratitude, he said, for the Christian family who first hosted him upon his arrival in London all those years before.

Of all his projects, it is the Weidenfeld-Hoffmann Scholarships and Leadership Programme that speaks most to George's legacy, according to its director Alexandra Henderson. Established in 2007, the project has provided more than 400 scholarships for students from emerging countries to sit for MA degrees at the University of Oxford. A large proportion of those participating come from Africa, the Caribbean, Asia and South America. Many have experienced conflict and trauma. 'I remember George chatting to the students at one event,' remembers Henderson, 'and he was talking about the importance of speaking to your opponents.' One of the students said, 'You can't possibly talk to your enemy.' To this George replied that this was exactly what he had done after the war. He had interviewed several senior Nazis and persuaded them to publish their stories. Hearing this, many of the students were shocked. How could he do that? To this, George answered that he wanted to understand more about how the Nazis thought and behaved. The students were deeply moved by this conversation. 'Nobody else was doing this kind of work at the time,' Henderson continues, 'combining moral philosophy with practical skills', adding, 'George was a huge believer that if you want to bring about meaningful change, you can't cut yourself off from your enemies.'

Next comes George's family. His legacy is perhaps best summed up by his grandson Rowan, Laura's second oldest child. Rowan is in his early forties, lives in Berlin, and runs Google's philanthropic arm in Europe, the Middle East and Africa. 'Opapa couldn't relate to young children,' Rowan Barnett says about his grandfather. 'It was only when I turned fifteen [in 1996] that we began to have a relationship.' He continues, 'As we got older and the University years drew nearer, so Opapa, a man of big ideas and big plans, could talk and challenge us to have bigger ideas and bigger plans – and we in turn as grandchildren, became much closer.' Later, as he moved into his twenties, Rowan began to see the multifaceted and multi-layered nature of his grandfather's personality, and 'he began to take on a role that he would go on to play to great effect in his life – one of a trusted mentor, a wise adviser, a loyal friend and an inspirer'.

Today, Rowan attributes his work in the philanthropic sector to George. He is also thankful to him for 'widening my horizons to Israel and beyond' and for his 'encouragement to embrace Germany'. Recently, Rowan and his wife provided a home to a Ukrainian family fleeing the war back home. For Rowan, this is a way to repay the debt owed after Britain provided a safe haven to his grandfather.

In one of their conversations, George told his grandson 'When death comes, I just won't be there.' Later, in a speech, Rowan would demur: 'You see, you live on in the things we have learnt from you and will continue to learn and in everything you have created. Not many people can say they have left the world in a better and grander place. You can.'

What about those who have no direct link with George Weidenfeld? What is his significance to them?

Perhaps most obviously, George's legacy can be seen in the extraordinary number of culturally significant books that were published during his association with Weidenfeld & Nicolson. During these sixty-seven years, first as co-founder/owner (1949–92) and then as chairman (1992–2016), the firm released more than 6,000 titles. From Vladimir Nabokov's *Lolita* to J. G. Farrell's *The Siege of Krishnapur* and Vikram Seth's *A Suitable Boy*. From Saul Bellow's *Herzog* to Jostein Gaarder's *Sophie's World* and Carlos Ruiz Zafón's *The Shadow of the Wind*. From *The Double Helix* by James Watson to Keith Richards' memoir *Life*, and *I Am Malala* by Malala Yousafzai. From *Unity Mitford: A Quest* by David Pryce-Jones and *Age of Revolution* by Eric Hobsbawm to Antony Beevor's *The Second World War* and Simon Sebag Montefiore's *Jerusalem*. And from Mary McCarthy's *The Group* to Bernhard Schlink's *The Reader* and Gillian Flynn's *Gone Girl*. Many, though not all, have stood the test of time and are likely to do so for decades to come. This is an astounding contribution to the world of literature and ideas.

Then there is his contribution to the battle for freedom of speech, his campaign against the obscenity laws and his support of authors whose voices might otherwise not have been heard. Maybe most important, however, is the publishing imprint named after him. Seventy-five years after its founding, Weidenfeld & Nicolson is as strong as ever.

Mathias Döpfner, the CEO of Axel Springer, works in one of the top floors of a gleaming, futuristic building in the centre of Berlin. Now in his fifties, he runs a global media empire with a cornucopia of publications including *Bild* (the highest-circulation newspaper in Europe), *Die Welt*, *Business Insider* and *Politico*.

Döpfner says that it had been while working with George on his regular column for the *Die Welt* newspaper that their personal relationship had developed. 'It transformed into a very, very, very close friendship,' reports Döpfner, 'where in the end, he used to say, "You are the son for me that I never had". I couldn't return that because I had a father. So, couldn't say "You are the father" that I didn't have. But in a way, he was for me always like . . . he was like a brother.'

Now, six years after the funeral at the Mount of Olives, Döpfner speaks about George's life, both the good and the bad. 'Everybody has a dark side and a bright side,' Döpfner says, adding, 'George was the opposite of cancel culture.' Then, speaking more generally as the head of a global media empire, he states, 'I'm worried about it today. It's a very topical political conversation. I find it super dangerous. I think it achieves the opposite. If you just cancel things, you have no critical discussion.'

'We simply got along so well, you know,' continues Döpfner, 'there was a degree of understanding intuitively, we were laughing in the same moment. We found the same things funny. We disliked the same people. We loved the same people.' They spoke almost every day. 'I still feel guided by him, so I know so well what he thought, what he would think,' he says. When Döpfner purchased *Politico* for more than $1 billion, he thought about George. 'He would have said "Come to London, we have to celebrate together", he would have loved it.'

Did Döpfner and George express their affection physically? Perhaps they hugged? Döpfner pauses for a moment and smiles. Yes, they hugged, he says, but that was not all. 'We held hands, that's when we were close,' he says. 'I remember that sometimes we sat for half an hour holding hands.'

In Mathias Döpfner, George Weidenfeld had found someone who could continue his publishing legacy. As head of the media powerhouse Axel Springer, the German executive embodies a deep commitment to the values that George held dear: free speech, democracy, a united Europe, the transatlantic alliance, a free-market economy and, perhaps most importantly of all, Israel.

More than this, with Mathias Döpfner it appears that George had secured the brother for which he had always yearned. The sibling he had missed as a child. The friend who would be loyal even after he, George, had left the room. It seems that at the end, the publisher was not as alone as he had so long feared.

ENDNOTES

INTRODUCTION

2 'At five foot nine...' Curiously, in his 1947, 1957, 1966 and 1976 British passports, George gave his height as 5 foot 11 inches. His 1985 passport gave his height at 1.8 metres. His daughter told me that in later life 'He did shrink very significantly'.

CHAPTER 1 – ARTHUR'S DIARY, 1919

7 'His mother, Rosa...' Her name was spelled variously. In Vienna, she was known as Rosa, Róza and Rozia. During her time in the UK she was known as Rose. As the story starts in Vienna I have gone with 'Rosa', and maintained this consistently.

10 '*Arthur's Diary...*' Rosa continued making entries until 30 April 1920. It was eighty pages long.

13 'as part of a documentary...' See the film *George Weidenfeld: Close Up* by Mathias Döpfner, Polyphon/NDR, 30 May 2009.

19 'In the summer of 1936, Arthur graduated from the gymnasium with top marks.' In spite of the fact that he had handed in a blank copy in maths in his *matura*. (Source: Laura Weidenfeld)

21 'They announced they were there to arrest him for fraud...' On 12 August 1954, Max submitted a compensation claim to the Austrian government, saying, 'I was arrested immediately after the Nazi seizure of power, both because of my Jewish ancestry and because of my known monarchist views.' According to the investigation carried out by a Vienna magistrate in 1955, Max was arrested by the financial police 'for fraud' and that somebody said that he had given money to a political organisation and aristocrats (i.e. a bribe), but nobody was willing to confirm this, so he was set free. (Source: Wr. Stadt und Landesarchiv)

CHAPTER 2 – THE GOEBBELS EXPERIMENT, 1942

27 'Regent Palace Hotel...' This hotel was established by my family, as was the Lyons Corner House that Arthur also frequented at this time. See my book, *Legacy*.

33 'Arthur' was too difficult...' For a while, George went by 'George Weiden' on the BBC and in articles he wrote for the *News Chronicle*.

34 'An avid reader since a boy...' I was told by several people that George did not read the books that he published. The rumour was rebuffed by many others who said he did read the books he was closely associated with but not of course each of the more than 6,000 released during his tenure. His long-time secretary Pat Kinsman called the claim that he never read books 'laughable'.

38 'Yes, I wrote a book...' *032c* magazine, 30 June 2011.

42 'To appear legitimate, Contact Books Limited...' Two other books published by Contact Books Limited include *American Interpretations* by David Mitrany and *France Between the Republics* by Dorothy M. Pickles. (Laura Barnett papers)

43 'some attention from the media...' *Winnipeg Free Press*, July 1946; *Observer*, 14 April 1946; London Letter, *Partisan Review*, Summer 1946.

43 'a second issue was released...' There would be eleven issues of *Contact* published by Contact Books Limited.

44 'George Orwell... in his London Letter...' *Partisan Review*, Summer 1946.

CHAPTER 3 – THE HEDGEHOG AND THE FOX, 1953

50 'revealing picture...' These reviews were included in a W&N advertisement published under the title 'Two Young Men' in the *New Statesman and Nation*, 15 May 1950.

55 'officially titled George Weidenfeld & Nicolson...' The first record I could find of the company being known by its shorter form 'Weidenfeld & Nicolson' was in the *Liverpool Echo* on 5 January 1950 in a review of *Unrequited Love* by Maxim Gorky. In 1959 letters were still being written on 'George Weidenfeld & Nicolson Limited' letterhead, though the 'George' was half the font size of the rest of the name.

56 'If a cable was received... NICOBAR...' The name NICOBAR was a contraction of Nigel Nicolson and Patrick Barrington, the latter being a short-term partner in the company. 'He came too late to add his name to the firm but he made the cable address'. (GW speech, Nigel Nicolson's eightieth birthday, 25 September 1997) The publisher also explained why 'Weidenfeld' came first in the firm's name: one of their early backers owned a company called Nicolson and Watson, and they didn't want there to be confusion between the two.

57 'She gathered...' By email, Antonia Fraser told me, 'The point of the Topolski story is that one of the two told a lie, and it was probably Topolski. I dare say he asked George to send a girl with various abilities, adding that she should be pretty. Not quite the same thing.'

58 'another cable to Berlin...' Letters in this chapter by permission of the Trustees of the Isaiah Berlin Literary Trust: Sandra Weidenfeld, 12 August 1969; Bernard Williams, 3 December 1973; Jacob Talmon, 29 January 1979; Leo Wieseltier, 3 January 1995; Rowland Burdon-Muller, mid-March 1961; Svetlana Peters, 15 March 1982.

59 'one published in *The Times*...' *The Times*, 23 December 1953.

63 'wiped clean...' Nigel would receive 2,000 shares in return for a £2,500 loan he had made of the same value.

63 'As part of the restructuring, a parent company...' By the 1980s, the structure was as follows: George Weidenfeld Holdings Ltd was the group's parent company which owned: Weidenfeld (Publishers) Limited, which in turn owned six companies:

1. George Weidenfeld & Nicolson published general fiction and non-fiction (WX), academic (WY), and co-edition illustrated books (WZ);
2. Arthur Barker Limited published sports books, biographies, hobbies, music and fiction (AB);
3. Artus Publishing Company Limited published Marks & Spencer books;
4. Weidenfeld & Nicolson Jerusalem Limited sold Hebrew books in Israel;
5. Contact Publications Limited published mass-market paperbacks, jointly owned by Macdonald Futura;
6. Frances Lincoln Publishers published illustrated co-edition projects.

There was a seventh company, Weidenfeld & Nicolson (World University Library) Publishing Company Limited (WUL), which published co-editions with European publishers.

64 'Nigel was hopeful that the publisher would keep this promise...' According to Juliet and Adam Nicolson, Nigel's children, George never made good on this promise, which had long been a source of family tension. Nigel was forgiving, they said, but their mother was embittered, believing that George had stolen from the family.

CHAPTER 4 – A YOUNG GIRL'S TOUCH, 1956

66 'She was also still in grief...' Maisie Victoria Sieff died on 11 September 1951 'on the way to Paddington Hospital London' (1952 Death Register). The engagement was announced exactly three months later in *The Times*, on 11 December 1951.

68 'Marks & Spencer would no longer order books...' Weidenfeld & Nicolson would once again publish M&S books starting in 1976 under the imprint Artus Publishing with the release of *Doctor Who and the Daleks* and *Brian Moore's Book of Soccer*.

69 '"In that case," Barbara had replied...' Much of the material for this chapter comes from Barbara Skelton's *Tears Before Bedtime*, along with the Princeton W&N archive, George's *Remembering My Good Friends*, and his interview with William Shawcross.

77 'George and Barbara filed for divorce...' *Daily Herald*, 30 January 1958; *Daily Mirror*, 21 June 1958; *The Times*, 16 September 1958.

CHAPTER 5 – LOLITA, 1959

81 'The publication of *Lolita*...' *Daily News*, 6 November 1959; *Newcastle Journal*, 6 November 1959; *Western Mail*, 7 November 1959; *Birmingham Post*, 10 November 1959. Next paragraph: *New York Times*, 7 November 1959.

83 'Nabokov wrote to George...' Much of the material in this chapter come from the New York Public Library Archive 'Nabokov and W&N letters 1-50'.

84 'letter to the editor...' *The Times*, 23 January 1959.

85 'According to a journalist from *The Times*...' *The Times*, 24 January 1959.

86 'George... wrote to his author in New York...' From the New York Public Library.

91 'would only say he worked in the Home Office...' George told different versions of this story. In a speech given to the Jewish Book Council on 20 March 1973, he said the man on the phone was a 'clerk in the office of the Director of Public Prosecutions', and at the end of the call he said, 'best of luck with *Lolita*'. (GW private archive, Speeches)

CHAPTER 6 – THE GROUP, 1963

99 'In May 1963, Mary McCarthy wrote to George...' Many of the documents in this chapter are found in the Princeton W&N archive, Box 193.

100 'Typical of the press coverage...' *The Times*, 7 November 1963.

103 'extensive in Australia...' *The Age*, 5 June 1964; *Ballarat Courier*, 16 March 1964; *Melbourne Herald*, 20 March 1964.

CHAPTER 7 – HERZOG, 1965

105 'On 10 September 1960... Barley Alison...' The source for this letter and many others in this chapter: University of Chicago Library, 'Alison Barley 1959–1976', Box 4, Folder 6. The source for other letters in this chapter: Princeton W&N archive, Saul Bellow, Box 361.

109 'their offices on Bond Street...' According to an office memo dated 10 April 1964, following a desk audit, 'all personnel should be moved to Bond Street and that Albermarle Street be closed down'. (Princeton W&N archive)

109 'most of the major English publishing houses...' Yet William Collins & Sons was based in Glasgow. Penguin's headquarters were in Harmondsworth, outside of London.

110 'Many years later, George would be asked by a German journalist...' Source: *Weltwoche* interview, May 2007.

115 '*Herzog* was published in September 1964...' *New York Times*, 20 September 1964; *Herald Tribune* quoted in chapter 1, *The Life of Saul Bellow* by Zachary Leader; *The Times*, 4 February 1965; *Tatler*, 10 February 1965.

122 'Enoch Powell...' The press connected Enoch Powell's new book with his infamous speech. The *Birmingham Post* (20 July 1968), wrote that 'The House of Lords has been in the news of late so has Mr Enoch Powell', continuing, 'combine the two and you might expect an exciting polemical mixture'. While in their review, the *Illustrated London News* (17 August 1968) made a specific reference to the River Tiber.

CHAPTER 8 – ██████████,1967

130 'Fred Praeger...' In a memo summarising their meeting at his office at 111 Fourth Avenue in New York on 10 February 1965, Praeger commented that 'George has lost 45 lbs and looks not only sylph-like but also more intellectual.' (Princeton W&N archive)

131 'In a subsequent *New York Times* article...' *New York Times*, 31 December 1974.

132 'In his comment reported...' *New York Times*, 8 May 1967.

132 'Was George aware...' There is some reason to believe that George had ongoing connections with various intelligence services. In addition to his relationship with Praeger and his association with *Encounter* magazine, many of his authors had been former spies. George himself had worked for the BBC monitoring service, a hotbed of espionage and counter-espionage. He travelled easily through the dining rooms of the good and the great of Washington DC, Paris, Bonn, Vienna, Tel Aviv and Rome. He spoke many languages, was fascinated by global politics, was fiercely anti-Communist and a great supporter of the transatlantic alliance. Yet, when the *New York Observer* asked if George 'worked undercover for the Israeli government', the publisher responded that the assertion was 'untrue, ludicrous and actionable. Repeat, actionable.' (Letter sent from George to Cynthia Cotts at the *New York Observer*, 12 October 1989, GW private archive)

133 'As part of the deal...' On 23 February 1970, George wrote to Senator Benton (owner of Encyclopedia Britannica) and Frederick Praeger (owner of Frederick Prager Inc. and Phaidon Presss) suggesting that they merge their companies with the proposed name: Weidenfeld, Phaidon, Praeger. On 27 May 1970, Benton declared 'I fear we don't have a deal.' (Princeton W&N archive)

CHAPTER 9 – THE DOUBLE HELIX, 1968

138 'bad tempered and unpleasant woman...' The material in this chapter comes from the Wellcome Trust, JDW/2/3/7/5, and the Princeton W&N archive, Box 194.

139 'HARVARD VETOES NOBEL WINNERS BOOK...' *The Times*, 16 February 1968.

CHAPTER 10 – MARY QUEEN OF SCOTS, 1969

146 'Nobody expected it to be a bestseller...' Antonia Fraser told me that the one person 'who saluted it as a bestseller and thus helped to create it as such was Jonathan Aitken, writing in the *Evening Standard*, where he worked'.

148 'She looks for all the world...' *New York Times*, 4 November 1966.

149 *'Mary Queen of Scots* was published...' *The Times*, 3 May 1969; *Birmingham Post*, 17 May 1969; *Illustrated London News*, 7 June 1969; and *New York Times*, 23 November 1969.

149 'overwhelming positive attention...' Articles: *The Times*, 3 May 1969; *Birmingham Post*, 17 May 1969; *Sunday Mirror*, 18 May 1969; and *New York Times*, 23 November 1969.

151 'in every way George was a gentleman...' In her obituary for the *Guardian*, 22 January 2016, entitled 'My Hero', Antonia Fraser wrote 'George loved women and women loved him back, particularly as he had the best chat-up line in the world at his disposal: "Have you ever thought of writing a book?"'

151 'relationship with women...' In his memoir *Another Life*, Michael Korda recalled attending a fancy-dress party at George's London flat. At some point, Korda was talking to the Irish author Cornelius Ryan when they were approached by the publisher. 'Tell me,' Cornelius Ryan asked George, 'how is it that a man like you is always surrounded by beautiful women? [...] I mean, let's be frank, boyo, you're fat, you're bald, what is it they see in you?' George paused for a moment. 'My dear Connie,' he replied. 'It's very simple. You see, in certain circles, I am known...' he paused again, 'as the "Nijinsky of cunnilingus".'

151 'Princess Herzeleide von Preussen, granddaughter...' In his interview with William Shawcross on 14 June 2012, George describes visiting Munich in 1951 or 1952 and spending time with Lali Horstmann, who he had been introduced to by Harold Nicolson. George told Shawcross that Horstmann was 'a very important figure in my life'. In 1953, George would publish her book *Nothing for Tears* – the story of Berlin during the Second World War and the first three years under the Russians – which he called 'remarkable', 'a delicacy' and 'one of the best books' he ever published. While in Munich, Lali Horstmann introduced him to Princess Herzeleide von Preussen (whose first name means 'sorrow of the heart') and her husband Prince Karl Biron von Curland. During his stay, George said that he took the princess to a nightclub and 'had an affair' with her.

153 'They called him "Popeye"...' In the late 1960s, George was visiting Vladimir Nabokov at the Palace Hotel in Montreux when his 'right eye suddenly protruded out of its socket'. Nabokov was 'both horrified and amused' while the publisher was in a 'stake of shock'. Soon after, George underwent eye surgery and the protrusion never happened again. (*Remembering My Good Friends*, p. 252)

CHAPTER 11 – THE GOVERNANCE OF BRITAIN, 1976

161 'the press reported one revelation after another...' Later, it would be revealed that one of the men on the list, Joseph Kagan, was convicted of fraud. Another, Eric Miller, was investigated for fraud, during which he committed suicide.

161 'Liverpool Echo...' *Liverpool Echo*, 28 May 1976.

163 'Upon its release...' *Birmingham Post*, 21 October 1976; *Sunday People*, 24 October 1976; *Birmingham Post*, 5 November 1976.

164 'disturbing conversation with Lady Falkender...' Letter from George to his lawyer written on 12 October 1983. (GW private archive)

165 'he told one listener...' George said this to Gina Thomas, who helped edit his autobiography.

CHAPTER 12 – UNITY MITFORD: A QUEST, 1976

170 'Tony Godwin...' In 1973 he left W&N to become co-publisher at Harcourt Brace Jovanovich Inc. in New York. He died three years later following an asthma attack at the age of fifty-six. In its obituary, *The Times* would call Godwin 'The single most influential personality in British publishing since the war.' In 1976, The Tony Godwin Memorial Trust was founded in his name. It was closed in 2017.

171 '"Carlos the Jackal"...' See the *Evening Standard*, 12 February 2008, and *Daily Mirror*, 31 December 1973.

173 'On 6 January 1974...' David Pryce-Jones told me that some of the letter's contents were 'a little bit of exaggeration' and that 'I wrote as I did to re-assure George. The pressure on him was intense and it would have been understandable if he had decided not to proceed with this book.' For instance, Pryce-Jones said, 'I am certain that the meeting with Diana was in a flat in Dolphin Square [London]', and 'I did get an agreement that we would meet again, but that was all I got. There was no question of showing her a draft.'

178 'critic Clive James...' 'Sir Oswald's Whoppers', *Observer*, 11 November 1976.

179 'sent a letter to the *Spectator*...' *Spectator*, 4 December 1976.

180 'Viscount Tony Lambton... a novel...' Under the headline LAMBTON FOR THE SLAUGHTER, the *Daily Mail* on 20 March 1979 wrote: 'It is a thinly disguised roman à clef and a central character, portrayed in less than endearing terms, bears an amazing resemblance to Weidenfeld.'

181 'There was a family tree, going back to a rabbi...' On 7 January 2011, David Pryce-Jones wrote to George congratulating him on his recent honour (Knight Grand Cross of the Order of the British Empire). He said that it had 'triggered a memory' of the time George had shown him the family tree and said that he had failed his ancestors. 'With all your achievements before their eyes,' Pryce-Jones said, 'it is unquestionable that every one of that family tree would be immensely, overwhelmingly, proud of you. As are all your friends.' Writing back four days later, George said that he was 'greatly moved' by Pryce-Jones's recollection and that he much appreciated their long friendship. (DPJ to GW, GW private papers)

CHAPTER 13 – YONI: HERO OF ENTEBBE, 1979

184 'introduced by a member of the London Jewish establishment...' This was Flora Solomon, who George described as 'a great woman in my life, a mother figure'. (William Shawcross interview with GW)

192 'According to one source ...' In February 1979, *Private Eye* reported the Israelis 'went bananas' when they saw a copy of *Yoni* and there had been 'nothing to stop George Weidenfeld from publishing Hastings' preferred version of the book'. 'Instead,' the magazine continued, the publisher 'completely gave in to the Israeli objections'.

192 'As a Zionist my purpose is to secure the survival of Israel ...' This quote and others come from a series of seven interviews that William Shawcross carried out with George Weidenfeld in 2012 and 2013. 'Towards the end of his life,' says Shawcross, 'I was privileged to be given the pleasure and responsibility by GW to discuss and record his extraordinary memories.'

193 'In early June 1984 ...' Moshe Raviv wrote the letter from the Israeli Embassy. Later, Raviv would be the Israeli ambassador to the United Kingdom. (GW private archive, Speeches)

CHAPTER 14 – IN THE EYE OF THE STORM, 1982

196 'Earlier that day, 4 March 1986, the *New York Times* ...' The story about Waldheim's wartime record was first broken by the Austrian newspaper *Profil* a day before, on 3 March 1986.

198 'Albert Speer ...' Later he told Daniel Johnson, editor of *Standpoint* magazine, that 'Speer was the only one I believed in ... because of his openness, his frankness and his remorse. But now I believe he was the worst, because he was so clever.' George then added that he had been 'fooled'. (*Standpoint*, September 2009)

199 '"Professor Speer," George asked ...' Story repeated in many of his speeches. (GW personal archive)

199 'Upon its release in 1970, *Inside the Third Reich* ...' *The Times*, 12 October 1970; *New York Times*, 23 August 1970; *Jewish Chronicle*, 14 May 1971.

203 'The first reviews were lukewarm ...' *New Statesman*, 10 January 1986; *TLS*, 17 January 1986; *Sunday Telegraph*, 19 January 1986; *New York Times*, 4 March 1986; *The Times*, 6 March 1986.

209 'It tarnished his reputation ...' On 5 May 2015, despite their differences decades earlier over Kurt Waldheim, George was given the Theodor Herzl Award by the World Jewish Congress. According to the WJC, 'The award recognises outstanding individuals who work to carry forward Herzl's ideals for a safer, more tolerant world for the Jewish people.'

CHAPTER 15 – MICK JAGGER, 1985

210 'George Weidenfeld made an offer ...' 'Lord Weidenfeld has pulled off the coup of the publishing year', *New York Post*, 31 July 1982.

210 'The price on the table was $2 million ...' Material from this chapter comes from the Princeton W&N archive, Box 275, and GW private papers, Box BS12188.

214 'Civilizations of the Holy Land by Paul Johnson...' On 29 June 2009, Johnson wrote to George in the run-up to his ninetieth birthday. 'You can look back on a remarkable panorama of first-class books beautifully and successfully published, over many decades, and to know truthfully that many of them would not have been written without your ideas, enthusiasm and encouragement. I have learned that enthusiasm is the most important gift of a publisher, for writers are often diffident, confused and un-self-confident and even cowardly people. Who need a leader who will give them the courage to go on with their lovely book. You have this ennobling quality to a unique degree, and that is why you have been the greatest publisher of our times.' (GW private archive)

214 'George had recruited Falkus...' According to Robin Denniston's obituary of Falkus in the *Independent* on 31 March 1995, 'The managerial problems at Weidenfeld were not dispelled by a healthier balance-sheet. Lines of command were obscured; and strong, talented personalities distorted good management. Falkus taught himself how to manage other people and draw the best from them, by encouragement, by enabling other voices to be heard, by a willingness to let others take the limelight, which – though not always appreciated at the time – led to a period of harmonious relationships and good publishing.'

216 'three pages of interview transcripts...' The publisher John Blake claimed to possess a 75,000-word version of Mick Jagger's autobiography. This he declared to be the 'the rock'n'roll equivalent of the Dead Sea Scrolls'. (*Spectator*, 18 February 2017)

221 'It would be impossible for me to exaggerate...' Letter sent on 4 November 1983 from Michael O'Mara, deputy chairman at Weidenfeld & Nicolson, to Mick Jagger, c/o Prince Loewenstein. (GW private archive)

223 'Coleman later reported...' The *Guardian*, 24 June 2021.

224 'The project could only continue...' On 10 May 1984 a column was published in the *Daily Express* under the headline 'no drugs, no sex and no good, Mick'. The article went on to say that 'Jagger's forthcoming autobiography is, not to put too fine a point on it, dull'. An article in the *Evening Standard* on 10 November 1985 titled HALL HOLDUP FOR JAGGER BIOGRAPHY suggested that the 'great Robert Sangster–Jerry Hall imbroglio' was playing havoc with the biography.

224 'the manuscript had been formally rejected...' In the summer of 1992 the writer and broadcaster David Sweetman wrote to George suggesting that he 'reopen the Mick Jagger project'. George forwarded this to Rupert Loewenstein, who responded, on 7 July 1992, 'I shall certainly take this up with Mick, though I feel he will find that this is still two or three years too soon.' (GW private archive)

225 'Jagger told the journalist Dave Simpson...' The *Guardian*, 24 June 2021.

225 'He had been "seduced", he said, by George Weidenfeld...' BBC Radio 6 Music with Matt Everitt on Wednesday 14 April 2021, as reported in the *Daily Mail*, 15 April 2021.

226 'It was a terrible odyssey...' The experience was not so terrible that it precluded Weidenfeld & Nicolson from publishing the book *According to the Rolling Stones* by Mick Jagger and the other members of the band in 2005.

226 'there was always this sense in the transcripts that Mick was holding back, or trying not to hurt anybody's feelings...' The *Guardian*, 24 June 2021.

CHAPTER 16 – CATCHER IN THE RYE II, 1987

229 'George had first met Ann...' Material from this chapter comes from the GW papers, Box BS12152, and the Princeton W&N archive, Box 61.

229 'I can't find words to thank you...' GW to AG, 17 September 1981. (GW private archive)

233 'Robert Stone's *Outerbridge Reach*...' Herman bought this at W&N NY but did not publish it until he was at Ticknor & Fields (Houghton). (JH letter to author)

233 'at least a week a month in New York...' According to his personal diary, George spent ninety-three days in America in 1985. In total that year he spent 197 days outside of England.

234 '"Lord Big"...' *Vanity Fair*, March 1986.

236 'After the meeting...' *Manhattan, inc.*, September 1986; *Publishers Weekly*, 25 April 1986.

237 'Princess Michael of Kent...' Juliet Nicolson told me about the time Princess Michael of Kent visited their New York office for the publication of her book. 'George was "sycophantic"', Juliet said. 'To the point that he would wear a red tie because that is the one she liked best. And then later on in the day, when things got tricky, he would say, "In God's name what are we doing publishing this woman's book?" So, I mean, yes, absolutely. A chameleon. With royalty and famous people, he would certainly do just whatever was required.' She then added, 'I never could quite identify who the man was, he was so many different things. Just baffling. I have not the faintest idea who he was, not really, not at the heart of it. He was like the weather,' she continued, 'he could change not within a day but within an hour.'

241 'I don't feel I've lost at least $15 million...' Reported in Liz Smith's column, *New York Daily News*, 1989.

243 'editor of the *Sunday Telegraph*...' The *Sunday Telegraph*, 10 September 1989.

243 'The name was apparently spoofing...' Adam McQueen, who wrote a history of *Private Eye*. McQueen told me that the name Snipcock & Tweed predated the strip. He then confirmed that it was 'apparently originally spoofing W&N', but then added that later the name became 'the standard [*Private*] *Eye* publisher in any jokes pieces about books'.

245 'In a letter to a friend from Texas...' From George to Dr Lars Gustafsson, 31 October 1989. (GW private archive)

245 'To counter the rumours...' On 25 May 1990, *Publishers Weekly* reported that George Weidenfeld was 'considerably irritated' by an article in the *Sunday Correspondent* which suggested that his business partnership with Ann Getty was about to come to an end in a 'divorce... with grave implications for Weidenfeld & Nicolson London'. The publisher told *PW* that this was 'all untrue'.

246 'there were no issues between them...' *Publishing News*, 25 May 1990.

246 'As for Mrs Getty, when asked...' The *New York Times*, 22 October 1989.

246 '*The Atlantic Monthly*... purchase Grove...' Morgan Entrekin, CEO and publisher of Grove Atlantic Books, told me he was extremely grateful to Ann Getty, who remained a shareholder until her death in 2020. She could have made more money selling Grove Weidenfeld to another company, he says, as it was a 'very reasonable deal'. Because of her decision to keep the press independent, they were able to 'right the ship' and soon started having some 'good successes', with books including *Sex and the City*, *Cold Mountain* and *Black Hawk Down*.

CHAPTER 17 – REMEMBERING MY GOOD FRIENDS, 1994

248 'In speeches to the House of Lords...' George did not regularly attend the House of Lords. In 2007, for example, he was present for just nine days. (2007 annual return, GW private archive)

249 'the German ambassador in London...' Letter from George to Peter Hartmann, 14 September 1994. (GW private archive)

250 'wrote Tony Blair...' Not all his introductions were so auspicious. On 27 March 1991 the publisher wrote to his good friend Barbara Walters. 'I am very economical with "letters of introduction",' he said. 'If I have asked Ghislaine Maxwell, daughter of the legendary Robert Maxwell, to telephone you, it is because I think you will find her a most amusing and charming person.' He sent similar letters of introduction on Ghislaine Maxwell's behalf to Lally Weymouth, columnist for the *Washington Post* and daughter of the paper's owner Katharine Graham, and the fashion designer Oscar de la Renta. A month later, Maxwell wrote to George saying that she had a 'really wonderful dinner' with Lally Weymouth and would reach out to the two other contacts upon her return to New York. (Letter from Tony Blair to George Weidenfeld, 7 June 1995. Both letters, GW private archive.)

253 'Their relationship had not fully recovered...' The relationship with Ann Getty was repaired sufficiently that George and Annabelle spent part of their honeymoon with the Gettys.

259 'News of the deal broke...' The agreement was actually signed on 11 June 1992.

261 'Just as the sun was setting...' Annabelle told me that she had been brought up Catholic and had converted to Judaism prior to the wedding.

265 'Maschler... "George is the best in the country at inventing books"...' Maschler then added, sourly, 'sometimes of course, his genius overflows into inventing books which ought never to have existed', *Sunday Telegraph*, 20 February 1983.

269 'Brian MacArthur...' Letter to George Weidenfeld dated 28 November 1990. (GW private archive)

269 'editor... was "bloody awful"...' Memo written by Adrian Laing at HarperCollins to Michael Fishwick and others, 28 November 1994. Presumably the editor of *The Times* was Peter Stothard. (GW private archive)

270 'At this time, Döpfner...' Döpfner told me that he and George had met for the first time a decade earlier for thirty minutes in the publisher's flat on Chelsea Embankment. Döpfner wished to invite George to speak to the organisation of journalists he was then working for.

CHAPTER 18 – LETTERS FROM OXFORD, 2004

273 'extraordinary parties with the A-list guests...' Two of those to be invited, for instance, were Prince Andrew and his wife Sarah. On 11 May 2001, Andrew wrote to George on Buckingham Palace letterhead thanking him for lunch the previous week. He said that he had not yet made a decision about the book they discussed on the Falklands and that he would be back from a trip at the month's end after which he would let the publisher know. 'We have a great many things on our plate at the present time and this is just one of the considerations.' (GW private papers)

273 'Katharine Graham...' On 2 September 1992, Graham wrote to George asking him to take care of Eugene Robinson, one of her journalists who was about to arrive in England. 'He and his wife Avis, who is an economist, are interesting people and looking forward to London,' she wrote. 'I hope you will help them in whatever way possible.' (GW private papers)

276 'The project was over...' The fallout proved ill-tempered. The agent Michael Sissons wrote that he had never been in a situation where one of two authors wanted a book to happen and the other didn't, calling it the 'messiest situation I've ever known' and described the publishers as 'dilatory'. For his part, Ben Buchan complained of 'going around in circles'. In the end, Frank Johnson was able to keep his advance while Hugh Trevor-Roper's estate returned three quarters of his. (Princeton W&N archive)

CHAPTER 19 – OBIT, 2016

283 'Annabelle was spending more and more time with the nonagenarian pianist Menahem Pressler...' According to George's 2015 diary, Annabelle's trips that year (some related to Menahem Pressler) included: 23–26 January in Switzerland; 5–7 February; 4–12 May in Boston; 20–30 July, Verbier; 1–3 August, Oxford; 3–7 October, Germany; 17–28 October, Germany; 15–20 December (destination unclear).

286 'Mount of Olives...' Jaqui Safra offered George the burial site on the Mount of Olives which is part of a whole area for the Safra family. There is also a place next to him for Annabelle.

288 'Annabelle received hundreds of letters of condolence...' Letters to Annabelle Weidenfeld from Angela Merkel, 21 January 2016, and Henry Kissinger, 27 June 2016 (AW private papers)

290 'they would rub their nose...' Annabelle told me that 'It all sprang from very early on in our relationship when George told me he could tell if I was happy or not by the position of my nose... up or down!!'

EPILOGUE

291 'During his lifetime, George was showered with awards...' These included: knighthood (1969); peerage (1976); honorary PhD, Ben-Gurion University (1984); Golden Knight's Cross with Star, Austria (1989); Chevalier, Légion d'Honneur, France (1990); German Knight's Commander's Cross (Badge & Star) of the Order of Merit, Germany (1991); honorary Senator of Rheinische Friedrich-Wilhelms-Universität, Germany (1996); honorary degree and magister, Diplomatic College, Vienna (1999); honorary Fellow of King's College London (2005); Italian Grand Office of the Order of Merit (2005); Teddy Kollek Life Achievement Award, Israel (2009); degree of Doctor of Letters, honoris causa, Oxford University (2010); Knight Grand Cross of the Order of the British Empire (2010); Bene Merito Honorary Distinction, Poland (2011).

291 'Weidenfeld-Hoffmann scholarships...' The scholarships were funded by the wealthy businessman André Hoffmann. He told me George 'had a very acute understanding of humans and humanity'; adding that George 'understood brilliantly today's main geopolitical issue i.e. the conflict between autocracy and democracy. In so doing he predicted Russia's war in Ukraine. Our joint conclusion was that strong leadership was needed for the planet and this was the origin of the Weidenfeld-Hoffmann Trust at Oxford university, which united us and makes me to this day exceptionally proud.'

292 'Leonard Blavatnik...' In a letter to George of 11 January 2011, congratulating him on receiving the Knight Grand Cross of the Order of the British Empire, Blavatnik wrote: 'I was especially delighted to see that No. 10 identified your efforts on behalf of the School of Government [...] I personally – as you know – will always owe you a special debt of gratitude for being both the spiritual founder and then the catalyst.' (GW private archive) Blavatnik told me that he first met the publisher around 2004 at a restaurant in London (George ate schnitzel). He was 'expecting an old man,' he said; instead 'George was full of energy and ideas.' Blavatnik added that 'we became quite close. He continued, 'George was not religious. Everything he did, he did for Israel and Jewish people, in the last decade of his life.'

BIBLIOGRAPHY

GEORGE WEIDENFELD

Amiel, Barbara, *Friends and Enemies: A Memoir* (Penguin Random House, 2020)
Curtis, John, ed., *Fifty Years of Publishing* (Weidenfeld & Nicolson, 1999)
Evans, Richard, *Eric Hobsbawm: A Life in History* (Little, Brown, 2019)
Gekoski, Rick, *Guarded by Dragons: Encounters with Rare Books and Rare People* (Constable, 2021)
Gross, Miriam, *An Almost English Life* (Short Books, 2012)
Holden, Anthony, *Based on a True Story* (Simon & Schuster, 2021)
Misc, *George Weidenfeld: A Seventieth Birthday Book* (private publication)
Nicolson, Harold, *Diaries and Letters 1930–1964, Condensed Edition* (HarperCollins, 1996)
Nicolson, Nigel, *Long Life: Memoirs* (Weidenfeld & Nicolson, 1997)
Nicolson, Nigel, *Portrait of a Marriage* (Weidenfeld & Nicolson, 1973)
Nicolson, Nigel, *Portrait of a Marriage – Illustrated Edition* (Weidenfeld & Nicolson, 1973)
Sington, Derrick, and Arthur Weidenfeld, *The Goebbels Experiment* (Yale, 1943)
Weidenfeld, George, *Remembering My Good Friends* (HarperCollins, 1995)

PUBLISHING

Abel, Richard, and Gordon Graham, *Immigrant Publishers* (Transaction, 2009)
Athill, Diana, *Stet: An Editor's Life* (Granta, 2000)
Attallah, Naim, *Memories: The Charms and Follies of a Lifetime's Publishing* (Quercus, 2020)

Caro, Robert, *Working: Researching, Interviewing, Writing* (Bodley Head, 2019)

Cerf, Bennett, *At Random: The Reminiscences of Bennet Cerf* (Random House, 1997)

Haycraft, Colin, *Maverick Publisher* (Duckworth, 1995)

Korda, Michael, *Another Life: A Memoir of Other People* (Dell Publishing, 2000)

Lee, Hermione, *Virginia Woolf* (Vintage, 1997)

Lewis, Jeremy, *Kindred Spirits: Adrift in Literary London* (Faber & Faber, 1995)

Lewis, Jeremy, *Penguin Special: The Life and Times of Allen Lane* (Penguin, 2005)

Lewis, Jeremy, *Grub Street Irregular: Scenes from Literary Life* (Harper Press, 2008)

Lourie, Alena and Norman, *Full Circle: A Family Memoir* (self-published, 2016)

Maschler, Tom, *Publisher* (Picador, 2005)

Rosenthal, Michael, *Barney: Grove Press and Barney Rosset* (Arcade, 2017)

Rosset, Barney, *Rosset* (OR, 2019)

Unwin, Stanley, *The Truth About Publishing* (George Allen & Unwin, 1960)

The following headings refer to the chapter titles. Books listed beneath each chapter title appear in the order in which they are referenced in the text.

THE HEDGEHOG AND THE FOX

Haldane, Charlotte, *Truth Will Out* (Weidenfeld & Nicolson, 1949)

Berlin, Isaiah, *The Hedgehog and the Fox* (Weidenfeld & Nicolson, 1953)

Ignatieff, Michael, *Isaiah Berlin* (Henry Holt, 1998)

Berlin, Isaiah, *Letters 1928–1946* (Cambridge, 2004)

Berlin, Isaiah, *Enlightening: Letters 1946–1960* (Chatto & Windus, 2009)

Berlin, Isaiah, *Building: Letters 1960–1975* (Chatto & Windus, 2013)

Berlin, Isaiah, *Affirming: Letters 1975–1997* (Chatto & Windus, 2015)

LOLITA

Nabokov, Vladimir, *Lolita* (Weidenfeld & Nicolson, 1955)

Nabokov, Vladimir, *The Annotated Lolita* (Penguin, 1970)

Connolly, Julian, *A Reader's Guide to Nabokov's Lolita* (Academic Studies Press, 2009)
Quigley, Jenny Minton, *Lolita in the Afterlife* (Vintage, 2021)

A YOUNG GIRL'S TOUCH

Skelton, Barbara, *A Young Girl's Touch: A Novel* (Weidenfeld & Nicolson, 1956)
Skelton, Barbara, *Weep No More* (Hamish Hamilton, 1989)
Skelton, Barbara, *Tears Before Bedtime* (Hamish Hamilton, 1989)

MARY QUEEN OF SCOTS

Fraser, Antonia, *My History: A Memoir of Growing Up* (Weidenfeld & Nicolson, 2015)
Fraser, Antonia, *Our Israeli Diary* (Oneworld, 2017)

THE GROUP

McCarthy, Mary, *The Group* (Weidenfeld & Nicolson, 1963)

HERZOG

Bellow, Saul, *Herzog* (Weidenfeld & Nicolson, 1965)
Bellow, Saul, *Mr Sammler's Planet* (Weidenfeld & Nicolson, 1970)
Atlas, James, *Bellow: A Biography* (Random House, 2000)
Leader, Zachary, *The Life of Saul Bellow: Love and Strife 1965–2005* (Knopf, 2018)

THE DOUBLE HELIX

Sayre, Anne, *Rosalind Franklin and DNA* (Norton, 1975)
Maddox, Brenda, *Rosalind Franklin: The Dark Lady of DNA* (HarperCollins, 2003)
Watson, James, *The Double Helix* (Weidenfeld & Nicolson, 1968)

███████

Stonor Saunders, Frances, *Who Paid the Piper: The CIA and the Cultural Cold War* (Granta, 1999)

THE GOVERNANCE OF BRITAIN

Falkender, Marcia, *Inside Number 10* (Weidenfeld & Nicolson, 1972)
Wilson, Harold, *The Governance of Britain* (Weidenfeld & Nicolson, 1976)

UNITY MITFORD

Pryce-Jones, David, *Unity Mitford: A Quest* (Weidenfeld & Nicolson, 1976)
Lambton, Anthony, *Elizabeth and Alexander* (Quartet, 1985)
Attallah, Naim, *Memories* (Quartet, 2007)

YONI

Hastings, Max, *Yoni: Hero of Entebbe* (Weidenfeld & Nicolson, 1979)
Eban, Abba, *The New Diplomacy* (Weidenfeld & Nicolson, 1983)
Silver, Eric, *Begin: A Biography* (Weidenfeld & Nicolson, 1984)
Hastings, Max, *Going to the Wars* (Macmillan, 2000)
Pfeffer, Anshel, *Bibi: The Turbulent Life and Times of Benjamin Netanyahu* (C. Hurst & Co., 2018)

IN THE EYE OF THE STORM

Hoess, Rudolf, *Commandant of Auschwitz* (Weidenfeld & Nicolson, 2000)
Speer, Albert, *Inside the Third Reich* (Weidenfeld & Nicolson, 1969)
Waldheim, Kurt, *In the Eye of the Storm* (Weidenfeld & Nicolson, 1986)
Rosenbaum, Eli, *Betrayal: The Untold Story of Kurt Waldheim* (St Martin's Press, 1993)
Sereny, Gitta, *Albert Speer: His Battle with Truth* (Macmillan, 1995)

MICK JAGGER

Sandford, Christopher, *Mick Jagger: Primitive Cool* (Victor Gollancz, 1993)
Mars-Jones, Adam, *Blind Bitter Happiness* (Chatto & Windus, 1997)

LETTERS FROM OXFORD

Graham, Katharine, *Personal History* (Weidenfeld & Nicolson, 1997)
Trevor-Roper, Hugh, *Letters from Oxford: Hugh Trevor-Roper to Bernard Berenson* (Weidenfeld & Nicolson, 2004)

ACKNOWLEDGEMENTS

To write this book, I was fortunate as the first researcher to be given access to the Weidenfeld & Nicolson corporate archive in Princeton University (403 boxes), along with George Weidenfeld's private papers in London (76 boxes). Faced with more than 750,000 pages, I spent many months going through the documents. In these, I came across forty years of the publisher's diaries (1975–2015), along with 120 speeches (from the House of Lords to Arianna Huffington's wedding in which he called her 'The gangly girl from Athens') and hundreds of corporate memos – from which photocopy machine to lease to personnel contracts to the organising of book shipments to the Frankfurt Book Fair. Also, buried deep amid the files, I found extraordinary letters between the publisher and some of literature's greatest English, American and French authors – Bellow, Capote, O'Brien, Drabble, de Beauvoir, Lévi-Strauss – and, tantalisingly, a scattering of unpublished manuscripts. So, I would like to thank the staff of the Special Collections at Firestone Library, Princeton University, who hosted me for a month and who gave me access to their record: 'Weidenfeld & Nicolson records 1917–2012 (mostly 1960–2005)'. I am also extremely grateful to Brit Felmberg, who helped me gain access to George's private papers that were housed for so many years at Crown Records in Bow, London. In addition, I wish to thank Weidenfeld & Nicolson for granting me permission to look through and quote from these documents.

While writing this book I relied on the help of numerous other archives that generously allowed me to review their papers, including: University of Chicago (Saul Bellow); University of Chicago (Barley Alison); Yale University (David Pryce-Jones and Henry Kissinger); Bodleian Library, Oxford University (Isaiah Berlin); United Nations (Kurt Waldheim); Library of Congress (Vladimir Nabokov archive); St John's College,

University of Cambridge (Cecil Beaton); Archives and Special Collections, Vassar College Library (Mary McCarthy); Victoria & Albert Museum archive (George Weidenfeld); Austrian State Archive, the Vienna Archive and Vienna's Jewish Archive (Arthur George, Rosa and Max Weidenfeld); York University archive (George Weidenfeld). Looking through these archives, I was also assisted by various experts, archivists and translators including Rosl Merdinger in Austria, Christoph Partsch and John Owen in Germany, and Sahar Seidl and Alastair Harden (*gaudeamus igitur*) in the UK.

Thank you to the authors and literary estates who gave permission to use their letters and writings: Barbara Amiel; Isaiah Berlin letters by permission of the Trustees of the Isaiah Berlin Literary Trust; Saul Bellow (The Wylie Agency); Henry Kissinger (The Wylie Agency); Mary McCarthy by permission of The Mary McCarthy Literary Trust; © Iris Murdoch used by permission of Curtis Brown Group Ltd; Vladimir Nabokov (The Wylie Agency); Harold Nicolson and Vita Sackville-West writings by permission of Juliet Nicolson; Nigel Nicolson by permission of Adam Nicolson; *Private Eye* magazine (www.private-eye.co.uk); Hugh Trevor-Roper by permission of © The Literary Estate of Lord Dacre of Glanton; James Watson letters by permission of James D. Wellcome Collection; George Weidenfeld's books, letters, speeches, articles and other copyright material by permission of Annabelle Weidenfeld and Laura Barnett.

During my research, I spoke with over 120 colleagues, friends, family members and other acquaintances of George Weidenfeld. There are too many to name here, but I do wish to extend my appreciation to some key individuals who not only shared their memories but helped me with my research, including: Rowan Barnett, Len Blavatnik, Tom Bower, Ben Buchan, Georgina Capel, Anthony Cheetham, Ruth Cheshin, Peter Conradi, Mary Dearborn, Mathias Döpfner, Malcolm Edwards, Gila Falkus, Brit Felmberg, Antonia Fraser, Flora Fraser, Rick Gekoski, Victoria Glendinning, Francis Gotto, Michael Gove, Martin Green, Miriam Gross, Henry Hardy, Belinda Harley, David and Dorothy Hartman, Sasha Havlicek, Alexandra Henderson, John Herman, Julia Hobsbawm, André Hoffmann, Anthony Holden, Aldine Honey, Allegra Huston, Pat Kinsman, Tzipi Livni, Jonathan Lourie, Alexandra MacCormick, Michael Maclay, Avishai Margalit, Adam Nicolson, Juliet Nicolson, Rebecca Nicolson,

Vanessa Nicolson, Michael Pakenham, Diana Phipps, David Pryce-Jones, Hella Pick, Mark Pottle, Ron Prosor, Gideon Reuveni, Gloria Richardson, Michael Rosenthal, Astrid Rosset, Hannah Rothschild, Stephan Sattler, Constance Sayre, Anne Sebba, Andrea Seibel, Don Skemer, Sally Strahan, Gina Thomas, Vanessa Thomas, Claire Tomalin and Gully Wells. And, importantly, to Hella Pick, who first suggested my name to Alan Samson to write this book and who has provided invaluable support during this project and, in turn, to Alan for opening so many doors and providing steady wisdom.

In particular, I am hugely grateful to George's daughter Laura Barnett for all her careful help and remembrances, and for opening up her family archive, including letters, photographs, newspaper cuttings and many other precious artefacts. As well as George's wife Annabelle Weidenfeld, whom I thank for her support and for so generously sharing her memories and photographs.

To my early readers: Anna Baring, Lucy Baring, Zam Baring, Niall Barton, Amanda Harding, Kate Harding, Lynn Medford and Amelia Wooldridge, thank you as always.

Thank you also to the team at Weidenfeld & Nicolson, in particular my editor Jenny Lord who guided this project with grace and wisdom, Jo Roberts-Miller for editorial assistance, Hannah Cox for production, Natalie Dawkins for picture research, Elizabeth Allen for publicity, Tom Nobel for marketing and Chevonne Elbourne for the fabulous cover design. And Sarah Chalfant, James Pullen and Claire Devine of The Wylie Agency for their constant support.

Finally, thanks to my wife Debora, who inspires me every day, and my daughter Sam, who is just starting out in publishing – which, as George would say, is a truly noble profession.

INDEX

Abe, Kōbō 122
Abraham, William Emmanuel 122
Ackroyd, Peter 241
Aitken, Jonathan 301
Alison, Barley 96, 97, 99–100, 101, 104, 105,
  106–7, 108, 111, 112, 113–14, 116, 117,
  119–20, 123–4, 180
Amiel, Barbara 152, 267
Amis, Martin 241
Andrew, Prince 308
anti-Semitism 18, 26, 46, 56, 126, 157, 164,
  169, 172, 176, 178, 179, 180, 268, 289
Answer, The, Kurt Waldheim 208
Applebaum, Anne 289
Aron, Raymond 34, 130, 131
Arthur Barker Ltd 299
Artus Publishing 299
Asimov, Isaac 59
Atallah, Naim 181
Atheneum Books 140
Athill, Diana 42, 65
Austria 7–24
  Anschluss (1938) 21–2, 26, 130, 266
  and the Holocaust 39–41, 206, 208–9
  Waldheim Affair 206–8
A World Restored, Henry Kissinger 76–7
Axel Springer 272, 294–5, 296
Ayer, A.J. 158, 214
A Young Girl's Touch, Barbara Skelton 69,
  71–2, 75

Bantam Books 219, 222, 224, 226
Barak, Ehud 187, 189
Barenboim, Daniel 281, 285
Barnett, Laura (née Weidenfeld: GW's
  daughter) 67, 68, 78–9, 127, 129, 167,
  171, 172, 269–70, 282, 285, 286
Barnett, Rowan (GW's grandson) 285, 286,
  293–4
Barrington, Patrick 62–3, 298
Barwich, Heinz 130, 131

BBC 27, 29–31, 32–3, 34, 41
Beales, Lance 41, 42
Beaton, Cecil 61, 129
Beauvoir, Simone de 118
Beckett, Samuel 116, 231, 236, 246
Beevor, Antony 294
Begley, Adam 244–5
Bellow, Saul 105–8, *108*, 111, 114–16, 117,
  118–22, 123–4, 294
Ben-Gurion, David 184, 195
Bennett, Daphne 239
Bentley, James 238
Berenson, Bernard 277
Berger, John 170
Berlin, Isaiah 49, 53–4, *54*, 60–1, 85, 129, 132,
  199, 252, 261, *262*
Bertelsmann 257, 272
Bessie, Simon Michael 140, 243
Bevin, Ernest 43
Black, Conrad 267
Blair, Tony 250
Blavatnik, Leonard 282, 292, 309
Blunden, Edmund 34
Bodley Head 47, 109, 257
Bonham Carter, Violet 51
Booker Prize 170
Borges, Jorge Luis 116
Bormann, Martin 198
Boyce, Max 214
Braden, Thomas W. 131–2
Bragg, Melvyn 178, 289
British publishing industry
  libel and copyright issues 137–40
  literary agents 36, 110, 125, 147
  new generation of publishers 109–10
  obscenity laws and 80–2, 83–4, 86, 87–8,
    89, 93–4
  paperback publishing 117
  post-war 47, 109, 110
  publisher–printer partnership 88
  readers' reports 96

serialisation 269
submission of books to publishers 96–7
Bruce, David 127
Buchan, Ben 275, 277–8, 279, 308
Burroughs, William 94, 230, 236
Bush, George H.W. 159–60

cancel culture 5, 295
Capote, Truman 3
Carter-Ruck, Peter 164
Castlereagh, Viscount 77
Catcher in the Rye, J. D. Salinger 227, 246–7
celebrity memoirs 214, 215–16
Cerf, Bennett 82
Charles, Prince of Wales (Charles III) 214
Chatwin, Bruce 264
Cheetham, Anthony 256, 258, 259, 273
Cheshin, Ruth 194
Churchill, Winston 31, 34, 128
CIA (Central Intelligence Agency) 131–2,
    133, 159, 160
Clay, Richard 88
Cleave, Maureen 211
Cohen, Sir John 172
Coleman, Barry 223, 226
Collins 47, 59, 108, 110, 257
Collins, Norman 34
Compton-Burnett, Ivy 116
Connell, Brian 202, 205
Connolly, Cyril 46, 69, 70–1, 73, 74, 99, 152
Contact Books Ltd 42–3, 44, 47, 157, 298
Contact magazine 41–4, 45–7
Conversations with George Weidenfeld,
    William Shawcross 282
Crawford, Joan 214
Crick, Francis 135, 137, 138, 139, 140, 141, 142,
    144, 145
Crossman, Richard 34, 43, 51, 158
Crow, Juliana 52
Crowned in a Far Country, Princess Michael
    of Kent 237–40
Curtis, John 188–9, 190–1, 212, 221, 259
Curtis Brown 147

Davenport, Nicholas 47
Davenport, Olga 47
Davenport-Hines, Richard 277, 279
David Higham Associates 147
Davis, Douglas 194
Dayan, Moshe 3, 184, 184
Delacorte Press 148, 149
Delfont, Bernard 161
Deutsch, André 41, 109, 110, 135, 256, 264

Devonshire, Deborah, Duchess of (née
    Mitford) 169, 176, 177
Dial Press 190, 192
Didion, Joan 3, 214
DNA structure, discovery of see Watson,
    James, Double Helix
Domingo, Placido 236
Dönitz, Carl 198
Döpfner, Mathias 270–1, 271, 284, 285, 286,
    289, 294–6, 308
Double Helix, The, James Watson 3, 134–45,
    143, 294
Drabble, Margaret 3, 96, 129, 170

Eban, Abba 184, 194
Eisenstein, Laura (GW's grandmother) 8,
    28, 29, 32, 38–9, 40, 40, 209, 266
Elizabeth II, Queen 187, 291
Empson, William 34
Encounter magazine 131–3
Encyclopedia Britannica 133, 211
Entebbe airport raid 182–3, 186, 187
Entrekin, Morgan 307
E.P. Dutton 256–7
Epstein, Joseph 122
Eshkol, Levi 193
European Economic Community (EEC)
    158, 159
Evans, Dwye 104

Falkus, Christopher 214–15, 305
Falkus, Gila 152
Farrell, J.G. 170, 294
fascism 168, 171, 178, 197
Felmberg, Brit 273, 287
Field, Peggy 161
Fishwick, Michael 265, 266
Fleming, Ian 75
Flick, Donatella and Gerd Rudolf 261
Flynn, Gillian 294
Forbes, Alastair 178–9, 267
Forsyth, Alastair 239
Frances Lincoln 299
Frankfurt Book Fair 255–6
Franklin, Rosalind 138, 144–5
Fraser, Antonia (née Pakenham) 3, 55, 56–7,
    70, 146–51, 150, 215, 268, 289, 298, 302
Fraser, Hugh 70, 146, 177
freedom of speech 3, 98, 102, 180, 231, 279
Freud, Caroline 69
Freud, Lucien 69
Freud, Sigmund 14
Friedman, Ina 191

Gaarder, Jostein 294
Gallimard 112, 116
García Márquez, Gabriel 264
Gaulle, Charles de 34, 170
Gazit, Yona 191
George Weidenfeld & Nicolson Ltd *see*
    Weidenfeld & Nicolson Ltd
German reunification 248–9, 253
Getty, Ann 1, 2, 227–8, *228*, 229, 230, 231,
    232, 233–4, 235, 236, 240, 241, 242,
    244–5, 246, 247, 252, 253–4, 259, 307
    investor in GW's publishing ventures 1,
    227, 230, 232, 241, 242, 254
Getty, Gordon 1, 229, 234
Gilbert, Martin 3, 194
Ginsberg, Allen 231, 236, 246
Glass, Eric 147
Glendinning, Victoria 153, 262–3
Godwin, Tony 149, 170, 303
Goebbels Experiment, The, Derrick Sington
    and Arthur Weidenfeld 34–8
Goethe, Johann Wolfgang von 50, 52
Goldsmith, James 161
Gombrowicz, Witold Marian 116
Gordon Walker, Patrick 34
Gorky, Maxim 50
Gove, Michael 281–2, 289, 308–9
Governance of Britain, The, Harold Wilson
    162–3
Grade, Lew 155, 161
Graham, Katharine 243, 273–4, 308
Green, Dan 227, 228, 233, 235–6, 239, 242
Greene, Graham 80, 109
Greene & Heaton 147
Gross, John 116, 178
Group, The, Mary McCarthy 3, 95–104, 110,
    265, 294
Grove Press 112, 116, 230–2, 234–7, 242
Grove Weidenfeld 242, 245–6, 247
Guinzburg, Thomas 112–3

Hachette 5, 257, 281
Haffner, Sebastian 43
Haines, Joe 161
Haldane, Charlotte 50, 52
Hamilton, Hamish 51
Hamlyn, Paul 109, 257
Hamshere, Cyril 122
HarperCollins 257, 263, 265, 267, 269
Harvard University Press 135, 137, 138, 139
Harwood, Ronald 289
Hastings, Hubert de Cronin 41
Hastings, Max 182, 183, 185–7, 192–3, 194, 195
Hatry, Clarence 44

Haydn, Hiram 140
Hayward, Brooke 221, 222–3
Heath, A.M. 147
Heath, Edward 83, 164, 243
Hecht, Ernest 109
Hedgehog and the Fox, The, Isaiah Berlin
    57–9, 61
Heinemann 47, 59, 95, 104, 108, 165, 257
Heinz, Drue 261
Heller, Joseph 264
Hellman, Lillian 105
Henderson, Alexandra 292, 293
Herman, John 227, 233, 242, 247
Herzl, Theodor 19, 184
Herzog, Isaac 289
Herzog, Saul Bellow 104, 108, 111–117, 120, 121
Hitchens, Christopher 267
Hitler, Adolf 18, 33, 59, 169, 173, *174*, 198, 199,
    274, 275
Hobsbawm, Eric 125
Hoess, Rudolf 198
Hoettl, Wilhelm 59
Hoffman, André 309
Holden, Anthony 211, 214
Holocaust 26, 39–41, 206, 208–9
Honey, Aldin 151
Horowitz, Isaiah Abraham 12–13
Horstmann, Lali 302
Huffington, Arianna 1, *228*, 314
Hughes, Emrys 84
Hunt, Howard 131

Inside the Third Reich, Albert Speer 199–200
In the Eye of the Storm, Kurt Waldheim
    196–7, 206
Isaacs, Rufus 183
Israel 182–4, 186–7, 191, 193–4, 251, 261–2,
    286–7

Jagger, Mick 210–13, *213*, 217–26, 229, 305
James, Clive 178
James Hanley, *Boy* 82
Jenkins, Roy 81, 91
John, Augustus 44
John Murray 36–7, 47, 59, 108, 110, 257
John Paul II, Pope 243, *244*, 281
Johnson, Frank 275, 276, 308
Johnson, Lady Bird 128
Johnson, Lyndon B. 3, 128
Johnson, Paul 214, 304–5
Jonathan Cape 109, 110, 198, 257, 264, 265

Kagan, Joseph 155, 302
Kaufman, Gerald 268

Kerouac, Jack 105, 231
Keswick, Henry and Tessa 251–2
Kinsman, Pat 152, 258, 260, 273, 283, 284, 288
Kissinger, Henry 1, 3, 76–7, 214, 242–3, 288
Knopf, Alfred A. 140
Koestler, Arthur 43
Kohl, Helmut 248–9, 250, *250*
Kollek, Teddy 129, 184, 194, 199, 207–8, 231, 251, 261, 262
Korda, Michael 302
Kundera, Milan 241
Kurtz, Harold 238

Lady Chatterley's Lover, D.H. Lawrence 81–2, 93, 230
Lambton, Viscount 176, 179, 180–1, 303
Lane, Allen 41, 48, 82, 85, 264
Laqueur, Walter 241
Laski, Harold 41
Lasky, Melvin 132, 133, 158
Lavender List affair 161, 164, 165
Lebowitz, Joyce 138, 139
Leech, Gerald 143
Leland, Marc 230, 235, 242
Letters From Oxford, Hugh Trevor-Roper 277–9
Lévi-Strauss, Claude 125
Levin, Bernard 2
Lewis, Damian 282
Life, Keith Richards 3
Litvinoff, Barnet 130, 131
Loewenstein, Prince Rupert 211, 221, 305
Lohr, Alexander 196
Lolita, Vladimir Nabokov 3, 79, 80–1, 82–94, *90*, 98, 110, 265, 294
Longford, Lady Elizabeth (Elizabeth Pakenham) 55, 146–7, 149, 150, *150*, 171
Longford, Lord 165
Long Life, Nigel Nicolson 276
Lourie, Jonathan 195, 272

MacArthur, Brian 269
Macaulay, Rose 51
McCarthy, Mary 95, *98*, 110, 116, 117, 118, 119, 128, 129, 132
MacCormick, Alexandra 153–4, 202, 203, 204–5, 208, 215–16
McElvoy, Anne 289
McEwan, Ian 241
MacLennan, Bud 222, 256
Macmillan, Harold 46
McQueen, Adam 306
Maddox, Brenda 144

Maddox, John 141
Mailer, Norman 3, 170
Major, John 269
Malcolm X 231, 246
Mandelson, Peter 289
Man in the Middle, Kurt Waldheim 202–5
Manningham-Buller, Reginald 83
Marecco, Anthony 62
Margaret, Princess 215–16
Marks, Sir Simon 51
Mars-Jones, Adam 211
Martin, Kingsley 43
Mary Queen of Scots, Annabelle Fraser 146, 147–50
Maschler, Tom 109, 121, 198, 264–5, 307
   see also Jonathan Cape
Maugham, W. Somerset 51
Maxwell, Ghislaine 307
Maxwell, Robert 109, 256
Mayer, Peter 264, 265, 282
Mazrui, Ali Al'amin 122
Meir, Golda 184
Merkel, Angela 288
Metternich, Klemens von 76, 77
Michael Joseph 162, 186
Michael of Kent, Princess 306
Miller, Arthur 105, 241
Miller, Eric 302
Miller, Henry 3, 94, 108, 125, 230, 246
Mishima, Yushio 116
Mitford, Jessica 169, 173
Mitford, Nancy 169, 171
Mitford, Pamela 169, 177
Mitford, Unity 168, 169, 173–81, *174*
Montefiore, Simon Sebag 294
Moore, Charles 289
Moore, Henry 158
Mortimer, Raymond 46, 51
Mosley, Diana, Lady (née Mitford) 168–9, 173, 175, 177
Mosley, Sir Oswald 168–9, 173, 175, 178
Mr Sammler's Planet, Saul Bellow 121–2, 123
Munro, D.H. 102
Murdoch, Iris 85, 86, 100
Murdoch, Rupert 243, 257, 259, 263
Murrow, Ed 43
Mussolini, Benito 50, 198

Nabokov, Vladimir 87, 90–1, 95, 128, 129, 187–8, 214, 302
Nazism 18, 19–20, 26, 27, 35, 41, 59, 168, 169, 171, 174, 176, 183, 196, 198, 293
Neil, Andrew 224
Netanyahu, Benzion 185–6, 189

Netanyahu, Benjamin 'Bibi' 186, 189, 190, 281
Netanyahu, Yonathan ('Yoni') 183, 185,
    188–92
Newman, Nick 243–4
Nicolson, Adam 299
Nicolson, Benedict 47, 63
Nicolson, Harold 45–6, 51, 80, 184, 241
Nicolson, Juliet 1–2, 227, 239, 306
Nicolson, Nigel 44–7, 45, 51, 62, 63–4, 66, 67,
    80, 82, 161–2, 243, 276, 299
  co-founds Weidenfeld & Nicolson 46–7,
    48
  death of 276
  Lolita affair 83–4, 85, 86–7, 90, 91, 93
  meets GW 44–6
  member of parliament 51, 83–4, 85, 87
Nicolson, Vanessa 153
Norman, Philip 211
Nuremberg Trials 41, 45, 62

O'Brien, Edna 3, 129, 158, 170
obscenity laws 80–2, 83–4, 86, 87–8, 89,
    93–4
Olympia Press 80
Orion Publishing Group 256, 258–9, 272,
    273, 281
Orwell, George 34, 43, 44, 51, 95
Orwell, Sonia 56–7, 95, 105
Osborne, George 282
Owen, David 289

Palestinian Liberation Organisation 171
Payson, Sandra (then Meyer; GW's 3rd wife)
    126–30, *127*, 155, 230, 260
Penguin Books 41, 47, 93, 108, 117, 120–1,
    149, 246, 257, 265
Penguin Random House 257
Peres, Shimon 183, 184, 194–5, 261, 282, 289
Personal History, Katharine Graham 273–4
Phillips, Melanie 288
Phipps Sternberg, Diana 126, 152
Pick, Hella 151, 282
Powell, Enoch 122–3, 300–1
Powell, Jonathan 282
Praeger, Frederick 130–1, 132, 133, 211, 230
Pressler, Menahem 283, 284, 289
Priestley, J.B. 106
Pritchett, V.S. 85, 91
Private Eye 163, 243–4, 304
Prix Formentor 108, 112, 113, 116–17
Prosor, Ron 193, 194
Pryce-Jones, Alan 46, 85
Pryce-Jones, David 129–30, 156, 167, 168,
    169–70, 173–6, 178, 181, 287–8, 289, 303

publishing industry
  bestseller lists 52–3
  mergers and consolidations 256–7
  New York publishing scene 228–9
  reputational damage 5
  see also British publishing industry
Pulitzer Prize 123, 274
Pusey, Nathan 138, 139

Quennell, Peter 51, 52, 85

Rabin, Yitzhak 184, 194
Random House 59, 82, 228, 246, 256, 257
Raviv, Moshe 304
Reed International 253, 257
Reinhardt, Max 109
Remembering My Good Friends (GW
    autobiography) 262, 263, 265–70
Renner, Karl 17
Ribbentrop, Joachim von 198
Richards, Keith 217, 294
Richardson, Gloria 50, 55, 56
Roberts, Kenny 223
Robinson, Eugene 308
Rosenfeld, André 130
Rosenthal, Tom 179–80
Rosset, Barney 230, 231, 235–7, 246
Rothschild, Edmund de 193
Rubinstein, Arthur 252
Rushdie, Salman 241
Ryan, Cornelius 302
Ryiah, Arthur 101
Ryle, John 211, 212–13, 217–25

Sacher, Harry 52
Sachs, Jonathan 287
Sackville-West, Vita 46, 47, 63, 80, 153
Safra, Jaqui 308
Salinger, J.D. 227–8, 246–7
Samson, Alan 281, 282, 288
Sanchez, Ilich Ramirez (Carlos the Jackal)
    171
Sanders, Tobi 224
Sansom, William 43
Saramago, José 241
Sartre, Jean-Paul 118
Satanic Verses, The, Salman Rushdie 265
Sayers, Connie 151–2
Sayre, Anne 144
Schacht, Hjalmar 50, 198
Schiele, Egon 167
Schlink, Bernard 294
Seaver, Dick 237
Sebba, Anne 289

Secker & Warburg 123, 179
Second World War 33-4, 39-41, 196-7
  Blitz 33
  declaration of 30-1
  end of 39
  Holocaust 26, 39-41, 206, 208-9
  Nazism *see* Nazism
  UK internment 31-2
Seth, Vikram 3, 294
Shamir, Yitzhak 249
Shand, James 89, 92
Shaw, George Bernard 44
Shawcross, William 192, 302, 304
Shelley, David 281
Shrimsley, Anthony 130
Sieff, Israel 51
Sieff, Jane (GW's 1st wife) 65-7, *66*, 68, 78,
  260, 278
Sieff, Marcus 193, 199, 261
Sieff, Teddy 65, 171-2, 230
Simon & Schuster 5, 219, 228, 233, 246
Sington, Derrick 35-6, 37
Sinowatz, Fred 206
Sissons, Michael 308
Sitwell, Edith 132
Skelton, Barbara (then Connolly: GW's 2nd
  wife) 69-76, *71*, 77-8, 152, 260
Snow, C.P. 158
Snowdon, Lord (Antony Armstrong-Jones)
  214, 216
Solomon, Flora 303
Sontag, Susan 241
Speer, Albert 198, 199-201, 304
Spender, Stephen 41, 85, 106, 129, 132, 133, 158
Stone, Robert 233
Stothard, Peter 307
Straus, Roger 245, 264
Szereszewski, Robert 130

Tanner, Tony 112
Thatcher, Margaret 155, 269
Thomas, Gina 263, 266, 267, 268, 283-4, 285
Thompson, Nicholas 55, 56, 62, 88, 99, 135,
  139, 140, 143
Tilling, Thomas 109
Tomalin, Clare 3
Topolski, Feliks 34, 57, 129, 273, 298
Toynbee, Arnold 43
Toynbee, Philip 41-2, 44
Trevor-Roper, Hugh 59, 132, 274-6, 308
Trump, Donald 1, 2

Updike, John 241
Ulysses, James Joyce 82

Unity Mitford: A Quest, David Pryce-Jones
  168, 170-1, 173-81, 294

Vaizey, Ed 289
Vargas Lhosa, Mario 241
Victor, Ed 256, 261, 268
Vidal, Gore 3
Viking Press 105, 113, 115, 228

Wade, James 190
Wagner, Richard 289
Waldheim, Kurt 196-7, *197*, 201-8, 209
Wallace, Thomas 179
Walsh, George 204
Walters, Barbara 1, 231-2, 243, 260
Warburg, Sigmund 268-9
Warhol, Andy 170
Warwick, Chris 215
Watson, Graham 147, 149, 190
Watson, James 134-5, 136-7, *136*, 138, 139-40,
  141-3, 144, 145, 294
Weidenfeld, Adele (GW's grandmother) 8,
  9, 28, 32, 38, 39, 40-1, *40*, 209
Weidenfeld, Annabelle (née Whitestone:
  GW's 4th wife) 251-2, 253, 256, 258,
  260-2, *262*, 266, 283, 284, 285, 286,
  288, 289-90, 308
Weidenfeld, George *16*, *24*, *66*, *118*, *127*, *150*,
  228, *244*, *250*, *262*, *280*
  anti-Semitic experiences 18, 179, 180, 268
  appearance 2, 55, 70, 74-5, 110
  awards and honours 155-7, 161-2, 163,
    164, 165-6, 249, 291, 309
  bar mitzvah 16-17
  BBC career 27, 29-31, 32-3, 34, 41
  birth and early life in Vienna 7-23, *12*,
    205-6, 266
  birthday celebrations 60, 128-9, 240-1,
    242-3
  chief of staff to Chaim Weizmann 184,
    184
  divorces 68, 73, 77-8, 155
  duel 19-21
  early love of books 14-15, 34, 298
  education 15-16, 19-20, 22-3
  emigrates from Austria to Britain 23-7
  fatherhood 67, *68*
  final days, death and funeral 283-9
  on his Jewish identity 261-2
  Jewish family background 9, 12-13, 181
  knighthood and peerage 155-7, *156*, 161-2,
    163, 164, 165-6, *166*
  launches *Contact* magazine 41-4
  legacy 291-4

INDEX

loneliness and insecurities 4, 15, 181,
279–80, 284, 290
marriages *see* Jane Sieff, Barbara Skelton,
Sandra Payson and Annabelle
Weidenfeld
memorial service and obituaries 287–9
miscellaneous projects and philanthropic
activities 265, 272, 292
name(s) 1, 9–10, 33
networking 3, 4, 34, 48, 125–6
obituaries 287–8
political preoccupations and activities 17,
48, 77, 157–61, 162–5, 248–50
in *Private Eye* 153–4
publishing career *see* Weidenfeld &
Nicolson Ltd
relationship with Israel 18–19, 183–4, 192,
193–4, 251, 261–2
teetotaller 50, 56, 109
unflattering comments on 60–1, 192, 234,
278–9, 291–2
wealth 259, 272
womanising 65, 68, 151–4, 302
Zionism 21, 184, 192, 195, 207
Weidenfeld, Jane (née Sieff: GW's 1st wife)
65–7, *66*, 68, 78, 260, 278
Weidenfeld, Max (GW's father) 7, 8, 9–10,
11–12, *12*, 13, 14, 17, 18, 21–2, 23, 27–8,
31–2, 34, 72, 75–6, 166, 206, 266, 297
Weidenfeld, Rosa (GW's mother) 7–8, 9, 10,
11, 12, *12*, 13, 17, 21, 22, 23, 28, 34, 72,
129, 266, 297
Weidenfeld, Sandra (née Payson, then
Meyer; GW's 3rd wife) 126–30, *127*,
155, 230, 260
Weidenfeld-Hoffmann Scholarships 292–3,
309
Weidenfeld & Nicolson Ltd 1–2, 49–64
author list 3, 294
authors of colour 122
Booker Prize-winning books 170
celebrity memoirs 214, 215–16
co-editions 61–2
extravagances 125–6
financial backers 230
financial pressures 51–2, 62, 125, 126,
229–30, 245, 247, 252–6, 258
first titles released 50
founding of 46–8
Grove Press acquisition 230–2, 234–7, 242
intelligence services connections 131–3,
301

Jagger autobiography debacle 210–13,
217–26, 229, 305
Lolita, publication of 3, 79, 80–1, 82–94,
90, 98, 265, 294
Nazi and fascist authors 59, 123, 193,
197–201, 278, 293
non-British and female authors 110
offices 49–50, 109, 134, 212, 280
publications *see specific authors*
publishes Praeger books 130–1
purchased by Orion 258–9
race issues 122–3
restructuring 62–3, 299
Weidenfeld & Nicolson New York 226,
227–30, 232–3, 237–40, 241–2, 244–5,
254
Weidenfeld Holdings Ltd 63, 133
Weidenfeld (Publishing) Ltd 63
Weizmann, Chaim 184, *184*
Well of Loneliness, The, Marguerite Radclyffe
Hall 81
Weymouth, Lally 307
Wheatland Corporation 230, 231, 233, 237,
241, 242, 254
Wheatland Foundation 241
White House Years, The, Henry Kissinger
214
Whitestone, Annabelle (GW's 4th wife)
251–2, 253, 256, 258, 260–2, 262, 266,
283, 284, 285, 286, 288, 289–90, 308
Whitney, John Hay 126
Whitney Payson, Joan 126
Wilkins, Maurice 135, 137, 138, 139, 144
Williams, Bernard 158
Williams, Marcia (Lady Falkender) 159, *159*,
160, 161, 164–5
Wilson, Harold 43, 155, 156, 157–8, 159, *159*,
160–1, 162–4, 180
Wilson, Thomas 135, 137, 140, 141
Wolfe, Tom 170
Woodruff, Douglas 86
Woolf, Virginia 46
Worden, Blair 277, 279
Worsthorne, Peregrine 243
Wyndham, Francis 116

Yoni: Hero of Entebbe, Max Hastings 185–7,
188–92, 281
Yousafzai, Malala 3, 294

Zafón, Carlos Ruiz 3, 294
Zionism 21, 184, 192, 195, 207

Thomas Harding is a bestselling author whose books have been translated into more than sixteen languages. He has written for the *Sunday Times*, the *Washington Post* and the *Guardian*, among other publications. His books include *Hanns and Rudolf*, which won the JQ-Wingate Prize for Non-Fiction; *The House by the Lake*, which was shortlisted for the Costa Biography Award; *Blood on the Page*, which won the Crime Writers' Association Golden Dagger Award for Non-Fiction; *Future History*, which was nominated for the German Youth Literature Aware, *The House by the Lake* (picture book), which was nominated for the Kate Greenaway Medal; and *White Debt*, which was longlisted for the Moore Prize for Human Rights Writing.